BIBLE DOCTRINE

FOR

OLDER CHILDREN

BOOK B

CHAPTERS 11-20

James W. Beeke

Illustrated by: William Van Dam

Bible Doctrine for Younger and Older Children
© 1984 by James W. Beeke

2008 Reprint Published by
Reformation Heritage Books
2965 Leonard St., NE
Grand Rapids, MI 49525
USA
616-977-0599 / Fax 616-285-3246
e-mail: orders@heritagebooks.org
website: www.heritagebooks.org

ISBN #s: *Bible Doctrine for...*
...Younger Children: Book A   978-1-60178-048-5
...Younger Children: Book B   978-1-60178-049-2
...Older Children: Book A   978-1-60178-050-8
...Older Children: Book B   978-1-60178-051-5

For additional Reformed literature, both new and used, request a free book list from Reformation Heritage Books at the above address.

PREFACE

. . . ACKNOWLEDGMENTS

Dear Friends,

The publication of **Bible Doctrine for Older Children, Books A and B,** is the result of the combined efforts of numerous people. It is not the product of one person.

I wish to sincerely thank everyone who helped in the following ways:

Administrative assistance throughout all phases of production —	Mrs. Jennie Luteyn and Mr. Bob Menger
Art Work —	Mr. William Van Dam
Proofreading for scriptural and doctrinal content —	Rev. J. R. Beeke, Rev. A.M. Den Boer, Rev. A. W. Verhoef, Elders J. Beeke, Sr., H. Bisschop, J. De Bruine, L. Den Boer, J. Den Bok, B. Elshout, G. Moerdyk, R. Wierks, and the NRC Book and Publishing Committee
General proofreading —	Mrs. Jacqueline Markus and the teaching faculty of Timothy Christian School
Typing, typesetting, layout, and printing —	Mrs. Arlene Hoefakker, Miss Lisa Neels and Mrs. Bernita Van Hierden
Use and critical review of the first draft edition —	Principals and teachers of the Netherlands Reformed Christian Schools throughout United States and Canada
Constant support and cooperation —	The NRC Synodical Education Committee members, the NRC Book and Publishing Committee, and the Timothy Christian School Board and faculty members
Understanding, patience, and loving assistance—	My wife, Ruth

Above all, may we together acknowledge the Lord who has graciously provided the opportunity and means to produce these textbooks. May He savingly apply the truths taught therein to the heart of their readers. May His Name receive all the honor and glory — for He is so worthy to be praised!

The need for simple, clear doctrinal teachings is very great. It is my sincere desire that the Lord will bless these books and use them as a means to clearly teach the truths of Scripture to our children. "That we henceforth be no more children, tossed to and fro, and carried about with every wind of doctrine, by the sleight of men, and cunning craftiness, whereby they lie in wait to deceive; but speaking the truth in love, may grow up into Him in all things, which is the Head, even Christ" (Ephesians 4:14-15).

Further, may God bless the study of biblical doctrine internally. Only through the inward working and application of the Holy Spirit will anyone ever be taught these truths in his soul. As Paul writes, "I have planted, Apollos watered; but God gave the increase. So then neither is he that planteth any thing, neither he that watereth; but God that giveth the increase" (1 Corinthians 3:6-7).

— J. W. Beeke

INTRODUCTION
TO EACH STUDENT

Dear Students,

Have you ever found a book which clearly explained things which you were very interested in learning? If so, you were probably excited and read the book you found eagerly and carefully.

The Bible is the most important book in the world. It was written by God and given to us to read. The Bible is God's Word; it teaches God's truths. These truths are called Bible doctrines. No other book contains such important and precious truths as the Bible. For this reason, you will need to read and study the Bible and its doctrines very carefully. The Bible is the greatest book you will ever receive, for it was written by God Himself.

As you continue to study Bible doctrine, do so seriously. Read and study each lesson carefully. Pray and ask God to teach you these truths in your heart and to bless them in your life. God can plant spiritual life within you and turn you from a deep love of sin to a true love of Him. He can also nourish spiritual life and cause it to grow and deepen within you.

May God bless you personally as you study various Bible doctrines through the means of using this two-book series entitled *Bible Doctrine for Older Children*.

TABLE OF CONTENTS

Book B
Chapters 11-20

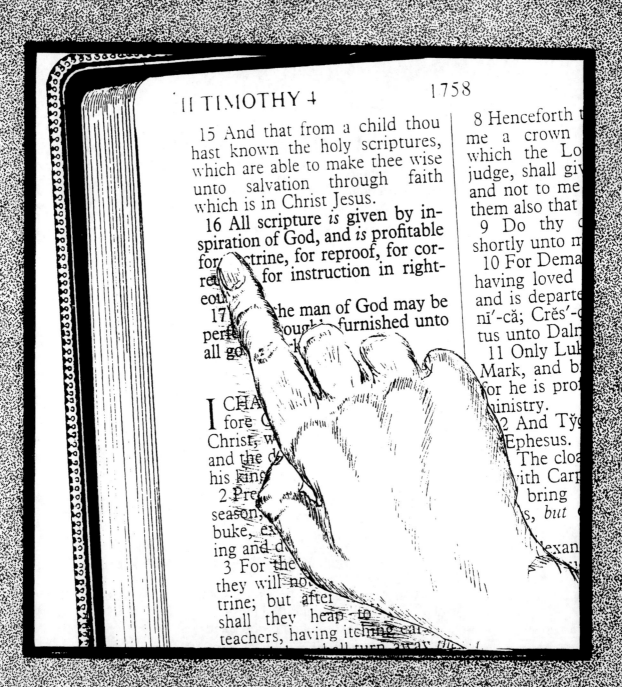

CHAPTER 11

**DOCTRINAL STANDARDS
CREEDS
FIVE POINTS OF CALVINISM**

VOCABULARY

1. **Doctrine** — A truth taught in God's Word
2. **Standard** — An official statement and explanation of the doctrines believed
3. **Unity** — Agreement; oneness
4. **Depravity** — The condition of being without any good; being full of sin and evil
5. **Unconditional** — Absolute; without any attached conditions
6. **Election** — An act of choosing or selecting; God's sovereign choice to graciously save certain sinners
7. **Atonement** — The act of making complete satisfaction or payment for an offense or wrongdoing
8. **Irresistible** — All-powerful; impossible to stop
9. **Perseverance** — The act of continuing; not falling away
10. **Saints** — The elect; the true Christians; the saved people of God

WHAT DO YOU THINK?

SIMPSON'S FOLLY

An ungodly man named Simpson once vowed to build a house upon the sand and live in it. He chose to build his house at the bottom of a cliff where the waves generally rolled in quite evenly and quickly each day. He brought large loads of expensive materials to the building site and did everything in his power to make his house safe from the waves. He was determined to prove wrong what God had said in His Word about the house that was built on the sand.

After some time, the house was built and furnished and it looked like a good solid dwelling. However, before Simpson could move in, the Word of God was fulfilled. "The floods came; and the winds blew, and beat upon that house; and it fell: and great was the fall of it."

Today, the remains of the house lie as a heap of ruins on the shore. This ruin proclaims both the truth of God's Word and the folly of the builder. Today it is known as "Simpson's Folly."

How can this story apply to our lives today? What must be our only foundation of truth? Upon what truth must we build "the house" of our hope?

— Adapted from **Ears for Little Gleaners**

WHAT DO YOU THINK?

A SOLDIER'S STANDARD

Years ago when wars were basically fought with hand weapons, the soldiers were organized into different groups called battalions. Each battalion had its own sign, usually a flag. This sign was called its **standard.** Each battalion had a soldier who held its flag high in the air. This person was called the **standard-bearer.**

When the army had to organize to march or regroup, the trumpet would sound, and each soldier would look for and line up behind his **standard.** The standard represented the group to which each soldier belonged and indicated where each had his place.

Why do we call the **Belgic Confession of Faith, Heidelberg Catechism,** and **Canons of Dordt** our doctrinal **"standards"**? How is the religious use of this word similar to its military use by former armies?

DOCTRINAL STANDARDS

God has graciously given His Word, the Bible to us. Because the Bible is God's Word, it is perfectly true and without any mistake. The truths taught in the Bible are called **doctrines.** To learn these doctrines, we must study the entire Bible and compare its various parts. Many false doctrines are also taught in the world today. Therefore, the Bible — the Word of God and not the ideas of man — must be our foundation, our basis when determining that which is true and false.

Our church forefathers saw how necessary and important it was to study the truths which are taught throughout the entire Bible. They grouped together and studied all of the various Bible portions which speak about the same truths, and then wrote clear, precise statements of doctrinal beliefs. These statements of biblical doctrine are called **doctrinal standards.** Doctrinal standards do not replace the Bible, but attempt to carefully and precisely state that which the entire Bible is teaching about each doctrine. Glance at the **Heidelberg Catechism**, which is printed in the back of your Psalter. This is one of our doctrinal standards. Why are there so many textual references printed on the right side of the page next to each question and answer? How do these texts reveal that the **Heidelberg Catechism** was carefully written from and based upon the truths of Scripture?

We, as Reformed churches, have the following three doctrinal standards:

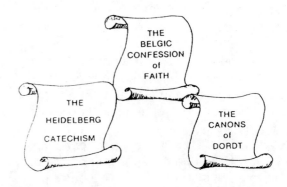

These doctrinal standards are often called the **Three Forms of Unity.** They clearly and officially

8

summarize various biblical doctrines which are believed and held to be true by the Reformed churches. They express the unity of faith found in the believers of these scriptural doctrines.

Our church forefathers found it necessary to write doctrinal standards for the following three reasons:

1. To confess
2. To instruct
3. To defend

Our doctrinal standards:

1. **Confess** to the world the truths that we believe the Word of God is teaching. The "Three Forms of Unity" confess the doctrinal beliefs of the Reformed churches.

WHAT DO YOU THINK?

THE BELGIC CONFESSION OF FAITH

The **Belgic Confession of Faith** was written by Guido de Bres in 1561, when he was 39 years old. It was packaged and thrown over the castle wall to be presented to King Philip II. Guido de Bres hoped that the persecution against the Protestants would be stopped if the king and the world would more clearly understand their beliefs. This did not happen, however, and Guido de Bres died as a martyr in 1567.

The **Belgic Confession of Faith** contains thirty-seven articles. This confession was approved as a doctrinal standard for the Reformed churches at the Synod of Dordt in 1618-1619.

What was the main purpose for writing the **Belgic Confession of Faith**: to confess, instruct, or defend?

WHAT DO YOU THINK?

THE HEIDELBERG CATECHISM

The **Heidelberg Catechism** was written in 1562. The main writers were Zacharias Ursinus, a twenty-eight-year-old professor of theology, and Caspar Olevianus, a twenty-six-year-old professor and minister in Heidelberg. The Catechism was written under the authorization and encouragement of Frederick III, Elector of the Palatinate, in Germany.

The **Heidelberg Catechism** was written in an "experiential order," the order in which true religion is experienced. This order is:
1. Misery
2. Deliverance
3. Thankfulness

The **Heidelberg Catechism** was also written in a personal manner using personal pronouns, such as "my", "you", and "your." Why do you think this was done?

What was the main purpose for writing the **Heidelberg Catechism**: to confess, instruct, or defend?

WHAT DO YOU THINK?

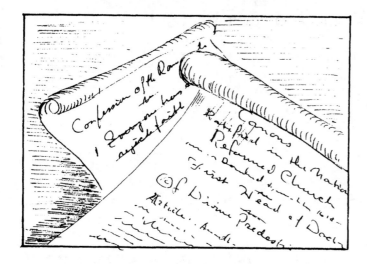

THE CANONS OF DORDT

The **Canons of Dordt** were written by the Synod of the Reformed Churches held in Dordrecht, a city in the Netherlands, in the years 1618 and 1619. The chairman of this synod was Johannes Bogerman.

A **"canon"** is a church law or standard. The **Canons of Dordt** were written to correct five false teachings of Jacobus Arminius, a Professor of Theology at the University of Leiden in the Netherlands. The followers of Arminius wrote a Remonstrance, a short confession of that which they believed. It contained the following five doctrinal errors:

1. Everyone has a free will to accept or reject faith.
2. God's election is based upon His foreknowledge of man's faith.
3. Christ died equally for everyone.
4. Man must cooperate with the Holy Spirit for God to work in his heart.
5. God's children can fall away and become unregenerated again.

The followers of Arminius were called "Remonstrants" because they believed in the five points of this Remonstrance. Our forefathers condemned these views and established the five points of Calvinism by writing the **Canons of Dordt** at this important synod meeting.

What was the main purpose for writing the **Canons of Dordt:** to confess, instruct, or defend?

2. **Instruct** us as church members in the doctrines in which we believe. Doctrinal standards help us to understand the basis upon which we believe that the Word of God is teaching these doctrines. They are a means to help us learn and increase our understanding of the doctrines of the Bible.

3. **Defend** the truth of God's Word from errors and wrong explanations which have entered into the church. Natural man is always trying to add to or subtract from the Bible. The church must continually defend all biblical doctrines from false teachings.

CREEDS

Creeds are statements of belief which often begin with the words "I believe..." Creeds differ from doctrinal standards in that little or no explanation is given, but only simple statements of belief are expressed.

Three creeds are believed and accepted as true statements of belief by all Christian churches. These three creeds are called:

1. The **Apostle's Creed**
2. The **Nicene Creed**
3. The **Athanasian Creed**

THE THREE CREEDS OF ALL CHRISTIAN CHURCHES

APOSTLES' CREED

I. I believe in God the Father, Almighty, Maker of heaven and earth:

II. And in Jesus Christ, His only begotten Son, our Lord:

III. Who was conceived by the Holy Ghost, born of the Virgin Mary:

IV. Suffered under Pontius Pilate; was crucified, dead, and buried: He descended into hell:

V. The third day He rose again from the dead:

VI. He ascended into heaven, and sitteth at the right hand of God the Father Almighty:

VII. From thence He shall come to judge the quick and the dead:

VIII. I believe in the Holy Ghost:

IX. I believe an holy catholic church: the communion of saints:

X. The forgiveness of sins:

XI. The resurrection of the body:

XII. And the life everlasting. AMEN.

NICENE CREED

I believe in one God, the Father Almighty, Maker of heaven and earth, and of all things visible and invisible.

And one Lord Jesus Christ, the only begotten Son of God, begotten of the Father before all worlds; God of God, Light of Light, very God of very God; begotten, not made, being of one substance with the Father, by whom all things were made.

Who, for us men for our salvation, came down, from heaven, and was incarnate by the Holy Spirit of the Virgin Mary, and was made man; and was crucified also for us under Pontius Pilate; He suffered and was bruised; and the third day He rose again, according to the Scriptures; and ascended into heaven, and sitteth on the right hand of the Father; and He shall come again, with glory, to judge the quick and the dead; whose kingdom shall have no end.

And I believe in the Holy Ghost, the Lord and Giver of Life; who proceedeth from the Father and the Son, who with the Father and the Son together is worshipped and glorified, who spake by the prophets.

And I believe one holy catholic and apostolic church. I acknowledge our baptism for the remission of sins; and I look for the resurrection of the dead, and the life of the world to come.

AMEN.

ATHANASIAN CREED

1. Whosoever will be saved, before all things it is necessary that he hold the catholic faith; 2. Which faith except every one do keep whole and undefiled, without doubt he shall perish everlastingly. 3. And the catholic faith is this: That we worship one God in Trinity, and Trinity in Unity; 4. Neither confounding the persons nor dividing the substance. 5. For there is one person of the Father, another of the Son, and another of the Holy Spirit. 6. But the Godhead of the Father, of the Son, and of the Holy Spirit is all one, the glory equal, the majesty co-eternal. 7. Such as the Father is, such is the Son, and such is the Holy Spirit. 8. The Father uncreate, the Son uncreate, and the Holy Spirit uncreate. 9. The Father incomprehensible, the Son incomprehensible, and the Holy Spirit incomprehensible. 10. The Father eternal, the Son eternal, and the Holy Spirit eternal. 11. And yet they are not three eternals but one eternal. 12. As also there are not three uncreated nor three incomprehensibles, but one uncreated and one incomprehensible. 13. So likewise the Father is almighty, the Son almighty, and the Holy Spirit almighty. 14. And yet they are not three almighties, but one almighty. 15. So the Father is God, the Son is God, and the Holy Spirit is God; 16. And yet they are not three Gods, but one God. 17. So likewise the Father is Lord, the Son Lord, and the Holy Spirit Lord; 18. And yet they are not three Lords but one Lord. 19. For like as we are compelled by the Christian verity to acknowledge every Person by himself to be God and Lord; 20. So are we forbidden by the catholic religion to say; There are three Gods or three Lords. 21. The Father is made of none, neither created nor begotten. 22. The Son is of the Father alone; not made nor created, but begotten. 23. The Holy Spirit is of the Father and of the Son; neither made, nor created, nor begotten, but proceeding. 24. So there is one Father, not three Fathers; one Son not three Sons; one Holy Spirit, not three Holy Spirits. 25. And in this Trinity none is afore or after another; none is greater or less than another. 26. But the whole three persons are co-eternal, and co-equal. 27. So that in all things, as aforesaid, the Unity in Trinity and the Trinity in Unity is to be worshipped. 28. He therefore that will be saved must thus think of the Trinity.

29. Furthermore it is necessary to everlasting salvation that he also believe rightly the incarnation of our Lord Jesus Christ. 30. For the right faith is that we believe and confess that our Lord Jesus Christ, the Son of God, is God and man. 31. God of the substance of the Father, begotten before the worlds; and man of substance of His mother, born in the world. 32. Perfect God and perfect man, of a reasonable soul and human flesh subsisting. 33. Equal to the Father as touching His Godhead, and inferior to the Father as touching His manhood. 34. Who, although He is God and man, yet He is not two, but one Christ. 35. One, not by conversion of the Godhead into flesh, but by taking of that manhood into God. 36. One altogether, not by confusion of substance, but by unity of person. 37. For as the reasonable soul and flesh is one man, so God and man is one Christ; 38. Who suffered for our salvation, descended into hell, rose again the third day from the dead; 39. He ascended into heaven, He sitteth on the right hand of the Father, God, Almighty; 40. From thence He shall come to judge the quick and the dead. 41. At whose coming all men shall rise again with their bodies; 42. and shall give account of their own works. 43. And they that have done good shall go into life everlasting, and they that have done evil into everlasting fire.

44. This is the catholic faith, which except a man believe faithfully, he cannot be saved.

JOHN CALVIN

The Five Points of Calvinism are named after John Calvin who was born in 1509. After his conversion to God, he became an important leader in the "Protestant Reformation" (the breaking away from many wrong doctrines and practices of the Roman Catholic Church and the returning to a clear teaching of scriptural truths). John Calvin wrote *Institutes of the Christian Religion* which became an important textbook in the churches of the Reformation.

Calvin served as the minister of the Protestant church in Geneva. He also was a professor at the college there, where hundreds of students and ministers of the Reformation came to be instructed. He guided the Reformation movement in several countries until his death in 1564.

We may be thankful yet today that God used John Calvin as an important means in establishing the Reformation and its teachings, which were based on a clear understanding of God's Word.

FIVE POINTS OF CALVINISM

The *"Five Points of Calvinism"* are:

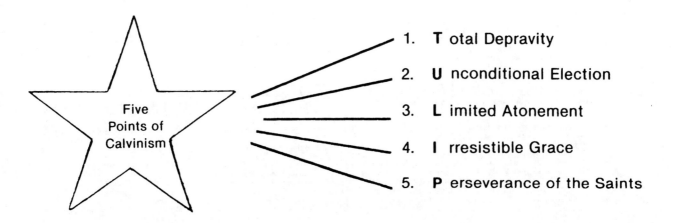

Five Points of Calvinism

1. **T** otal Depravity
2. **U** nconditional Election
3. **L** imited Atonement
4. **I** rresistible Grace
5. **P** erseverance of the Saints

Look at the first letter of each of these five points. Can you think of an easy way to remember the order of the "Five Points of Calvinism"?

Each one of these five reflects an important biblical truth or doctrine. It is important for us to study each one individually and carefully.

TOTAL DEPRAVITY

Depravity is the condition of being without any good — being full of sin and evil. Since our deep fall in Paradise, everyone has become totally depraved. Before the fall, man was created loving God and others.

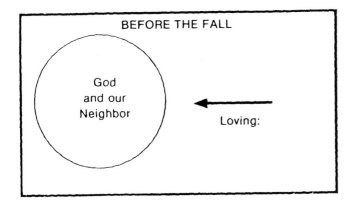

After our fall in Paradise, however, we have become totally depraved. We are now born facing the opposite direction — loving self, sin, world, and Satan.

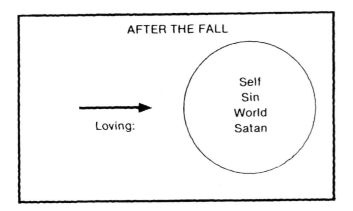

This truth is a very sad one. Every person is now born **spiritually dead.** Man is born **totally depraved.** By nature, no one loves or serves God, but each person loves and serves himself. By nature, no one can do any spiritual good because his heart desires to love and serve self, sin, world, and Satan rather than God and his neighbor. Everyone needs to be converted; his heart and life need to be turned around in order to love and serve God again.

WHAT DO YOU THINK?

"I CANNOT DO THAT WHICH I SHOULD"

Mr. Peters hired several men to work for him on his large farm. One day Sam came to work completely drunk. When Mr. Peters asked Sam to take down several bales of hay to feed the animals, Sam **could not.** When Sam was asked to plow a certain field, he **could not.**

To make matters worse, Sam accused Mr. Peters of being cruel and unreasonable because he was asking him to do things which he was **not able to do.**

What do you think? Was Mr. Peters or Sam right in this situation? Why?

By nature, we too can try to argue like Sam. We can try to accuse God and say, "God is unfair. He is asking me to do things which I **cannot** do."

We forget that we have made ourselves unable, and by nature, we do not want to change our condition either.

Who is guilty when I **cannot** serve God as I should? Why?

13

And GOD saw that the **wickedness of man was great** in the earth, and that every imagination of the thoughts of his heart was only evil continually.

— Genesis 6:5

But we are all as an unclean thing, and **all our righteousnesses are as filthy rags.**

— Isaiah 64:6a

The LORD looked down from heaven upon the children of men to see if there were any that did understand, and seek God.

They are all gone aside, they are all together become filthy: **there is none that doeth good, no, not one.**

— Psalm 14:2-3

We are unable to convert ourselves because we are totally depraved, but God is able to turn us. Therefore we must earnestly and continually ask the Lord for this. We must seek for conversion through prayer and the reading of and listening to God's Word at home, school, and church.

The **heart is deceitful** above all things, **and desperately wicked:** who can know it?

— Jeremiah 17:9

For out of the heart proceed **evil thoughts, murders, adulteries, fornication, thefts, false witness, blasphemies.**

— Matthew 15:19

UNCONDITIONAL ELECTION

God could have justly left all of the human race in its fallen, depraved, and lost condition. If the Lord would have done this, then there would be no hope of salvation for us, our parents, grandparents, relatives, or friends. There would then be no need for a Bible, church, or Christian school for there would be no possibility of salvation. But, what a wonder! God chose to freely elect certain sinners, plant new spiritual life in them, and turn their hearts toward loving Him.

"To **elect**" means "to choose." God chose to save certain lost sinners and He chose these people **unconditionally.** This means that the chosen people were not any better than other people. The elected persons did not have a better heart than others. All people are totally depraved, but God unconditionally elected to save some.

God's choosing to save some guilty sinners reveals His great love and mercy; God's choosing to punish other sinners for their sins reveals His holy justice and great hatred for sin.

Salvation is entirely from and freely given by God. Therefore, we must actively seek and ask Him for it.

For He saith to Moses, **I will have mercy on whom I will have mercy,** and I will have compassion on whom I will have compassion.

So then it is not of him that willeth, nor of him that runneth, but **of God that sheweth mercy.**

— Romans 9:15-16

According as He hath **chosen us** in Him before the foundation of the world, that we should be holy and without blame before Him in love:

Having predestinated us unto the adoption of children by Jesus Christ to Himself, according to the good pleasure of His will.

— Ephesians 1:4-5

Ye have not chosen Me, but **I have chosen you.**

— John 15:16a

14

LIMITED ATONEMENT

"To **atone**" is to pay the full price or make complete satisfaction for a wrongdoing. If you were playing softball with your younger brother and he hit the ball so far that it crashed through your neighbor's window, then a wrong has been done. But, if you went to your neighbor and paid the full cost for replacing the window with your own money, then you would have **atoned** for the wrongdoing of your brother.

Jesus Christ has atoned for all the sins of His people. He has paid the full price for sin, a price so great that He had to die on the cross to fully pay it.

Christ's **atonement** is **limited.** This means that He did not die to actually pay for every person's sin, but He died to fully pay the price for those whom His Father had elected to save.

There is no disagreement in God. The sinners whom God the Father elected to save are the same sinners for whom the Son died and in whom the Holy Spirit works salvation.

I pray for them: *I pray not for the world, but for them which Thou hast given Me;* for they are Thine.
— John 17:9

He shall see of the travail of His soul, and shall be satisfied: by His knowledge shall My righteous Servant justify **many;** for He shall bear **their** iniquities.
— Isaiah 53:11

For this is My blood of the new testament, which is shed for **many** for the remission of sins.
— Matthew 26:28

WHAT DO YOU THINK?

"IT IS ALL OF GOD SO I WILL DO NOTHING!"

Imagine meeting a farmer who said, "I cannot make one seed grow; only God can do that. God has also determined in His plan whether my family and I will have food, shelter, and clothing in this coming year. Nothing I do or not do can change God's plan. Since everything depends upon God and I cannot change His plan, I will sit back and do nothing." If this man never went out to prepare or plant his fields and had no harvest, who is at fault — God or this man? Why?

You may think that this man was very foolish. Yet there are people in church who reason the same way spiritually. They think, "I cannot give myself spiritual life. I cannot convert myself. Only God can do that. God has also determined if I am elected or not. Nothing that I do or do not do will change that. Since everything depends upon God, I will sit back and do nothing."

If this person never actively uses the means of grace and never seeks God through prayer, Bible reading, carefully listening in church, school and home when the Bible is read and explained, who is at fault when this person is lost? Why?

Both of these people separate God's end from His means. **Both** the means and end are part of God's plan. Why is it wrong to separate these two parts? Even though everything is in God's plan, why are we fully responsible for all of our actions?

WHAT DO YOU THINK?

A MERCIFUL JUDGE FALSELY ACCUSED

Imagine the following taking place in the life of an old, experienced judge. One day a young man was brought into court who had stolen and wasted $50,000. The judge felt sorry for the young man, but had to sentence him justly. He therefore sentenced him to pay back the $50,000 and to serve two years in prison.

After sentencing the young man, the judge, out of free grace, said to the court, "I will pay the full sentence of this young man; I will pay his debt and serve his prison term for him. This man is free." The judge then paid the full price, stepped down from his office, put aside his robe, and served the young man's complete prison term.

After two years, when the judge returned to his office, some people spoke harshly about him. They complained and said, "Why doesn't he do this for more people? Why only for this one?"

What do you think of these accusations? Were they being fair to this judge? Why or why not? What should their attitude be when considering what this judge did?

There can be people who hold similar harsh thoughts of God. "Why doesn't He save more people?" they ask. To understand this properly, we must see that God is perfectly free and just not to save any. It is only due to God's wonderful mercy and grace that even **one** person is saved! The price which Jesus Christ had to pay to forgive one sinner is much more than that which the judge in the story had to pay.

When we speak of God's payment for and salvation of sinners, what should our attitude be?

IRRESISTIBLE GRACE

To show **grace** or mercy is to show love, pity, and forgiveness to someone who does not deserve it. **Irresistible** means all-powerful; that which is too powerful to be stopped.

The Holy Spirit works God's grace **irresistibly** in the hearts of all those whom God the Father elected and for whom God the Son atoned. Being totally depraved sinners, people try to resist and fight against the work of God in their hearts. However, the Holy Spirit works irresistibly — each elect sinner will be regenerated and converted. Their wills shall be turned so that their deepest desires shall be to love and serve God. This turning of the hearts of the elect is not an accomplishment of their own strength or desire, but it is the result of the irresistible power of the Holy Spirit who enters and dwells in their hearts.

> And a certain woman named Lydia, a seller of purple, of the city of Thyatira, which worshipped God, heard us: **whose heart the Lord opened,** that she attended unto the things which were spoken of Paul.
> — Acts 16:14

> For **it is God which worketh in you both to will** and **to do** of His good pleasure.
> — Philippians 2:13

> For **by grace are ye saved** through faith; and that not of yourselves: **it is the gift of God.**
> — Ephesians 2:8

PERSEVERANCE OF THE SAINTS

"Perseverance" is the act of continuing; not stopping or falling away. **"Saints"** are the children of God, those who are elected, atoned for, regenerated, and converted by God. **Perseverance of the saints** teaches the truth that those who are regenerated by God shall be preserved in that state forever. Those who are once saved by God shall never go lost again.

The **totally depraved** sinners who are **unconditionally elected** by God the Father, who are purchased by the **limited atonement** of Jesus Christ, and who are regenerated through the **irresistible grace** of the Holy Spirit, will also **persevere** as God's children forever.

16

Those who are saved by God will have their spiritual ups and downs as long as they live on this earth. Their sins will cause God's felt presence to disappear, but their regenerated state is certain; they will remain children of God forever. They may be unfaithful children, but God will remain their faithful Father forever. They do not persevere as children of God through their own faithfulness, but by the power of God.

Who are **kept by the power of God** through faith unto salvation ready to be revealed in the last time.

— I Peter 1:5

And I give unto them eternal life; and **they shall never perish,** neither shall any man pluck them out of My hand.

— John 10:28

Being confident of this very thing, that He which hath begun a good work in you **will perform it until the day of Jesus Christ.**

— Philippians 1:6

The **Five Points of Calvinism** teach five important truths of God's Word. All five show that salvation is entirely the work of God and not the work of man. Since the fall, we do not like the truth of these doctrines, for we would rather have a religion in which we can earn something toward our own salvation. True religion, however, remains "God exalted to the highest, and man humbled to the lowest."

WHAT DO YOU THINK?

THE SUN BEHIND CLOUDS

Have you ever played outside on a cold wintry day with the sun shining brightly in the sky? Suddenly the sun disappears behind a cloud. What happens? Is it correct to say that the sun is not there anymore? No, it is still there, but a cloud has moved between you and the sun. This makes a felt difference, for you do not feel and see the warmth and brightness of the sun in the same way you previously did. You grow colder.

This is a picture of that which happens in the lives of God's people. When they sin, they feel a separation from God's presence. A cloud comes between God and them. God has not left them, for He remains faithful. They will always remain His children. But they cannot see His brightness nor walk in His warmth as they did formerly.

God shall preserve His children forever, but they still sin at a great price. Their sins bring a felt separation between God and them into their lives.

Why is this a great price to pay?

MEMORIZATION QUESTIONS
Ephesians 2:1-9

CHECKING YOUR READING

1. Fill in the following information for each of our three doctrinal standards:

    Doctrinal Standard: **Author(s):**   **Sections:**

    a. _____   _____   _____

    b. _____   _____   _____

    c. _____   _____   _____

2. What is a "doctrinal standard?" _____

    _____

    _____

3. Describe three reasons why doctrinal standards are necessary:

    a. _____

        _____

    b. _____

        _____

    c. _____

        _____

4. What are the three Reformed doctrinal standards often called? _____

    _____

    Why?_____

5. a. What are the three main parts of the **Heidelberg Catechism**?

        1. _____

        2. _____

        3. _____

    b. Why is the order of these three divisions called an "experiential" order?

        _____

        _____

6. Name the three creeds which are believed and confessed by all Christian churches:

    a. _____

    b. _____

    c. _____

CHECKING YOUR READING

7. Name the Five Points of Calvinism and clearly explain that which is meant by each:

   a. _____ — _____
   _____

   b. _____ — _____
   _____

   c. _____ — _____
   _____

   d. _____ — _____
   _____

   e. _____ — _____
   _____

8. What hint can help you to remember the order of the Five Points of Calvinism? _____
   _____

▄▄▄▄▄▄ EXTRA CHALLENGE QUESTIONS ▄▄▄▄▄▄

1. From the story *"I Cannot Do That Which I Should,"* who is guilty when I cannot serve God as I should — God or myself? Why?_____
   _____

2. From the story *"It is All of God . . . So I Will Do Nothing!",* explain how God's election and

   unchangeable plan does not remove my responsibility to actively use His means of grace: _____
   _____
   _____

3. Match each doctrinal standard with the main purpose for which it was written:

Doctrinal Standard	Purpose
The *Heidelberg Catechism*	To Confess
The *Canons of Dordt*	To Instruct
The *Belgic Confession*	To Defend

4. How do the Five Points of Calvinism:

   a. Exalt God to the highest? _____
   _____

   b. Humble man to the lowest? _____
   _____

CHAPTER 12

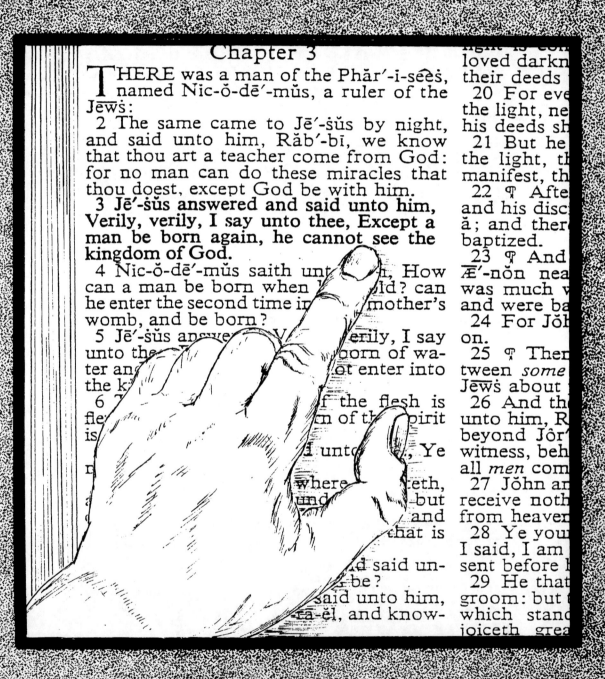

Chapter 3

THERE was a man of the Phăr'-i-sēēś, named Nic-ŏ-dē'-mŭs, a ruler of the Jēwś:

2 The same came to Jē'-śŭs by night, and said unto him, Răb'-bī, we know that thou art a teacher come from God: for no man can do these miracles that thou doest, except God be with him.

3 Jē'-śŭs answered and said unto him, Verily, verily, I say unto thee, Except a man be born again, he cannot see the kingdom of God.

4 Nic-ŏ-dē'-mŭs saith unt   h, How can a man be born when   ld? can he enter the second time i   mother's womb, and be born?

5 Jē'-śŭs answe   V   erily, I say unto the   orn of wa-ter an   t enter into the k

6   f the flesh is fle   n of t   pirit is

where   eth,
und   but
and
hat is

d said un-
be?
said unto him,
rā-ĕl, and know-

light is co
loved darkn
their deeds

20 For eve
the light, ne
his deeds sh

21 But he
the light, th
manifest, th

22 ¶ Afte
and his disc
ă; and there
baptized.

23 ¶ And
Æ'-nŏn nea
was much v
and were ba

24 For Jŏh
on.

25 ¶ Ther
tween some
Jēwś about

26 And th
unto him, R
beyond Jôr'
witness, beh
all men com

27 Jŏhn an
receive noth
from heaven

28 Ye you
I said, I am
sent before

29 He that
groom: but
which stand
joiceth grea

CALLING
REGENERATION
CONVERSION

VOCABULARY

1. **Outward or external call** — God's call to all who hear His Word to repent and believe

2. **Inward or internal call** — The irresistible or all-powerful call by the Holy Spirit through the Word of God which works salvation in the hearts of those who are saved

3. **Regeneration** — The planting of new spiritual life by God in the heart of a spiritually dead sinner

4. **Heart (soul)** — The deepest part of a person which lives forever; from where a person's deepest loves, desires, motives, and thoughts arise

5. **Born again** — The spiritual rebirth of a person; a spiritually dead sinner receiving new spiritual life from God

6. **Conversion** — Repentance and faith; the turning of a person by God from sin to God

7. **Temptation** — An attraction which often leads to sin

8. **Repentance** — A true sorrowing for and striving to flee from sin

9. **Mortification** — A conquering or subduing of one's desires or feelings

10. **Quickening** — A making alive or active; a reviving

CALLING

God's Word teaches us many lessons concerning the doctrine of salvation. Salvation includes the following six items:

1. Calling
2. Regeneration
3. Conversion
4. Faith
5. Justification
6. Sanctification

God created man upright and in His own image — in knowledge, righteousness, and holiness. Man was created to love God and his neighbor. Through our deep fall into sin, we have lost the beautiful uprightness and sinlessness we had in Paradise. Yet God graciously chose not to leave all fallen people in their sinful condition as He could justly have done. God calls to certain people through His Word to turn from their sinful ways unto Him. This **calling** of God to all who hear His Word is named God's **"outward or external call."**

GOD'S OUTWARD CALL

Look unto Me, and be ye saved, all the ends of the earth; for I am God, and there is none else.
— Isaiah 45:22

O earth, earth, earth, *hear the Word of the LORD.*
— Jeremiah 22:29

Seek ye the LORD while He may be found, *call* ye upon Him while He is near:
Let the wicked *forsake* his way, and the unrighteous man his thoughts: and let him *return* unto the LORD; and He will have mercy upon him; and to our God, for He will abundantly pardon.
— Isaiah 55:6-7

And the Spirit and the bride say, Come. And *let him that heareth say, Come.* And let him that is athirst come. And whosoever will, let him take the water of life freely.
— Revelation 22:17

21

God calls us when we hear the preaching of His Word in church, read the Bible at home, or study God's Word at school.

This outward or external call of God is urgent and sincere. God's external call warns us to turn from our sins and invites us to seek for our salvation from sin in Jesus Christ. Not listening to God's warning or refusing God's invitation is a very serious sin. Read **The Parable of the Marriage of the Kings's Son** in the "What Do You Think?" on this page. What will the result be of ignoring or refusing God's outward call?

I have sent also unto you all my servants the prophets, rising up early and sending them, saying, **Return ye now every man from his evil way,** and amend your doings, and go not after other gods to serve them, and ye shall dwell in the land which I have given to you and to your fathers: **but ye have not inclined your ear, nor hearkened unto me.**
— Jeremiah 35:15

Because **I have called, and ye refused;** I have stretched out My hand, and no man regarded:

But ye have set at nought all My counsel, and would none of My reproof:

I also will laugh at your calamity; I will mock when your fear cometh.
— Proverbs 1:24-26

For John came neither eating nor drinking, and they say, he hath a devil.

The Son of Man came eating and drinking, and they say, Behold a man gluttonous, and a winebibber, a friend of publicans and sinners.
— Matthew 11:18-19a

What did our church forefathers believe about the sincerity of God's outward call? Read the **Canons of Dordt,** Articles 8 and 9 of the Third and Fourth Heads of Doctrine:

Article 8. As many as are called by the gospel, are unfeignedly (sincerely) called. For God hath most earnestly and truly declared in His Word, what will be acceptable to Him; namely, that all who are called, should comply (agree) with the invitation. He, moreover, seriously promises eternal life, and rest, to as many as shall come to Him, and believe on Him.

Article 9. It is not the fault of the gospel, nor of Christ, offered therein, nor of God, who calls men by the gospel, and confers upon (gives) them various gifts, that those who are called by the ministry of the Word, refuse to come, and be converted: the fault lies in themselves; some of whom when called, regardless of their danger, reject the Word of life; others, though they receive it, suffer (allow) it not to make a lasting impression on their heart; therefore, their joy, arising only from a temporary faith, soon vanishes, and they fall away; while others choke the seed of the word by perplexing cares, and the pleasures of this world, and produce no fruit. — This our Savior teaches in the parable of the sower. Matt. 13.

Read the following two stories, **Herrings For Nothing** and **Not Now — But Later!** One story illustrates the **sincerity** and the other the **urgency** of God's call. Which story clearly pictures each of these truths?

WHAT DO YOU THINK?

"HERRINGS FOR NOTHING"

One bitterly cold winter day, I was walking on a street in London where many of the people who came to hear me preach lived. The wind was blowing strongly and snow was falling rapidly. As it began to get dark, a man with a basket on his head came down the street calling, "Herrings! Three for a penny! Good, cheap herrings! Three for a penny!" I stopped to watch this man as he passed up and down the street trying in vain to sell his fish. At last, he came to where I stood, set his basket down, and said, "Sir, these are very good fish and my price is very low. I have walked for more than a mile, but nobody has bought any!"

"I am not surprised," I answered.

Astonished by my answer, he said, "But why, Sir?"

"Many people here have no work, and many are starving. Some families do not have a single penny."

"Then I have made a mistake. I knew they were poor so I only charged a penny for three fish. But if they do not even have a penny, then I had better try to sell my fish elsewhere!"

"How much do you want for the entire lot?" I asked.

He looked at me, then down at his fish. His face twisted from the effort of a long mental calculation. At last, he asked with a grin, "Do you mean profit included, Sir?"

When I nodded, he said, "I'll be happy to settle for four shillings." After I paid him, he said, "Thank you very much, Sir! Now what shall I do with them?"

"Just walk down the middle of the road and shout, 'Herrings for free! Come and get herrings for nothing!' " I answered.

He looked at me curiously to see if I was serious, but when I insisted that I meant what I said, he set the basket back on his head and went down the street shouting, "Herrings for free! Good herrings for nothing!"

As I watched, a tall woman looked out of her window. "Here you are, Ma'am," he called. "Herrings for nothing! Come and take some." The woman shook her head, not believing what he said, and turned away.

Thinking the woman to be very foolish, the man continued till he saw a young girl. "Here my dear. Take these fish to your mother. Tell her they are for nothing." But the girl was afraid and ran inside. So the man continued making his way through the snow till he reached the end of the street; but his trip was in vain. No one accepted his offer of free fish.

Finally, he returned to the place where I stood. He set down his basket and exploded, "What a bunch of fools! When you gave me money for herrings you didn't want, I thought you were foolish, but now I think all the people on this street are too! What will I do with all these fish, if you don't want them and they won't have them?"

"Let's try again," I answered. "I'll call this time."

When the people heard my voice, which they knew very well, they came out immediately. Men, women, and children were soon eagerly reaching for the welcome food. The fish seller and I quickly handed three fish to as many people as we could until the fish were gone. But there were still more people waiting than those who had received fish.

In front of the disappointed crowd stood the tall woman. She bitterly lashed out saying, "Why aren't there any for me? Aren't I as good as the others and my children just as hungry as theirs?"

Before I could answer, the fish seller pointed at her and said, "Why, Sir! That's the woman I offered them to first, but she turned away."

"But," cried the angry woman, "I didn't believe that you meant it!"

"Then you can just do without for your unbelief," he retorted. "Good night, and thank you, Sir!"

Possibly you can smile at what took place in this true story, but are we not just as unbelieving as they? In fact, we are ten thousand times worse. The unbelief of these people only cost them an empty stomach, but what does a sinner's unbelief of God's offer of salvation cost? God has sent His Word and messengers to us for years to offer pardon freely. Salvation paid for by another! He has sent you the most loving, tender, and inviting offers of grace, and how have you answered? Have you, like the woman, turned away in scornful unbelief?

Why is it so serious if we do not believe and if we reject God's outward call? Is God's outward call sincere? Why is no person before regeneration interested in God's offer?

Salvation in Jesus Christ is of free grace — it is without money or price. Yet, those who are saved by Christ also serve Him as their new King. What "price" does this require in daily life? Why would natural (unregenerated) man not be interested in paying this "price?" How does this truth make accepting salvation in Christ different from simply "accepting fish" as it took place in this story?

— An Unknown Minister

Adapted from The NRC Banner of Truth

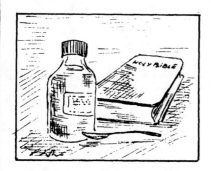

NOT NOW — BUT LATER!

One day a serious Christian doctor called to see an old man whom he had frequently visited. The doctor had often spoken faithfully to old John and his wife about their soul's condition, but without any apparent results. Old John listened attentively and said he agreed with the truth explained to him, but always seemed to want to avoid the deeper personal truth of the matter. He would willingly admit that he was a sinner and that he needed to be saved. He would even say that he intended to seek the Savior some day. He wished to be saved, but it was plain that this was only a desire to escape the punishment of hell. He intended to prepare for heaven, but was putting it off for a "more convenient season."

Now John was suffering from bronchitis. He was in no serious danger, but felt painfully weak and ill. The doctor examined him and promised to prepare some medicine which they could send someone to pick up. He was about to say "good-bye" when John's wife asked, "When must John take the medicine, Doctor?"

"I will put the directions on the label," replied the doctor. Then, turning to his patient, he said, "Let me see; you are not very ill; suppose you begin to take the medicine a month from today?"

John, who had begun to cough to show how much he needed the medicine, almost choked. "A month from today!" he sputtered at last with his wife practically echoing his words.

"Yes, why not? Is that too soon?"

"Too soon! Why, Sir, I may be dead then," groaned old John.

"Quite true," agreed the doctor, "but you must remember that you are not very bad yet. Still, perhaps you had better begin in a week's time."

"But, Sir!" cried John greatly puzzled and troubled, "I beg your pardon, Sir, but I might not live a week!"

"That is very true," the doctor agreed, "but probably you will, and the medicine will be in the house. It will keep, and should you find yourself getting worse, you could take some then." He eyed the old man calmly as though there were nothing at all strange in the directions he was giving.

John groaned; never had his doctor dealt with him in such a strange manner! As if giving in somewhat, the doctor added, "If you should feel worse tomorrow, you might even begin then."

"Sir," the old man almost shouted desperately, "I may be dead tomorrow! Oh Sir," he went on more quietly, for indeed his throat and chest were painful, "I hope you won't be angry with me, nor think me ungrateful. You've always been good to me, but you know, Sir, I don't want to get worse. I believe the medicine is good, but it will do me no good while it is in the bottle. It is foolish and senseless to put off taking it, isn't it?"

"When would you suggest to begin then, John?"

"Well, Sir, I thought you'd tell me to begin today."

"Begin today, by all means," said the doctor, and for the first time he smiled. "I only wanted to show you how foolish your own reasoning is when you delay asking for the more valuable medicine which the Great Physician has provided for your sin-sick soul. Just think how long you have neglected His remedy! For years you have turned away from it. You have said to yourself, 'Next week or next year, or when I am about to die, I will seek the Lord, any time rather than the present.' And yet today is the only time you are sure of. God's offer is only for 'today.' 'Now is the accepted time; behold, now is the day of salvation.' The remedy is near, but it will do you no good unless it is given to you. It is so foolish to put off the asking for this even until tomorrow."

Old John's eyes were full of tears as he pressed the hand of his kind friend. "I never saw it this way before," he whispered.

Why is it so foolish to put off God's outward call? Why is it so dangerous to delay and plan to seek God at a later time?

— Adapted from *The NRC Banner of Truth*

God's outward call is very important and necessary; all people should stop and turn to the Lord upon hearing it. But, our hearts are so stubbornly sinful and spiritually dead that to penetrate our hearts we need an all-powerful call of God. We need God's **inward or internal call.** God's inward call is His irresistible call by the Holy Spirit through His Word. When the Holy Spirit applies the Word of God with Divine power in the heart of a sinner, that person is stopped upon his sinful way. God, sin, and his need to be saved become real! These become his deepest needs.

When God inwardly calls a sinner, He not only stops a person through the application of His Word, but He also plants new spiritual life in his soul. We call this implanting of new spiritual life "**regeneration.**"

REGENERATION

Man was created by God to love, serve, and glorify Him. In doing this, man would also live in true love and concern for his neighbor.

MAN IN PARADISE

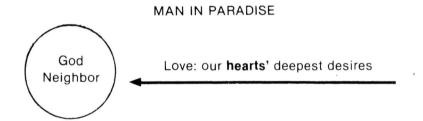

In our sinful fall in Paradise, we chose to reverse this God-created order. We chose to love and serve self, sin, the world, and Satan, instead of God.

MAN — NOW BORN AS A FALLEN SINNER

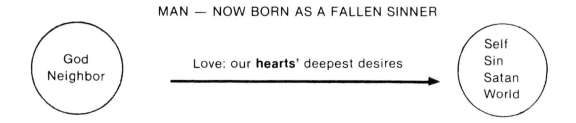

Since our fall, we are born with reversed wills. Our wills are active, but in the wrong direction. We are spiritually alive to sin, but spiritually dead to God. We are in a most serious and sad condition.

To make matters worse, we do not even want to change; we love serving self, sin, and world. We enjoy being a slave of Satan! By nature, we fight against being freed from the slavery of sin.

Therefore, we all need God to call us with His all-powerful, inward call. We need God to stop us upon our sinful way which leads to eternal destruction. We need God to *regenerate* us. *Regeneration* is the planting of new spiritual life by God in the heart of a spiritually dead sinner. This experience in the life of a person is called "being **born again**."

In regeneration, or when a person is born again, God plants three precious jewels in the heart: faith, hope, and love. God restores the basic parts of His image, which man lost in his sinful fall, in the person: true knowledge, righteousness, and holiness.

WHAT DO YOU THINK?

HARD WORK FOR TERRIBLE WAGES!

A minister of the gospel once made use of the following example in one of his sermons. "Suppose," he said, "that a person went to a blacksmith and said, 'Sir, I would like you to make a very long, heavy chain. Have it ready by next week and I will pay you cash for it!'

The blacksmith was busy with other work, but in order to earn the extra money, he began to make the chain. After working hard for many days, he finally finished it.

The man returned and asked, 'Have you made the chain?'

'Yes Sir, here it is.'

'That is very well done; a good chain, but it is not long enough.'

'Why, it is just the length you told me to make it!'

'Yes, I know, but I have decided to have it much longer than at first; work on it another week; I will then call and pay you for it.'

Feeling thus flattered with praise, and encouraged by the promise of full reward for his labor, the blacksmith worked on, adding link to link, until the appointed time when his employer called again. As before, he praised his work, but still insisted that the chain was too short.

'But,' replied the blacksmith, 'I can do no more; my iron is used up, and so is my strength. I need the pay for what I have done, and can do no more till I have it.'

'Oh, I think you have the means of adding a few links more; then the chain will be long enough for my purpose, and you will be fully rewarded for all your hard work!'

With his remaining strength and his last few scraps of iron he added the last link of which he was capable. The man returned and said to him, 'The chain is a good one; you have worked hard and long to make it; I see that you can do no more, and now you shall have your full wages.' But instead of paying him cash, he took the chain, bound the workman hand and foot with it, and cast him into his own furnace of fire!"

"Such," said the preacher, "is the wages of sin! It promises much, but its reward is death; and each sin is an additional link to that chain which will bind the sinner in the prison-house of hell."

If this man had been warned of what would happen, he would not have continued to make more links for the chain, would he? But what if you clearly warned him and he answered, "Leave me alone; I enjoy my work; I'll do what I think is best!" — how would you feel? Would his condition not be doubly sad?

This is man's picture since our sinful fall and yet, by nature, we do not want to be delivered from it. In answer to the question, "What is the greatest misery?" Rev Ledeboer wrote, "Not to feel our misery." Why is this answer true?

— Adapted from *The Shorter Catechism Illustrated*

Regeneration, the implantation of new spiritual life in a spiritually dead sinner, is a free gift of God. God graciously stops a sinner upon his sinful course with His irresistible, inward call and implants a "new heart": new loves, desires, purposes, and motives in his life in regeneration. Since regeneration is a work of God, we must actively seek, knock, ask, and beg the Lord for this gift. This can be done by prayerfully using the means of grace which God has given. In His Word, God often commands us to seek Him.

Salvation is purely a gift of God's grace	*God commands us to actively seek Him for this gift*
No man can come to Me, **except the Father** which hath sent Me **draw him:** and I will raise him up at the last day. — John 6:44	**Seek** ye the LORD while He may be found, **call** ye upon Him while He is near: Let the wicked forsake his way, and the unrighteous man his thoughts: and let him **return** unto the LORD, and He will have mercy upon him; and to our God, for He will abundantly pardon. — Isaiah 55:6-7
So then it is not of him that willeth, nor of him that runneth, but **of God that sheweth mercy.** — Romans 9:16	And I say unto you, **Ask,** and it shall be given you; **seek,** and ye shall find; **knock,** and it shall be opened unto you. For every one that asketh receiveth; and he that seeketh findeth; and to him that knocketh it shall be opened. — Luke 11:9-10
Who hath saved us, and called us with an holy calling, not according to our works, but **according to His own purpose and grace,** which was given us in Christ Jesus before the world began, — II Timothy 1:9	Behold I stand at the door, and knock: if any man **hear my voice, and open the door,** I will come in to him, and will sup with him, and he with Me. — Revelation 3:20

WHAT DO YOU THINK?
BLIND BARTIMAEUS

Read the story of Blind Bartimaeus:

And they came to Jericho: and as He went out of Jericho with His disciples and a great number of people, blind Bartimaeus, the son of Timaeus, sat by the highway side begging.

And when he heard that it was Jesus of Nazareth, he began to cry out, and say, Jesus, Thou son of David, have mercy on me.

And many charged him that he should hold his peace: but he cried the more a great deal, Thou son of David, have mercy on me.

And Jesus stood still, and commanded him to be called. And they call the blind man, saying unto him, Be of good comfort, rise; He calleth thee.

And he, casting away his garment, rose, and came to Jesus.

And Jesus answered and said unto him, What wilt thou that I should do unto thee? The blind man said unto him, Lord, that I might receive my sight.

And Jesus said unto him, Go thy way; thy faith hath made thee whole. And immediately he received his sight, and followed Jesus in the way.

— Mark 10:46-52

Are we spiritually blind? Can we cure ourselves? Where should we place ourselves? Where does Jesus "pass by" today? How should we follow Bartimaeus' example in verse 48? Can you find misery, deliverance, and thankfulness in this story? How does this story picture the manner in which a person is cured from spiritual blindness?

CONVERSION

Conversion is always connected to and flows out from regeneration. When God regenerates a soul, He also converts that person. *"Conversion"* means to change over or to turn around. When God implants new spiritual life in the heart of a person, He turns him around. That person now loves what he formerly hated, and hates what he formerly loved. Before conversion, his deepest desires were to serve and please himself. He loved to sin, and wanted more of the world. He hated God, His demands, and His law, because he wanted to serve himself rather than God. Now that he has received a new heart from God, his deepest motives, desires, and loves are completely changed. Now he hates his former selfish love of self; he fights against sin and the **temptations** of the world. Now his heart's desire is to love, serve, and honor God.

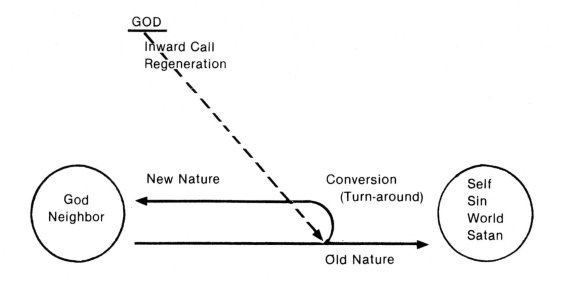

Create in me a clean heart, O God; and *renew a right spirit* within me.
— Psalm 51:10

And *I will give them an heart to know Me,* that I am the LORD: and they shall be My people, and I will be their God: for they shall *return unto Me with their whole heart.*
— Jeremiah 24:7

A *new heart also will I give you,* and a new spirit will I put within you: and I will take away the stony heart out of your flesh, and I will give you an heart of flesh.
And I will put My spirit within you, and cause you to *walk in My statutes,* and ye shall keep My judgments, and do them.
— Ezekiel 36:26-27

And said, Verily I say unto you, Except ye *be converted,* and become as little children, ye shall not enter into the kingdom of heaven.
— Matthew 18:3

Jesus answered and said unto him, Verily, verily, I say unto thee, Except a man *be born again,* he cannot see the kingdom of God.
— John 3:3

Therefore if any man be in Christ, *he is a new creature:* old things are passed away; behold, all things are become new.
— II Corinthians 5:17

And you hath He *quickened,* who were dead in trespasses and sins.
— Ephesians 2:1

WHAT DO YOU THINK?

THE DIRTY CUP

"Please hurry," Nancy's father urged, "just wash the outside — that will be fine."

Nancy stared at the dirty cups she had to wash. "Just wash the outside," she thought, "I can't do that!"

"Dad," she answered, "look at the inside of these cups — they're dirty. I can't only wash the outside."

"Look," her father replied, "just make sure that the outside is clean; who looks at the inside anyway?"

Nancy was stunned. "Dad, I can't!" she exclaimed. "No one will ever want to use them again!" With a thoroughly puzzled expression, she stared at her father.

Her father smiled. "Nancy, I wanted to teach you something," he said. "Some people believe that religion is only washing the outside of 'the cup.' Do you think God would ever be pleased with only a clean outward appearance?"

Nancy understood her father's question and example. God instructed the prophet Samuel in the same truth when Samuel was sent to anoint one of the sons of Jesse to be king. We read in 1 Samuel 16:7b, "For the LORD seeth not as man seeth; for man looketh on the outward appearance, but the LORD looketh on the heart." Is true conversion only an outward change in a person's life? Why not?

What did the Lord Jesus mean when He said in Matthew 23:27, "Woe unto you, scribes and Pharisees,

hypocrites! for ye are like unto whited sepulchres, which indeed appear beautiful outward, but are within full of dead men's bones, and of all uncleanness." What does this teach us about true conversion? Why is the turning of a person's heart necessary in true conversion? If a person's heart is turned from a deepest love of serving self, sin, world, and Satan, to serving God, how will this be noticeable in his motives, thoughts, emotions, words, and actions?

WHAT DO YOU THINK?

"WHAT THEN?"

"Well, your college course is finished!" said an old college professor.

"Yes," the young man answered, "I graduate today."

"And then?"

"Oh, I shall go into business, marry a fine woman, make a lot of money, and make my way up in the world."

"And then?"

"Then I shall retire, travel, and take life easy."

"And then?"

"Well...then I shall have to die, I suppose."

"And then?"

The young man had no answer, and was left speechless.

A certain rich man, whom the Lord had prospered, said within himself, "Soul, thou hast much goods laid up for many years; take thine ease, eat, drink, and be merry. But God said unto him, **Thou fool,** This night thy soul shall be required of thee; then whose shall those things be, which thou hast provided?" (Luke 12:16-20).

Why is the question: "Am I regenerated?" the most important question for each of us? Are you concerned about this question? Why are we also fools if all our plans and riches are in this world?

— Adapted from *The NRC Banner of Truth*

There are two natures in the heart of a person after regeneration: the **old nature** and the **new nature.** The old nature desires to love and serve self, sin, world, and Satan, but the new nature desires to love God and others. These two natures are constantly at war with each other; they try to pull the person in opposite directions. Sometimes the old nature has the upper hand; at other times, the new nature, by God's grace, has more strength. The continual battle between these two natures produces a spiritual warfare in the hearts of all regenerated people. The following drawings picture this truth:

HEART OF AN *UNREGENERATED* PERSON

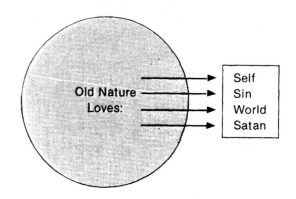

HEART OF A *REGENERATED* PERSON

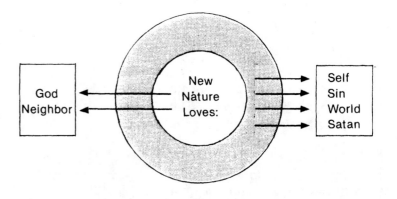

In a regenerated person's heart the new nature reflects his deepest longings and desires, and is the center of his being. In the future this new nature will obtain a complete victory. When a regenerated person dies, his old nature remains dead in the grave, but his new nature will live forever with God.

WHAT DO YOU THINK?

REV. SPURGEON'S CONVERSION

Rev. Charles H. Spurgeon was a famous Baptist minister in England. As a young teenager he was in great distress for approximately five years concerning his sins and sinful heart. The Holy Spirit was convicting him of his lost condition.

Rev. Spurgeon describes his experience in this way: "I thought the sun was blotted out of my sky, that I had so sinned against God that there was no hope for me. I prayed — the Lord knows how I prayed — but I never had a glimpse of an answer that I knew of. I searched the Word of God: the promises were more alarming than the threatenings. I read the privileges of the people of God, but with the fullest persuasion that they were not for me. The secret of my distress was this: I did not know the gospel. I was in a Christian land; I had Christian parents: but I did not understand the freeness and simplicity of the gospel."

One Sunday morning, Charles walked into a small church building. Due to a severe snowstorm, the minister who was scheduled to preach did not arrive. Another man, a poor shoemaker who could not read or write, but who often preached on Sundays, arose to preach.

He chose as his text these words about Christ in Isaiah 45:22, "Look unto Me, and be ye saved, all the ends of the

earth." He continued to repeat this text as he preached. Seeing Charles listening to him, and recognizing him to be a stranger, he said, "Young man, you look very miserable. And you will always be miserable — miserable in life, and miserable in death — if you do not obey my text!"

God blessed these words and the often repeated text to the heart of Rev. Spurgeon. God opened his soul's eyes to see that salvation was posssible for the "ends of the earth," for the chief of sinners — yes, even for him! He experienced deliverance in Jesus Christ.

Rev. Spurgeon's heart was won over to God in true thankfulness. He served the Lord diligently as a faithful minister for many years and preached to thousands and thousands of people. His entire life revealed his true conversion to the Lord.

Can you find the marks of misery, deliverance, and thankfulness in the conversion experience of Rev. Spurgeon? If a person's conversion is true, how will repentance and faith be seen in his life? Jesus said, "For the tree is known by his fruit," in Matthew 12:33. What did Jesus mean with this expression? What does this teach us about true conversion?

WHAT DO YOU THINK?

A NARROW WAY

There is a way that leads to death,
   A way that many go,
In spite of all that Wisdom saith
   Of sin and endless woe.

The way is smooth, and fair, and broad,
   'Tis pleasant to the sight;
But woe to those who take this road;
   It leads to endless night.

A narrow way there likewise is,
   That leads to joys above;
But few, alas! do travel this,
   'Tis not the way they love.

How blest are they whose feet are found
   In wisdom's sacred way!
They soon shall reach the happy ground,
   And there forever stay.

— *Gadsby Selection*

Upon which road are you traveling? Which group is wise and which is foolish?

Conversion contains two parts: **repentance** and *faith.* This can be pictured by the turning of a sphere or globe. When the sphere is turned it is being turned away from and at the same time toward something. Repentance is turning *away* from loving and serving self, sin, world, and Satan; faith is turning *toward* God.

Repentance

Turning *away* from:

| Self |
| Sin |
| World |
| Satan |

Faith

Turning *toward:*

| God |

True repentance also contains two parts: a *true sorrow* of the heart for all sin and a *sincere striving* to increasingly hate and flee from sin. *True* repentance is different from *outward* repentance. Outward repentance also experiences "sorrow", but it is a sorrow because of the punishment and results of sin. True repentance is a sorrowing and fleeing from sin itself. Read Cain's repentance in Genesis 4:13-14.

Is Cain's repentance outward or true repentance? Which mark of outward repentance is present? Name two marks of true repentance that are missing.

Repentance is sometimes called **the mortification** *of the old nature,* and faith **the quickening** *or enlivening of the new nature.* Why are both repentance and faith necessary parts of true conversion?

> And Cain said unto the LORD, My punishment is greater than I can bear.
> Behold, Thou hast driven me out this day from the face of the earth; and from Thy face shall I be hid; and I shall be a fugitive and a vagabond in the earth; and it shall come to pass, that every one that findeth me shall slay me.
> — Genesis 4:13-14

MEMORIZATION QUESTIONS

1. What did Jesus teach the people?
   The holiness of God and the duty of man.

2. How does God's holiness appear from the doctrine of Jesus?
   By His teaching that the least thought against God's law is sin.

3. What does Jesus teach about our duty?
   That we must love God above all, and our neighbor as ourselves.

4. What if we do not do so?
   Then we deserve punishment of hell fire.

5. Why did Jesus teach this?
   To convince us that we are "lost sinners."

6. Is this conviction necessary?
   Certainly, for Jesus came to save only the lost.

7. Are then all the lost saved?
   No: only those who believe in Him, and who repent.

8. What does Jesus mean thereby to "believe in Him."
   To know the Lord Jesus and to trust Him.

9. But what is it to repent?
   To again obey God and Jesus out of love.

10. Did Jesus teach that we could do this of ourselves?
    No; He promised the Holy Spirit.

11. What then does the Holy Spirit do?
    The Holy Spirit works all things: faith as well as repentance.

— *Dyksterhuis Catechism: Lesson XXXI*

CHECKING YOUR READING

1. What is God's **outward call?** _____
   _____
   _____

2. What important lesson can you learn about God's **outward call** from reading the following stories?

   a. **"Herrings for Nothing"** — _____
      _____

   b. **Not Now — But Later!** — _____
      _____

   c. **The Parable of the Marriage of the King's Son** — _____
      _____

3. Why will no one respond to God's **outward call** and turn to the Lord unless God stops him with His **inward call?**
   _____
   _____
   _____

4. What is:

   a. Regeneration? — _____
      _____

   b. Conversion? — _____
      _____

5. Why are regeneration and conversion absolutely necessary for each person? Why is this so important? _____
   _____
   _____

6. In the heart of a converted person, what is meant by his:

   a. Old nature? — _____
      _____

   b. New nature? — _____
      _____

CHECKING YOUR READING

7. Describe the **spiritual warfare** which is continually taking place in the heart of a converted person: _____

   _____

8. When will this spiritual warfare end? Why? _____

   _____

9. Name the two parts of **true conversion:**

   a. _____   b. _____

10. Describe two characteristics of **true repentance:**

    a. _____

    b. _____

11. How does **true repentance** differ from **outward repentance?**

    a. True repentance — _____

       _____

    b. Outward repentance — _____

       _____

▬▬▬▬▬ EXTRA CHALLENGE QUESTIONS ▬▬▬▬▬

1. From the story **The Dirty Cup,** explain why true conversion must be from the heart:

   _____

   _____

2. Referring to **Rev. Spurgeon's Conversion,** how will repentance and faith be seen in the life of a converted person? _____

   _____

3. Why are "the mortification of the old nature" and "the quickening of the new nature" both necessary parts of true conversion? _____

   _____

   _____

4. Read Romans 7:18 and 19. What is Paul saying about his own heart in these verses? _____

   _____

5. God's Word tells me that I must seek God; at the same time it tells me that, by nature, I cannot seek God in the right way. What must I do then? _____

   _____

   _____

TESTING YOUR KNOWLEDGE

1. What three purposes do our doctrinal standards serve? Explain each purpose.

   a. _____
   _____

   b. _____
   _____

   c. _____
   _____

2. What name is often given to these three doctrinal standards? _____

   Why is this an appropriate name? _____

   _____

3. a. Why was the **Belgic Confession of Faith** written? _____

   _____

   b. How many articles does it contain? _____

4. a. What are the three main parts of the **Heidelberg Catechism**?

      1. _____

      2. _____

      3. _____

   b. What do these three parts describe? _____

   _____

   c. How is the **Heidelberg Catechism** further divided? _____

   Why?_____

5. Why are all people born totally depraved?_____

   _____

6. Why is unconditional election the only hope of salvation for spiritually dead sinners?

   _____

   _____

7. Since salvation is all of God, what must **we** do? _____

   _____

   _____

TESTING YOUR KNOWLEDGE

8. Name the Five Points of Calvinism:

   a. _____   d. _____

   b. _____   e. _____

   c. _____

9. How is God's outward call different from God's inward call?

   a. Outward call — _____

   _____

   b. Inward call — _____

   _____

10. a. Is God's outward call sincere? _____ What does this mean for

   us? _____

   b. Can only God's outward call save us? _____ Why or why not?

   _____

11. Why do we all need God to regenerate us; why can we not turn to God of ourselves?

   _____

   _____

12. How is a person's life after conversion different from his life before conversion?

   _____

13. Which two natures are "at war" in the heart of a converted person, and in which direction is each nature pulling?

   Natures   **Directions**

   a. _____   _____

   b. _____   _____

14. What do we call the following two parts of conversion?

   a. The turning **away from?** _____

   b. The turning **toward?** _____

15. Why is only **outward repentance** not true repentance? How do they differ?_____

   _____

   _____

CROSSWORD PUZZLE

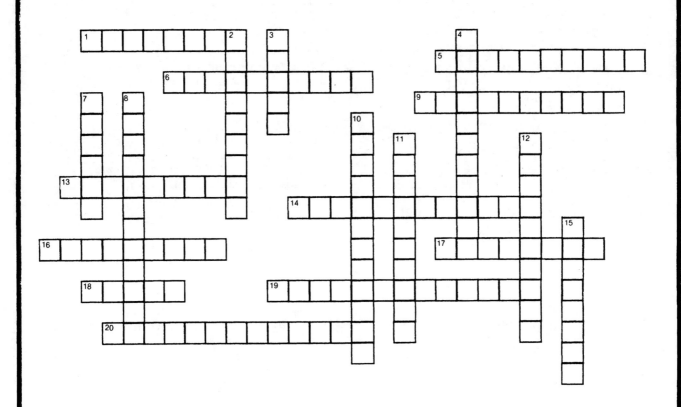

Across

1. An official statement and explanation of the doctrines believed
5. A making alive or active; a reviving
6. An attraction which often leads to sin
9. The irresistible call by the Holy Spirit through the Word of God which works salvation in the hearts of those who are saved
13. The act of making complete satisfaction or payment for an offence or wrong-doing.
14. The act of continuing; not falling away
16. The spiritual rebirth of a sinner
17. God's sovereign choice to graciously save certain sinners
18. Agreement; oneness
19. A conquering or subduing of one's feelings and desires
20. Absolute; without any attached conditions

Down

2. The condition of being without any good; full of sin
3. The deepest part of a person which lives forever; from where the deepest desires, motives, and thoughts of a person arise
4. God's call to all who hear His Word to repent and believe
7. The elect; the true Christians; the saved people of God
8. The planting of new spiritual life by God in the heart of a spiritually dead sinner
10. All-powerful; impossible to stop
11. Repentance and faith; the turning of a person by God from sin to God
12. A true sorrowing for and a striving to flee from sin
15. A truth taught in God's Word

38

BIBLE STUDY QUESTIONS

Read the following chapters and write out the verse or verses which most clearly teach the following doctrinal truths:

1. Total Depravity —

   Jeremiah 17:_____ — _____

   _____

   _____

2. Unconditional Election —

   John 15:_____ — _____

   _____

   _____

3. God's outward call —

   Isaiah 55:_____ — (two verses) _____

   _____

   _____

   _____

4. The necessity of personal conversion —

   Matthew 18:_____ — _____

   _____

   _____

   John 3:_____ — _____

   _____

PROJECT IDEAS

1. Write out a report on our three doctrinal standards and the men who wrote them.

2. Construct a poster which names and explains our three doctrinal standards.

3. Make a chart which clearly teaches the Five Points of Calvinism; use several proof texts for each point.

4. Draw a poster which portrays regeneration and conversion.

5. Design a poster which pictures the heart of an unregenerated person and the old and new natures in a regenerated person's heart.

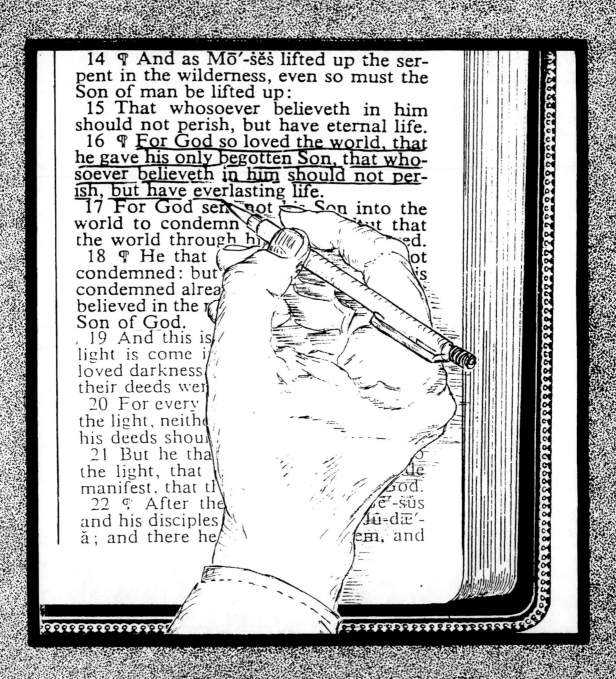

14 ¶ And as Mō'-šěš lifted up the serpent in the wilderness, even so must the Son of man be lifted up:

15 That whosoever believeth in him should not perish, but have eternal life.

16 ¶ For God so loved the world, that he gave his only begotten Son, that whosoever believeth in him should not perish, but have everlasting life.

17 For God sent not his Son into the world to condemn but that the world through h ed.

18 ¶ He that ot condemned: but is condemned alrea believed in the Son of God.

19 And this is light is come i loved darkness their deeds wer

20 For every the light, neith his deeds shou

21 But he tha the light, that de manifest, that th God.

22 ¶ After the ē-šŭs and his disciples Ju-dæ'-ă; and there he em, and

FAITH
TYPES OF FAITH

1. **Knowledge of Faith** — A knowing of Jesus Christ and God's way of salvation through Him
2. **Agreement of Faith** — Assent or consent; an agreeing with God's truth and way of salvation
3. **Trusting of Faith** — Confidence; a resting in Jesus Christ and a placing of full hope and expectation in Him
4. **Historical Faith** — A belief in and confession of the truths of the Bible with the mind only
5. **Temporary Faith** — A belief in and confession of the truth for a time with the mind and emotions
6. **Miraculous Faith** — A belief that a miracle will be done by or for us
7. **True Saving Faith** — A belief and trust in God through the saving renewal and conversion of mind, emotions, and heart
8. **Misery** — The extremely deep, lost, and miserable condition sinners are in because of their sin and separation from God
9. **Deliverance** — Salvation from the greatest evil and entrance into the greatest good through Jesus Christ
10. **Thankfulness** — Gratitude; a sincere desire to know, honor, and serve God from a spirit of love to God for His merciful deliverance

FAITH

Faith is the knowing of, agreeing with, and trusting in someone. If we know someone, believe him to be sincere, and trust him, we have *faith* in this person.

Read the story, **Believing and Trusting,** on this page, and the story, **You . . . in the Wheelbarrow!** on the next page. How is *trusting* more than just *knowing* and *agreeing*? Faith has three parts:

1. **Knowledge**
2. **Agreement** (Assent or Consent)
3. **Trust** (Confidence)

Therefore, to believe in someone we must: know something of the person, believe that he is telling us the truth, and trust him.

WHAT DO YOU THINK?

BELIEVING AND TRUSTING

There was a severe drought some years ago in the northern part of England. The situation became so severe that if it did not rain within a week, the crops would be totally lost. Due to this urgent need, it was decided to have a special prayer service for rain in one of the local churches.

As the minister of this congregation was approaching his church, he saw a little girl walking ahead of him, carrying an umbrella. He caught up with the girl and asked her, "My little girl, why are you carrying an umbrella to church on such a hot day?"

Turning and looking into his face, the girl answered, "We are going to ask God to send rain today. I want to be ready."

The minister testified in his sermon that the faith of this girl put him to shame.

How did this girl show more than just "knowledge"? How can we see "trusting" in her faith?

— Adapted from *The NRC Banner of Truth*

WHAT DO YOU THINK?

YOU. . . IN THE WHEELBARROW!

While we do not believe that it is right to take our lives in our own hands or place ourselves in unnecessary risks, yet the following story clearly illustrates the differences between knowledge only or knowledge, agreement, and trust when we speak of faith or believing.

A world-famous acrobat secured a cable across the Niagara River Gorge. This gorge is very wide and deep. A rough river rushes through the canyon several hundred feet below.

A large crowd gathered to see this famous tightrope walker cross the Niagara Gorge by walking on this cable.

First, the acrobat stood on the cable, facing the crowd, and shouted, "Who believes that I can walk across this gorge on this cable and return?" The crowd *knew* that he was a famous tightrope walker and they called back that they believed he could.

When the acrobat returned, he threw down his balance rod, had a wheelbarrow lifted up onto the cable and called to the crowd, "Who believes that I can walk across this cable and back pushing this wheelbarrow?" The crowd again expressed their belief in him.

When he returned, the acrobat said, "Who believes that I can walk across this cable pushing my wheelbarrow with a person in it?" Many waved their hands and shouted that they "believed." "Okay," said the acrobat to a "believing" man in the front, "you . . . into the wheelbarrow!"

The man stood motionless in shocked silence. He then refused to step into the wheelbarrow.

How are *agreement* and *trust* deeper than just *knowledge*? How was this "believer's" faith tested? How would this test reveal whether his faith was true or not?

What can this story teach us about faith or believing in Jesus Christ? How is true faith more than just knowledge?

WHAT DO YOU THINK?

THE CANAANITISH WOMAN
Read the story of the Canaanitish woman found in *Matthew 15:21-28*·

Then Jesus went thence, and departed into the coasts of Tyre and Sidon.

And, behold, a woman of Canaan came out of the same coasts, and cried unto Him, saying, Have mercy on me, O Lord, Thou son of David; my daughter is grievously vexed with a devil.

But He answered her not a word. And His disciples came and besought Him, saying, Send her away; for she crieth after us.

But He answered and said, I am not sent but unto the lost sheep of the house of Israel.

Then came she and worshipped Him, saying, Lord, help me.

But He answered and said, It is not meet to take the children's bread, and to cast it to dogs.

And she said, Truth, Lord: yet the dogs eat of the crumbs which fall from their masters' table.

Then Jesus answered and said unto her, O woman, great is thy faith: be it unto thee even as thou wilt. And her daughter was made whole from that very hour.

Can you find the three necessary parts of faith which were given to this woman?

Where can you see knowledge? Where can you discover agreement? Where can you find trust?

WHAT DO YOU THINK?

ASA, KING OF JUDAH

Read these two stories about Asa:

II Chronicles 14:9-12

And there came out against them Zerah the Ethiopian with an host of a thousand thousand, and three hundred chariots; and came unto Mareshah.

Then Asa went out against him, and they set the battle in array in the valley of Zephathah at Mareshah.

And Asa cried unto the LORD his God, and said, LORD, it is nothing with Thee to help, whether with many, or with them that have no power: help us, O LORD our God; for we rest on Thee, and in Thy Name we go against this multitude. O LORD, Thou art our God; let not man prevail against Thee.

So the LORD smote the Ethiopians before Asa, and before Judah; and the Ethiopians fled.

II Chronicles 16:1-5

In the six and thirtieth year of the reign of Asa, Baasha king of Israel came up against Judah, and built Ramah, to the intent that he might let none go out or come in to Asa king of Judah.

Then Asa brought out silver and gold out of the treasures of the house of the LORD and of the king's house, and sent to Benhadad king of Syria, that dwelt at Damascus, saying,

There is a league between me and thee, as there was between my father and thy father: behold, I have sent thee silver and gold; go, break thy league with Baasha king of Israel, that he may depart from me.

And Benhadad hearkened unto King Asa, and sent the captains of his armies against the cities of Israel; and they smote Ijon, and Dan, and Abelmaim, and all the store cities of Naphtali.

How can we see faith in God in the one account, and faith in man in the other? Where did Asa place his trust in each example?

TYPES OF FAITH

The Bible speaks of four types of faith:

1. Historical Faith

2. Temporary Faith

3. Miraculous Faith

4. True Saving Faith

The root word of historical is "history." **Historical faith** is a believing that the facts and history of the Bible are true. A person with only historical faith knows of God and His Word and believes that that which is written in the Bible is true. But historical faith only involves a person's mind. There is no deep interest or need in this person's life for the salvation of which the Bible is speaking.

Each of you has probably received historical faith and believes that the Bible is a true book. Historical faith is good for we all need to know God's Word and to believe that it is true. We need to continually learn more about the truths of the Bible, but more than only historical faith is necessary for salvation. We also need true saving faith.

Historical faith can be compared to the crowd that watched the tightrope walker. They had heard of him and believed that he could cross the gorge, but they had no personal interest or involvement in this crossing. It would only become personal for them in their life's experience if they were to be placed into the wheelbarrow and actually cross the canyon!

Through our deep fall in Paradise and our daily sins, a deep gorge, a great separation, has been made between God — our righteous Creator, and us — a sinful people. There is only one way for sinners to be brought across this deep gorge of separation unto God and that is through faith in Jesus Christ.

WHAT DO YOU THINK?

PAUL ADDRESSING KING AGRIPPA

When speaking to King Agrippa, Paul asked, and stated:

"King Agrippa, **believest** thou the prophets? I know that thou **believest.**"
— Acts 26:27

King Agrippa answered in verse 28:

Almost thou persuadest me to be a Christian.

King Agrippa believed in his mind the history of Jesus. But he did not have a heartfelt concern and need to be delivered from his sin through the saving work of Jesus Christ. What type of faith did King Agrippa have?

What type of faith is referred to in the following verses?

And every one that **heareth** these sayings of Mine, **and doeth them not,** shall be likened unto a foolish man, which built his house upon the sand:
And the rain descended, and the floods came, and the winds blew, and beat upon that house; and it fell: and great was the fall of it.
— Matthew 7:26-27

Thou **believest** that there is one God; thou doest well: the devils also believe, and tremble.
— James 2:19

WHAT DO YOU THINK?

THE FAITH OF RUTH AND ORPAH

When Naomi desired to return to the land of Israel, both of her daughters-in-law wanted to go with her. Both Ruth and Orpah confessed, "Surely we will return with thee unto thy people." It seemed as though both girls sincerely meant this, for they both said this to Naomi with tears. This belief and desire was not only in their minds, but also in their emotions.

However, when they came to the border, to the final test, and when Orpah heard Naomi tell her of all that she would have to sacrifice and leave behind if she went over the border into Israel, then she went back to Moab. She returned to her former people and gods.

Ruth did not go back, however, even though she had to sacrifice all of the same things as Orpah. Instead, Ruth said to Naomi:

> Intreat me not to leave thee, or to return from following after thee: for whither thou goest, I will go; and where thou lodgest, I will lodge: thy people shall be my people, and thy God my God:
> Where thou diest, will I die, and there will I be buried: the LORD do so to me, and more also, if ought but death part thee and me.
> — Ruth 1:16-17

What do you think? What type of faith did Orpah have? What type of faith did Ruth have?

What type of faith is spoken about by the Lord Jesus in the following verses?

> But he that received the seed into stony places, the same is he that heareth the Word, and anon with joy receiveth it;
> Yet hath he not root in himself, but dureth for a while: for when tribulation or persecution ariseth because of the Word, by and by he is offended.
> — Matthew 13:20-21

We need to be personally awakened to truly see our miserable and sinful condition. Then we will see and feel the terrible condition we are in; being separated from God and lying under His condemnation. Then we will begin to experience a deep need, concern, and personal interest in the only Savior who can safely bring lost sinners across the deep gorge of separation.

This deep personal need for and experience of deliverance through Jesus Christ is missing in the life of a person with only historical faith.

Temporary faith is deeper than historical faith for it involves not only the mind, but also the conscience and feelings of the person. However, temporary faith does not last. The person may experience joy in believing and confessing the truth, and for a time it may appear to be true saving faith. However, later on temporary faith disappears, especially if the person must suffer or sacrifice something for the truth.

Temporary faith involves the mind and feelings of the person, but not his whole heart. It is like a person who appears interested in stepping into the wheelbarrow, but at the last moment turns back.

Temporary faith differs from true saving faith in the following five ways. Temporary faith:

1. Usually springs up quickly and grows rapidly

2. Appears to be free from doubts and fears

3. Causes the person to become more proud instead of humble

4. Does not result in a conversion of heart

5. Only lasts for a time

44

The root word of miraculous is "miracle." **Miraculous faith** is a belief that a miracle will be done by or for me. A person may possess miraculous faith without having true saving faith. He may be interested only in a special physical deliverance, but not in spiritual deliverance from sin. Neither does a person with only miraculous faith have a deep personal need to be brought across the great gorge of separation, from death in sin to life in God.

True saving faith differs from the three other types of faith we have studied. Only in true saving faith is the heart renewed. Only in true saving faith is the entire person with mind, emotions, and heart converted and turned from loving sin to serving God.

True saving faith is planted by God in a person's heart in the moment of regeneration. This person is then turned or converted to God. His conversion and true saving faith is experienced in a way of:

1. Misery

2. Deliverance

3. Thankfulness

When God regenerates someone, that person begins to feel his sin and **misery,** and starts to realize how far he has departed from God. He begins to see how holy and just God is and how sinful he is. He starts to understand how great a separation there is between God and his soul because of his sin.

He tries to improve his condition by overcoming sin, but the more he tries, the more sin he begins to see. He discovers

WHAT DO YOU THINK?

"WHERE ARE THE NINE?"

On a certain occasion, Jesus entered a village where ten lepers met Him. They all "lifted up their voices, and cried, 'Jesus, Master, have mercy on us.' " Jesus instructed them to travel to the priests, and on their way they would be healed. They all believed the words of Jesus and went to see the priests. As they walked, they were all healed. However, we read in the Bible:

> And one of them, when he saw that he was healed, turned back, and with a loud voice glorified God,
> And fell down on his face at His feet, giving Him thanks: and he was a Samaritan.
> And Jesus answering said, Were there not ten cleansed? but where are the nine?
> There are not found that returned to give glory to God, save this stranger.
> — Luke 17:15-18

Only one leper was truly thankful and needed Jesus after he was healed from his bodily disease. He returned and fell at Jesus' feet to praise Him. All ten believed that Jesus could heal their bodies. What type of faith did the ten lepers have? What type of faith do we see in the returning Samaritan?

Why type of faith is spoken of in the following verses?

> And though I have the gift of prophecy, and understand all mysteries, and all knowledge; and though I have all faith, so that I could remove mountains, and have not charity, I am nothing.
> — I Corinthians 13:2

> Not every one that saith unto Me, Lord, Lord, shall enter into the kingdom of heaven; but he that doeth the will of My Father which is in heaven.
> Many will say to Me in that day, Lord, Lord, have we not prophesied in Thy Name? and in Thy Name have cast out devils? and in Thy Name done many wonderful works?
> And then will I profess unto them, I never knew you: depart from Me, ye that work iniquity.
> — Matthew 7:21-23

45

WHAT DO YOU THINK?

I MUST BE IN THE LIFEBOAT!

Have you ever traveled on a large ferry or ship? As you walked around the ship, did you value or treasure the lifeboats which were stored on the ship? You will probably answer, "I knew they were on the ship, but I hardly even noticed them; I only saw them in passing."

But what would happen, do you think, if you were traveling far from the sight of land and the following events took place? As you were traveling, suddenly the ship's engine exploded with a blast that blew a large hole in the side of the ship. The hole cannot be repaired and the ship steadily fills with water! The rear part of the ship is now sinking under the water. Soon the rest of the boat will follow — it is only a matter of time! What would you think of the lifeboats now? Would you value or treasure them? You certainly would! In fact, they would now be the most important thing in your life; you must get into a lifeboat or you will perish!

What made the difference — you didn't value the lifeboats before, so why are they so important to you now? The lifeboats did not change. But now you experienced a felt need for a lifeboat and you could not survive without it.

This is a picture of what takes place spiritually in true conversion. We have heard of the Savior, Jesus Christ. But, by nature, we pay little or no attention to Him. We do not really need, cry out for, nor see the great value of Jesus Christ until we realize and experience that our lives are sinking and that we are lost without Him.

Why is it necessary to know *misery* before experiencing *deliverance* in a person's life?

that he does not only *do* certain sins, but that he *is* sin in the sight of God. His heart with its desires and motices are all sinful in God's sight. He tries to find a way to cross the great valley of separation from God, but he cannot. Everything he tries only makes his case worse instead of better, for God is perfectly holy and cannot have any fellowship with sin.

Yet, this sinner cannot remain separated from God either, for it has become a reality for him that God will justly punish all sinners. He discovers that he must cross the great gorge between God and his soul, but he cannot. His deep misery now becomes real to him and causes him true heartfelt sorrow.

When all is lost from his side, God opens his spiritual eyes to look in faith outside of himself for **deliverance.** He begins to see the Savior, Jesus Christ, in a new way, for now he has a deeply-felt need for this Savior in his life.

He begins to *know* Jesus Christ as He is presented in God's Word. He sees such a precious Person in Jesus and such a wonderfulness in His salvation. He learns that Jesus Christ is able to carry him, a totally lost sinner, across the deep gorge and bring him safely to the other side. This knowledge is not just in his mind or memory, as it is in historical faith, but it is experiential. It is known, felt, and experienced in his life with deep interest and concern of heart.

He also begins to *agree* with God's way of salvation. He is brought as a poor, needy, helpless and begging sinner to ask and plead for complete salvation in Jesus Christ. Before this, he was too proud; but now he accepts the just punishment he deserves. He prays to Jesus Christ to save him, even though he is and feels himself to be a totally unworthy sinner. He now sees and believes that Jesus *can* save him, but *will* He?

Finally, this person begins to *trust* in this Savior. He begins to hope, believe, and trust that Jesus Christ will save him. He places his life and salvation in Jesus Christ by faith. He clings to Christ to carry him across the gorge of separation. His only hope and trust is in Jesus. Jesus Christ is now everything and he is nothing in his experience of salvation.

All such sinners who have been made poor and needy in themselves, but who may also place all their hope and faith in Jesus Christ, shall be delivered by the Savior. Jesus Christ shall safely bring them across the great gorge of separation, delivering them from sin and death and bring them unto God and eternal life.

When a person experiences something of God's deliverance in Jesus Christ, he will be filled with true **thankfulness.**

WHAT DO YOU THINK?

MISERY, DELIVERANCE, AND THANKFULNESS

Can you find the experience of misery, deliverance, and thankfulness described in the following biblical examples?

Psalm 40:2-3

He brought me up also out of an horrible pit, out of the miry clay, and set my feet upon a rock; and established my goings.

And He hath put a new song in my mouth, even praise unto our God: many shall see it, and fear, and shall trust in the LORD.

Psalm 50:15

And call upon Me in the day of trouble: I will deliver thee, and thou shalt glorify Me.

Romans 7:24-25a

O wretched man that I am! who shall deliver me from the body of this death?

I thank God through Jesus Christ our Lord.

Ephesians 5:8

For ye were sometimes darkness, but now are ye light in the Lord: walk as children of light.

Can you find misery, deliverance, and thankfulness in the life of the Ethiopian eunuch? Read Acts 8:26-39 in your Bible.

What did you find in verses 26-31?

What did you locate in verses 32-38?

What did you discover in verse 39?

WHAT DO YOU THINK?

LOST!

One cold wintry afternoon, Willie was sent to deliver a message for his parents. He had to walk about three miles, and as he started out, the snow began to fall very fast. However, Willie bravely hurried on. At last he was able to deliver his message and was soon on his way home again.

As he started back, Willie walked as fast as he could, but the snow fell faster and began blowing into drifts. To make matters worse, night was beginning to fall and he still was far from home. The snow was soon more than knee-deep, making it very difficult to continue. As darkness fell, Willie could no longer see where he was going, and soon strayed from the path. He was lost!

Willie stumbled on through the horrible darkness, fighting his way against the bitterly cold wind and blinding snow. However, no matter how he tried, he could not find his path again. He no longer had any idea where he was going, and his strength was beginning to fail as he struggled on through the storm.

Suddenly, Willie fell into a deep hollow which had drifted full of snow. There he lay up to his chest in snow, unable to get out. The more he struggled, the deeper he sank. To make matters even worse, Willie realized that the snow was becoming deeper all the time. Soon it would cover him entirely! All hope of escape seemed to be cut off, and there was only one thing left to do — cry for help! Willie's half-choked voice began to call — "Lost! Lost! Lost!" Not knowing whether anyone would be able to hear him, Willie continued calling as loudly as he could with his failing strength.

When Willie did not return home, his parents became very worried. His father decided to go out and search for him. He soon found how impossible it was to find anything in the dark, stormy night. After searching in vain for more than an hour, the father was thoroughly exhausted and began to fear that he would have to give poor Willie up as lost. But listen! He heard a faint sound in the distance: "Lost! Lost! Lost!" Could it be true, or was it the echo of his own thoughts? He listened carefully and heard the voice again — more distinctly this time. "Lost! Lost! Lost!" It was Willie's voice. Joyfully the father shouted to Willie to keep calling so he could follow the sound. He soon found the treacherous hollow where poor Willie was helplessly trapped, and with much time and great effort, he rescued his dear son who had so narrowly escaped death. Great joy and thankfulness flooded through Willie when he was rescued and safely returned to his home. Never before had his humble home looked so inviting nor his parents seemed so dear to him.

Willie's experience in this true story can serve as a picture of the spiritual experience of conversion. When God begins to work savingly in people's hearts, they begin to see their sinfulness and to fight against it. But eventually their sin overpowers them and they experience their totally lost condition. They need to be saved and cannot save themselves. All their efforts only sink them deeper in the pit of sin. Then they begin to cry and call in prayer, "Help! Lost! Lost! Lost!" What surprise, joy, and love is experienced when God the Father finds His lost children, when they are delivered through Jesus Christ! What thankfulness fills their hearts when they are saved and restored!

Some people experience conversion in a short and sudden way, as Paul in the Bible. For others it is more slow and gradual as with Timothy. The length of time does not matter, but the reality of conversion is of prime importance. We must experience conversion — it must be real in our lives. Conversion is experienced in a way of misery, deliverance, and thankfulness. Can you find the experience of these three items in Willie's experience? How can this be compared with misery, deliverance, and thankfulness being experienced in true conversion to God?

— Adapted from *Religious Stories for Young and Old: Volume IV*

His heart will overflow with love unto God who saved such a poor, rebellious, and hell-worthy sinner as he is. The desire of his heart will be to love, serve, and honor God. He will desire to live more and more perfectly; to walk according to God's will and to do that which pleases the Lord. He desires to follow God's will and law, not only because he is required to, but, because he wants to. He can never sufficiently repay the Lord for all the goodness and mercy which God has shown toward him.

Can you relate to this experience of true saving faith? Do you know something of misery, deliverance, and thankfulness in your life? We need to know, in the experience of our hearts, something of the knowing of, agreeing with, and trusting in Jesus Christ which is found in true saving faith.

This is God's plan and method of saving lost sinners — there is no other way!

Neither is there salvation in any other: for there is none other name under heaven given among men, whereby we must be saved.
— Acts 4:12

And that *no man can say that Jesus is the Lord, but by the Holy Ghost.*
— I Corinthians 12:3b

So then *faith cometh* by hearing, and hearing *by the Word of God.*
— Romans 10:17

True saving faith is planted and strengthened by the Holy Spirit through the means of the Word of God. Do you often ask God to bless His Word to your heart?

WHAT DO YOU THINK?

THE THREE THINGS NECESSARY TO KNOW

Read **Question and Answer 2** of the **Heidelberg Catechism:**

> Q.2 How many things are necessary for thee to know, that thou, enjoying this comfort, mayest live and die happily?
> A. Three; the first, how great my sins and miseries are; the second, how I may be delivered from all my sins and miseries; the third, how I shall express my gratitude to God for such deliverance.

What are the **three things** mentioned in this answer. **How** must we know these three things? What are the three main parts of the **Heidelberg Catechism**? Why is it divided in this manner?

Read the three parts of true self-examination as they are described in the **Form for the Administration of the Lord's Supper:**

> **First.** That every one consider by himself, his sins and the curse due to him for them, to the end that he may abhor and humble himself before God: considering that the wrath of God against sin is so great, that (rather than it should go unpunished) He hath punished the same in His beloved Son Jesus Christ, with the bitter and shameful death of the cross.

> **Secondly.** That every one examine his own heart, whether he doth believe this faithful promise of God, that all his sins are forgiven him only for the sake of the passion and death of Jesus Christ, and that the perfect righteousness of Christ is imputed and freely given him as his own, yea, so perfectly, as if he had satisfied in his own person for all his sins, and fulfilled all righteousness.

> **Thirdly.** That every one examine his own conscience, whether he purposeth henceforth to show true thankfulness to God in his whole life, and to walk uprightly before Him; as also, whether he hath laid aside unfeignedly all enmity, hatred, and envy, and doth firmly resolve henceforward to walk in true love and peace with his neighbor.

What are the three things being described in this form?

49

WHAT DO YOU THINK?

THE HIGHLAND KITCHEN MAID

Many years ago a minister was traveling to a large city in Scotland. One evening he stopped at a small inn, hoping to continue his journey the following day. As was his custom when staying at an inn, he called the family together for worship. When the family was gathered, the minister asked if everyone in the house was present. The landlord answered, "Yes."

"Everyone?" asked the minister again.

"Yes," answered the landlord. "Everyone is here except the kitchen maid, but she is so dirty that we did not call her."

"Please call her," answered the minister. "She also has a precious soul." When the landlord still hesitated, the minister stated, "We will wait until she comes." The girl was finally called, and the service began.

After the service, the minister spoke to the little girl privately and found that she did not know anything about spiritual things.

"Who made you?" he asked.

"I don't know."

"Do you know that you have a soul?"

"No, I never heard that before. What is a soul?"

"Do you ever pray?"

"I don't know what you mean."

Finally the minister said, "I am going to Edinburgh and I will buy you a beautiful scarf if you promise to say a short prayer each morning and evening. The prayer has only four words. Just pray, 'Lord, show me myself.' If you promise to pray this prayer, I will bring you the scarf."

The girl was delighted at the thought of the scarf. The prayer was short and easy to say, so she gave her promise gladly. The minister continued on his journey the next day, but did not forget the little girl.

Some time later the minister returned to the inn and again called the family to worship. Again the little girl was absent, but for a different reason. When he asked about her, the mistress said, "Oh, Reverend! Ever since you were here she has been of little help. She only sits and cries day and night, and by now she is so weak that she must stay in bed."

"Oh, please let me see the poor girl at once!" he exclaimed. They led him to a place beneath the stairs where the girl lay upon a straw bed.

"Well, my child," said the minister, here is the scarf which I have brought you from Edinburgh. I hope you have done what you promised, and said the prayer that I taught you."

"Oh no, Sir, I can never take your present. You taught me a prayer that God has answered in an awful way; He has shown me myself, and, oh, what a sight that is! Oh Reverend, what shall I do?"

It was very clear that the Holy Spirit had taught the little girl of her sinful misery. The minister spoke to her about Jesus Christ who came to seek and to save lost sinners, and taught her another short prayer. It was — "Lord, show me Thyself." The next morning he was once again on his way.

Many years passed by before the minister heard of the little girl again. When he was old, a woman came to his home to see him. She said, "You will not know me, but I am that little girl in the inn where you stayed as you traveled to Edinburgh many years ago. You taught me two short prayers. By the first I was brought to feel my need of a Savior; by the second I was led to behold that Savior Himself. I have traveled far to see you to tell you with my own lips the glorious things which, by your means, the Lord has been pleased to do for my soul."

What prayer did God bless to teach this girl of her misery? to teach her deliverance? Do you ask the Lord to "show you yourself" and to "show you Himself" — the Lord Jesus Christ?

— Adapted from *The NRC Banner of Truth*

God plants true saving faith in the hearts of His people in regeneration. God's children also need the Holy Spirit to exercise this faith after regeneration. If God would leave them over to themselves, then their old, doubting, sinful nature would quickly get the upper hand. Their old nature causes them to sin and keeps them from serving God perfectly. Do you remember the pictures and explanations of this truth given in Chapter Twelve?

How can you see the old and the new nature at spiritual war in the daily experience of the Apostle Paul in the following verses?

> For that which I do I allow not; for *what I would, that do I not*; but *what I hate, that do I.*
> — Romans 7:15

> For the *good* that I would *I do not*: but the *evil* which I would not, that *I do.*
> — Romans 7:19

Is this struggle also taking place in your life?

WHAT DO YOU THINK?

THE SAME ELIJAH?

Read the following verses about Elijah on Mount Carmel.

I Kings 18:21-22, 38, 40

And Elijah came unto all the people and said, How long halt ye between two opinions? if the LORD be God, follow Him: but if Baal, then follow him. And the people answered him not a word.

Then said Elijah unto the people, I, even I only, remain a prophet of the LORD; but Baal's prophets are four hundred and fifty men.

Then the fire of the LORD fell, and consumed the burnt sacrifice, and the wood, and the stones, and the dust, and licked up the water that was in the trench.

And Elijah said unto them, Take the prophets of Baal; let not one of them escape. And they took them: and Elijah brought them down to the brook Kishon, and slew them there.

How are these verses very different from that which we read in:

I Kings 19:1-3?

And Ahab told Jezebel all that Elijah had done, and withal how he had slain all the prophets with the sword.

Then Jezebel sent a messenger unto Elijah, saying, So let the gods do to me, and more also, if I make not thy life as the life of one of them by tomorrow about this time.

And when he saw that, he arose, and went for his life, and came to Beersheba, which belongeth to Judah, and left his servant there.

Is the same man being described in both of these chapters? Why is he so full of faith one day, and so fearful the next? How can this be?

MEMORIZATION QUESTIONS

Faith

1. By what do we become partakers of all that Christ obtained?
   Only by a true faith in Him (John 3:36).
2. May we believe in Christ?
   Yes indeed; because God commands us to (I John 3:23).
3. Can we then believe of ourselves?
   No; it is a gift of God, which He graciously bestows (Philippians 1:29).
4. How does God work this faith?
   God opens the heart by His Word and Spirit.
5. What do we then do?
   Then we attend to those things spoken to us by God in His Word (Acts 16:14).
6. Whom then, do we learn to know from the Word of God?
   We then learn to know Christ as the only and complete Savior (I Corinthians 1:30).
7. What do we then desire?
   To be saved by that Savior only.
8. What do we receive through this true faith?
   Forgiveness of all our sins, a new heart, and eternal life.
9. What constrains us to believe in Christ thus?
   The knowledge of our sins and misery, and the love of Christ.
10. Does the love of Christ excite us to love Him also?
    Yes, we love Him because He first loved us (I John 4:19).

— Donner's Catechism: Lesson XIV

CHECKING YOUR READING

1. Name and define the four types of faith found in the Word of God:
   a. _____ — _____

   _____

   b. _____ — _____

   _____

   _____

   c. _____ — _____

   _____

   d. _____ — _____

   _____

2. How is temporary faith:
   a. Deeper than historical faith?_____

   _____

   _____

   b. Different from true saving faith? _____

   _____

   _____

3. Define the three parts of faith as they are found in true saving faith:
   a. Knowledge — _____

   _____

   _____

   b. Agreement (Assent or Consent) — _____

   _____

   _____

   c. Trust (Confidence) — _____

   _____

   _____

4. What are the three parts of true religious experience?
   a. _____
   b. _____
   c. _____

CHECKING YOUR READING

5. Why must misery be experienced before deliverance or thankfulness?

   _____

   _____

   _____

6. a. Who works true saving faith in a person's heart? _____

   b. By what means does He work this faith? _____

   _____

7. a. What are the three main parts of the **Heidelberg Catechism**?

      1. _____ 2. _____ 3. _____

   b. Why is the Catechism divided in this manner? _____

   _____

━━━━━━━━ EXTRA CHALLENGE QUESTIONS ━━━━━━━━

1. From the story **You . . . In the Wheelbarrow,** when speaking of faith, explain how agreement and trust are deeper than only knowledge:_____

   _____

   _____

2. From the story **The Same Elijah?,** explain how it is possible for Elijah to be so strong and bold in faith one day and so fearful the next: _____

   _____

   _____

3. Read the Parable of the Sower in Matthew 13:3-9. What type of faith is described in:

   a. Verses 5-6? _____

   b. Verse 7? _____

   c. Verse 8? _____

4. God's children not only need God to plant true saving faith in their hearts, but also to strengthen and exercise their faith daily. Why?_____

   _____

   _____

CHAPTER 14

1773   HEBREWS 9

of goats, and the ashes of an heifer sprinkling the unclean, sanctifieth to the purifying of the flesh:

14 How much more shall the blood of Christ, who through the eternal Spirit offered himself without spot to God, purge your conscience from dead works to serve the living God?

15 And for this cause he is the mediator of the new testament, that by means of death, for the redemption of the transgressions that were under the first testament, they which are called might receive the promise of eternal inheritance.

JUSTIFICATION
SANCTIFICATION

VOCABULARY

1. **Sentence** — A judge's pronouncement of a guilty person's punishment

2. **Substitute** — One who takes the place of another

3. **Justification** — God's gift of the forgiveness of the guilt of sin and the right to eternal life for Christ's sake

4. **Adoption** — The legal act of bringing a child into one's family as his own

5. **Assurance** — The state of having full confidence

6. **Dedicated** — Set apart for a religious or special purpose

7. **Sanctification** — God's gift of the washing away of the pollution of sin and of dedication unto Him for Christ's sake

8. **Purify** — To wash; to cleanse from the pollution of sin

9. **Enlivening** — Giving life to; making more active

10. **Gradual** — Changing by steps or degrees; changing little by little

JUSTIFICATION

WHAT DO YOU THINK?

DECLARED FREE!

Robert was a poor, twelve-year-old orphan. His father and mother had died in an accident and he had recently found a place to live on a nice farm close to his town. After school he helped with various chores on this farm.

One afternoon Robert was driving the tractor in a field behind the barn. As he came to the top of a hill, he saw a nest of young birds on the ground just ahead of him. He stopped the tractor, jumped off, and ran to the nest to have a closer look.

When he turned to walk back to the tractor, he panicked. The tractor was rolling down the hill and picking up speed as it went. He had forgotten to set the brake! Robert ran at full speed after the tractor, but he could not catch it. He yelled and screamed but it did not help. Robert could see a car coming on the road below. He yelled again . . . but it was too late! The tractor crashed directly into the side of the car.

Poor Robert was taken to court. After the judge heard the entire story, he had to declare Robert guilty. Robert had not set the tractor's brake, and therefore it was his fault. The damages to the car totalled $4,500 and Robert did not have a dollar with which to pay. What could he do? He could not pay and yet he must!

Just as the judge was ready to sentence him, a stranger stepped forward and spoke to the judge. "Your Honor, I have heard the boy's case," he said, "and I will pay the full amount for him. You may charge the entire $4,500 to my account." With that, the stranger wrote out a check for the full price.

The judge accepted the check and said, "I declare this young man free!"

How do you think Robert felt? What spiritual truth concerning a guilty sinner is pictured in this story? Can you also see how the work of Jesus Christ as Savior is pictured here? We will see this more clearly as we study this chapter on "justification."

Since our deep fall, all our us are more guilty and in greater debt than Robert in the story, **Declared Free.** We continually sin more intentionally than Robert did, and are in debt for a far greater amount than he was. We have an infinite debt from our original sin in Paradise and from our daily sins in thoughts, words, and actions.

Neither do we have anything with which to pay. By nature we only sin more and more; even our best deeds are full of sin in God's sight. What will our **sentence** be? The Bible tells us that "the wages of sin is death." We deserve eternal death in hell for our sins.

Is there not any hope for us then? From our side there is not, but from God's side there is! The Lord Jesus was willing to suffer and die to pay the full price for the sins of His people. Jesus gives a full payment to His Father, the Heavenly Judge, who then pronounces "free" all those for whom Christ fully paid.

The heart is deceitful above all things, and desperately wicked: who can know it?
— Jeremiah 17:9

But we are all as an unclean thing, and *all our righteousnesses are as filthy rags.*
— Isaiah 64:6a

For *the wages of sin is death.*
— Romans 6:23a

For it is written, *Cursed is every one that continueth not in all things* which are written in the Book of the law to do them.
— Galatians 3:10b

Then shall He say also unto them on the left hand, *Depart from Me, ye cursed, into everlasting fire,* prepared for the devil and his angels.
— Matthew 25:41

But He was wounded for our transgressions, He was bruised for our iniquities: the chastisement of our peace was upon Him; and *with His stripes we are healed.*
— Isaiah 53:5

Even as the Son of man came not to be ministered unto, but to minister, and *to give His life a ransom for many.*
— Matthew 20:28

For this is My blood of the new testament, which is *shed for many* for the remission of sins.
— Matthew 26:28

Who was delivered for our offences, and was *raised again for our justification.*
— Romans 4:25

Christ hath redeemed us from the curse of the law, being made a curse for us: for it is written, *Cursed* is every one that hangeth on a tree.
— Galatians 3:13

This can be pictured as follows:

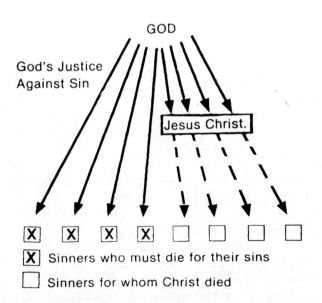

X Sinners who must die for their sins

☐ Sinners for whom Christ died

God does not forget nor overlook any sin, not even the sin of His people. God's children are spoken free because the Lord Jesus Christ

bore the full wrath of God against their sins for them. He took their place as a most wonderful **Substitute!** When God's children are spoken "free" on the basis of Christ's merits, this is called their **justification.**

Justification has two parts:

1. The forgiveness of all the guilt of sin

2. The right to eternal life through **adoption** by God as His child

> That they may receive *forgiveness* of sins, and *inheritance* among them which are sanctified by faith that is in Me.
> — Acts 26:18b

What a wonder it is for a poor sinner to learn that all the guilt of his sin is paid; that he is completely forgiven and granted a right to eternal life as a child of God! He will now enter heaven when he actually deserves hell! All this is possible for sinners because of God's free grace! Are you asking for or have you received this most precious gift?

WHAT DO YOU THINK?

ANIMAL SACRIFICES

In the Old Testament we often read of animals being killed and sacrificed. Think of the sacrifices of Abel, Noah, Abraham, Moses, the Tabernacle worship, Samuel, David, Solomon, the Temple worship, and several other examples.

Could a person's sins be forgiven by the blood of an animal? To whom did all these sacrifices point? To what did this blood-shedding refer? Only on the basis of which sacrifice can a sinner be justified? Why?

WHAT DO YOU THINK?

FROM ORPHAN TO PRINCE!

A poor orphan boy lived in a large city. He tried for several days to find a home and job, but could not. He barely managed to stay alive by stealing food here or there in the outdoor market of the city.

One morning, however, he was caught by the owner of a vegetable stand. "Ah-hah! I got you, you little rascal and thief!" he yelled. "Come people, help me teach this little thief a lesson!"

A crowd gathered and the poor, crying orphan boy was dragged up onto a large platform to receive a severe, public beating.

Suddenly everyone stopped and stepped aside. The king of the country walked forward to the stand. He had observed what was happening and now stepped forward. "I wish to adopt this boy as my own," he stated. "Here is more than enough money to cover your loss," he said to the vegetable seller.

The orphan boy was taken to the palace and, as an adopted son of the king, received all the rights and privileges of a prince.

How do you think this orphan boy felt? How do God's people receive an even greater change of condition than this boy in their justification?

WHAT DO YOU THINK?

A LIVING PIPELINE

Imagine a large oil field lying under a certain town. The people in the town are very poor and starving. They would be able to provide for all their needs and become rich if they had possession of the oil which is located under their town.

What two things do they need?
1) They need to know that the oil is there
2) They need to be connected to the oil by a pipeline in order to receive it

Jesus Christ is a far richer source of spiritual wealth than a natural oil field and we are much poorer spiritually than these town people are materially. What two things do we need?
1) We need to know of Christ and His rich salvation
2) We need to be personally connected to Him by a "living pipeline" of true saving faith

What blessings would we receive from being connected to the Lord Jesus Christ by true saving faith? In what important way is the pipeline used in this example different from true saving faith?

Having predestinated us *unto the adoption of children by Jesus Christ* to Himself, according to the good pleasure of His will,

To the praise of the glory of His grace, wherein He hath made us accepted in the beloved.

In whom we have redemption through His blood, the forgiveness of sins, according to the riches of His grace.
— Ephesians 1:5-7

The Lord Jesus has paid the full price for many sinners with His suffering and death. There is an infinitely rich, never-ending supply of salvation in Jesus Christ. However, this will not be of personal benefit to a person if he is not connected to Him.

How can a person be connected to Jesus Christ and receive His benefits? This can only happen through true saving faith. This can be pictured in the following manner:

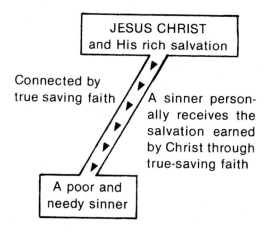

Study this diagram. A poor sinner is saved and justified because of Jesus Christ and the rich salvation earned by Him. A sinner is not saved *because* of his faith, but *by* faith. He is connected to Christ by faith and receives from Christ the salvation of which he stands in need. He is justified on the basis of the merits of Christ and receives these wonderful benefits by faith.

Therefore being *justified by faith,* we have peace with God through our Lord Jesus Christ.
— Romans 5:1

Even the righteousness of God which is *by faith of Jesus Christ* unto all and upon all them that believe: for there is no difference.
— Romans 3:22

And the Scripture, foreseeing that God would *justify* the heathen *through faith,* preached before the gospel unto Abraham, saying, In thee shall all nations be blessed.
— Galatians 3:8

Where does the *Heidelberg Catechism* emphasize the fact that sinners are not saved **because** of their faith, but **by** the faith they received from God? Who is their righteousness?

Do you see the great need for true saving faith in your life? Do you continually ask God for this? Have you received this faith from God? The suffering and death of Christ has no personal value for us unless we are connected to Him by true saving faith.

The Bible speaks of a *five-fold justification* for God's people. This is clearly shown in the chart below:

BY FAITH

The *Heidelberg Catechism*: Lord's Day XXIII

Q.59.   But what doth it profit thee now that thou believest all this?
A.   That I am righteous in Christ, before God, and an heir of eternal life.

Q.60.   How art thou righteous before God?
A.   Only by a true faith in Jesus Christ; so that, though my conscience accuse me, that I have grossly transgressed all the commandments of God, and kept none of them, and am still inclined to all evil; notwithstanding, God, without any merit of mine, but only of mere grace, grants and imputes to me, the perfect satisfaction, righteousness and holiness of Christ; even so, as if I never had had, nor committed any sin: yea, as if I had fully accomplished all that obedience which Christ has accomplished for me; inasmuch as I embrace such benefit with a believing heart.

Q. 61.   Why sayest thou, that thou art righteous by faith only?
A.   Not that I am acceptable to God, on account of the worthiness of my faith; but because only the satisfaction, righteousness, and holiness of Christ, is my righteousness before God; and that I cannot receive and apply the same to myself any other way than by faith only.

FIVE—FOLD JUSTIFICATION		
BEFORE FAITH	1) **From Eternity** in God's election election	Who hath saved us, and called us with an holy calling, not according to our works, but *according to His own purpose and grace, which was given us in Christ Jesus before the world began.* — II Timothy 1:9
	2) In the **Resurrection of Christ**	Who was delivered for our offences, and was *raised again for our justification.* — Romans 4:25
BY FAITH	3) In the **Moment of Regeneration**	Moreover whom He did predestinate, them *He also called: and whom He called, them He also justified:* and whom He justified, them He also glorified. — Romans 8:30
	4) In the **Court of One's Conscience**	But ye have received the Spirit of adoption, whereby we cry, Abba, Father. *The Spirit itself beareth witness with our spirit, that we are the children of God.* — Romans 8:15b-16
IN PUBLIC	5) On the **Final Judgment Day**	Henceforth there is laid up for me *a crown of righteousness, which the Lord, the righteous judge, shall give me at that day:* and not to me only, but unto all them also that love His appearing. — II Timothy 4:8

All of God's children are justified: from eternity, in the resurrection of Christ, when they are regenerated, and will be publically justified on the final Judgment Day. However, not all of God's children experience justification in their own consciences; not all have the personal **assurance** that they are justified children of God.

WHAT DO YOU THINK?

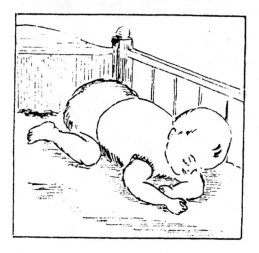

A HUMAN BEING . . . BUT NOT KNOWING IT

If you would ask this baby, "Are you a human being?" — what will she answer? She will not know. She cannot tell you if she is a human being or not because she has not reached the level of understanding required to know and say what she is. Is she a human being, however? You will answer, "Of course she is! She just isn't mature enough to tell you yet."

God's spiritual children also differ in spiritual maturity. Some are babes in grace; they do not know certainly nor can they testify with assurance that they are saved children of God. Are they children of God, however? How can we know? We can know from the scriptural marks of spiritual life. What is the first sign of human life when a baby is born? How is this the same in spiritual life?

> As newborn babes, desire the sincere milk of the Word, that ye may grow thereby.
> — I Peter 2:2

Read the following statement: "A child of God must be justified, but not necessarily know that he is justified. He must be a child of God, but not necessarily assured of it." Why is this statement true?

Sometimes they can have more hope of this than at other times. Sometimes they can believe they are children of God and other times not. All God's children must seek the Lord and use the means to grow in faith, but not all have the assurance of their personal justification.

> And we desire that every one of you do shew the same diligence to **the full assurance** of hope unto the end:
> That ye be not slothful, but followers of them who through faith and patience inherit the promises.
> — Hebrews 6:11-12

> Wherefore the rather, brethren, give diligence to **make your calling and election sure:** for if ye do these things, ye shall never fall.
> — II Peter 1:10

The foundation or basis of justification is found entirely in the work of the Lord Jesus Christ, not in the work of man. God demands a perfect righteousness which even the most holy child of God does not have.

> Knowing that a man is not **justified** by the works of the law, but **by the faith of Jesus Christ,** even we have believed in Jesus Christ, that we might be justified by the faith of Christ, and not by the works of the law: for by the works of the law shall no flesh be justified.
> — Galatians 2:16

> For by grace are ye **saved through faith;** and that not of yourselves: it is the gift of God:
> Not of works, lest any man should boast.
> — Ephesians 2:8-9

A person who is justified by God does not begin to live carelessly because all his sins are forgiven. The opposite is true. He now desires to love and serve God from a deep feeling of thankfulness for such a wonderful and gracious deliverance. He wants to live more holily, flee from the pollution of sin, do good works, and be more and more **dedicated** unto God. This process is called **"sanctification."** Sanctification is always connected to justification. These two cannot be separated, but always go together. Both are God's work for and in His people.

SANCTIFICATION

The word "sanctify" means to cleanse, **purify**, separate, and dedicate to God. Sanctification refers to God's children being washed by God from the filthiness and pollution of sin and becoming more and more holy through the work of His Spirit. Sanctification and justification are both gifts of God to His chosen people.

Sanctification includes two parts:

1. The continual **dying** of the **old nature**
2. The continual **enlivening** of the **new nature**

Husbands, love your wives, even as Christ also loved the Church, and gave Himself for it;

That He might **sanctify** and cleanse it **with the washing of water** by the Word,

That He might present it to Himself a glorious Church, not having spot, or wrinkle, or any such thing; but that it should be holy and without blemish.

— Ephesians 5:25-27

1) Turning **away** from:

| Sin |
| World |
| Self |
| Satan |

2) Turning **toward:**

| God |
| Neighbor |

Sanctification grows out of conversion. If a person's heart is turned toward God in conversion, then his deepest desire is to flee from sin and do that which is pleasing to God. Conversion and sanctification can be pictured by turning a globe. When we turn a globe, it turns **away** from something and turns **toward** something else at the same time. Conversion is the turning; sanctification is the result of the turning — living a life according to God's commandments.

Sanctification is different from justification in the following ways:

1. Justification removes the **guilt** of sin; sanctification removes the **pollution** of sin.

2. Justification is an act of God **outside** of the person; sanctification is an act of God **inside** the person.

3. Justification is **instant and complete;** sanctification is **gradual and lifelong.**

How much more shall the **blood of Christ**, who through the eternal Spirit offered Himself without spot to God, **purge** your conscience from dead works to serve the living God?
— Hebrews 9:14

Sanctification is a gradual, lifelong experience in the hearts of God's children. There are two natures in the hearts of those who are converted. Do you remember this drawing?

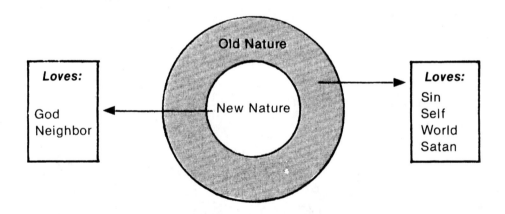

God the Holy Spirit works sanctification in the hearts of all true believers and causes them to grow in faith. The Holy Spirit works through means to produce this growing in faith. God's children are commanded to fight against sin and actively use the means of grace which God has provided. They must avoid sinful: places, temptations, company, worldly lusts, selfish desires, and all other types of yielding to sin. Instead, true believers must actively read and study their Bibles, listen attentively to the preaching of God's Word, sincerely ask God's blessing in prayer, seek the company of other children of God, and use all the means of grace that the Lord has given them. God the Holy Spirit will graciously bless the use of these means of grace to increase their growth in sanctification.

WHAT DO YOU THINK?

BEWARE OF BAD FRIENDS

Once again, Will had gone down to the docks to see Sam Jones. He knew his mother was probably worried about him, but Will was becoming more and more attracted to Sam's invitation to go to sea.

Sam was a wild boy with rebellious ideas who often used rough language, but he told Will of the wonderful things he had seen in far-away lands. "Come on, Will," he urged. "My Dad is the skipper and I know he will take you. Think of how much fun we could have together!"

"But Mother won't let me go," Will answered. "Besides, Captain Downe says I'm too young."

Sam's reply was an oath filled with rough language. Yet Will would not admit to himself that Sam was bad company for him, and kept visiting the docks in spite of the warning voice of his conscience.

At home, Will told his mother, "I want to go to sea. Sam's father is willing to take me on."

"Oh, Will!" his mother cried. "You are all I have. I cannot part with you yet!"

"I'll have to go sometime," Will grumbled. He refused to think about his mother. She was a widow and in poor health. She needed all the love and support he could give her. But that interfered with his longing to go to sea with Sam. Consequently, he was not as pleasant to his mother as he should have been, and would often answer her roughly or not do that which she asked. His mother

became very worried and brought her concerns before the Lord. She often prayed, "Lord, I am afraid that Will is under bad influence. Please keep my boy from going astray."

One Saturday evening Will sat up late watching his mother. "Oh, Mother!" he said. "All you do is stitch, stitch, stitch! You will wear yourself out."

"I don't mind as long as you are here," she replied smiling.

Will shut his book and went to bed. "If only I could go to sea," he muttered, "at least I could earn something so she would not have to work so hard."

The next morning, Will awoke with the warm sun shining on him and the clean clothes which his mother had laid out for him. How fresh and neat they looked; and there too was his mother's work from the previous night, a new pair of pants which she had finished for him to wear to church.

"How good and dear Mother is!" he exclaimed, and again his eyes returned to the clothes. Somehow they brought out his mother's love and care as never before. In a wonderful way Will's heart and conscience were touched. Tears filled his eyes;

not proud, angry, wilful tears because he could not have his own way; but sweet, penitent tears for grieving such a love as hers. "I will never, never hurt her by going to sea, or even by mentioning it again," he decided, and he kept his promise.

Not long after this, he went to work for a carpenter. One day Sam Jones came to see him. In his usual rough language he told Will that he had found a place for him. "You must come now," he said. "Run away tonight."

"No," said Will. "My duty and decision is to stay at home with my mother, and that is final." When Sam saw that Will's mind was made up, he went away. It was not hard for Will to get rid of bad company once he decided to.

A year later, Will's mother died. He felt that he could never thank God enough for speaking to his conscience on that sunny, Sunday morning, and keeping him at home! It was the beginning of the best year of his life when he was happy doing all he could for his dear mother.

Is it important what types of people we have for friends? Why? Why can this be an important means to promote or hinder a person's growth in sanctification?

— Adapted from *The NRC Banner of Truth*

WHAT DO YOU THINK?

CAN YOU ASK GOD'S BLESSING ON IT?

Elizabeth had been brought up by God-fearing parents. Yet here she was, getting ready for a dance. Dressed in a fancy gown, she inspected herself in the mirror once more. Then seeing her mother, she turned and said, "Why, Mother! What makes you look so sad? The big night is here at last. Come and help me arrange this rose in my hair. Don't you think I look nice tonight?"

Her mother sighed and kissed her cheek. As she said goodbye to her daughter, she whispered, "Can you ask God's blessing on the dance, Elizabeth?" The excited girl paused to give her a thoughtful glance before hurrying out the door.

Elizabeth came home earlier than usual that night. Her mother came down to meet her, but found that Elizabeth had gone directly to her room. As she approached Elizabeth's door, she suddenly stopped. She could hear Elizabeth's voice — she was praying! "Hear my prayer, oh Lord, I beseech Thee, and let my cry come before Thee."

Finally her mother could not wait any longer. She knocked and entered her room. "Oh Mother!" Elizabeth cried. "I had to come home early. All evening I danced with the merriest and laughed with the loudest, but there was an arrow in my heart. All evening I have had the words 'God's blessing on the dance!' ringing in my ears. Oh! If only the Lord will forgive the past! If He will yet receive me, I will lay my whole heart on His altar."

They knelt together and asked God to bless and strengthen the impression Elizabeth had received. God answered this prayer and later among God's children, Elizabeth set a humble, meek, and modest example.

Why is the title of this story such an important question in sanctification? Are the types of places we attend important? Why?

— Adapted from *The NRC Banner of Truth*

Satan hates God and His work. He is continually trying to interfere, ruin, or delay God's work. Satan will also try to tempt and lead God's people into sin. Therefore God warns us in His Word to be on our guard against Satan and all his tricks and devices.

Be sober, be vigilant; because your adversary the **devil,** as a roaring lion, walketh about, **seeking whom he may devour.**
— I Peter 5:8

The **statutes of the LORD** are right, **rejoicing the heart:** the commandment of the LORD is pure, enlightening the eyes.
— Psalm 19:8

I have **rejoiced** in the way of Thy **testimonies,** as much as in all riches.
I will meditate in Thy precepts, and have respect unto Thy ways.
I will **delight myself in Thy statutes:** I will not forget Thy Word.
— Psalm 119:14-16

Lest **Satan should get an advantage of us:** for we are not ignorant of his devices.
— II Corinthians 2:11

Sanctification reveals itself in good works. If we love someone, then we want to do what pleases that person. God's children love God and desire to do that which is pleasing to Him.

We can know that which is pleasing to God from God's Word and law. It is the heart's desire of all God's children to live perfectly for the Lord and to do His will entirely. They love God's law and desire to keep His commandments; not only because they are **required** to, but because they **want** to.

WHAT DO YOU THINK?

AN ENEMY IN DISGUISE

"I will stand guard tonight," announced Hugh, a brave young soldier. A shocked silence followed his announcement. They were fighting a war with the Indians and on each of the four previous nights, the guard on duty had been killed. Now Hugh had offered to take the dangerous position of guard for that night. At last one of his friends spoke. "You will be number five!" he said, breaking the stunned silence.

"Oh, don't worry," Hugh replied. "I have orders to shoot anything that moves, and you can be sure that even if it is only a bird, I'll do it!"

That night as he stood guard, Hugh could not help picturing the faces of his four dead friends. His senses were very sharp as he realized the great danger he was now in. His post was on a small hill, and between him and the distant forest was a stretch of partially-cleared land. Hugh remained alert through the long hours of the night but no sign of life broke the stillness.

As dawn began to steal across the sky, Hugh almost felt disappointed that nothing had happened to share with his friends. At the same time he idly watched as a wild hog

left the safety of the forest. It seemed to be picking up food as it gradually came closer. Hugh paid little attention to the animal until, when it was quite close already, he remembered his orders to shoot **anything** that moved.

"Well," he thought, "I must follow orders, even though the beast is hardly worth the bullet." So thinking, he took careful aim at the hog and fired.

The sharp cry of a wounded Indian broke the stillness which brought two other soldiers charging to the spot. They discovered that an Indian had cleverly disguised himself as a wild hog and had nearly succeeded in coming close enough to kill guard number five.

Hugh was filled with deep gratitude and thankfulness to God when he saw how narrowly he had escaped death. He had been saved by the wonderful providence and mercy of God.

This story of natural war can be used as an example of spiritual warfare in the hearts of God's children. Who is their enemy? Why do they have to be on their guard all the time? What are some of Satan's disguises and tricks? Why must we strive to kill all sins and temptations?

— Adapted from **The NRC Banner of Truth**

God's people love God more than anything else and wish to live entirely for the Lord.

Due to our sinful nature, which remains with us until we die, it is not possible for anyone, not even God's most holy child, to live perfectly in this life. Everyone sins, but God's children experience a heartfelt sorrow for their sin and a sincere desire to strive to avoid sin in the future.

If we say that **we have no sin, we deceive ourselves,** and the truth is not in us.

— I John 1:8

For the **good** that I would **I do not:** but the **evil** which I would not, that **I do.**

— Romans 7:19

God the Holy Spirit leads His children in a way of spiritual growth. There is a growing in sanctification in the lives of true believers. However, as the Holy Spirit reveals more of their sinful hearts unto them, they become more humble. They cannot trust or rest in themselves nor in their works. Their experience directs them outside of themselves to seek their spiritual life and strength continually in Jesus Christ. More and more they learn that without God, they can do nothing but sin. Sanctification is a "plant" which grows roots downward concerning themselves to bring forth fruits upward to God. The more self is humbled, the more God is exalted in their lives. The Apostle Paul testified of this when he wrote: "When I am weak, then am I strong" (II Corinthians 12:10b).

One day all of God's children shall obtain a complete victory over sin. When they die, their old natures with all their sinful desires shall remain in the grave; but their new natures which desire to love, serve, honor, and glorify God perfectly, shall live and be with God forever. Then they shall fully receive the desire of their hearts to be with God and live fully dedicated lives unto Him!

Is this your desire? Or do you still desire to serve yourself, sin, and the world? Those who desire to die as God's people must also learn, by the gracious work of the Holy Spirit in their hearts, to live as God's people.

Do you know something of this? Do you earnestly ask and seek for this?

WHAT DO YOU THINK?

THE BLOOD AND WATER

When a priest walked into the courtyard of the tabernacle, he first came to the Brazen Altar of Burnt Offerings where he had to kill the sacrifice. He then walked to the Brazen Laver where he had to wash before approaching the presence of God in the sanctuary building. To what do the Brazen Altar of Burnt Offerings and the Brazen Laver point? How is this a picture of that which we studied in this lesson? Are the two items pictured by the altar and laver also necessary to approach unto God today?

MEMORIZATION QUESTIONS

1. What does the love of faith work in us?
    An upright and earnest desire to turn from our sins unto God (Lamentations 5:21).

2. Wherein does true repentence consist?
    In the first place; it is a godly sorrow for and a fleeing from sin (2 Corinthians 7:10).

3. What is it in the second place?
    An earnest striving after and a doing of all that which is pleasing unto God (Psalm 119:97).

4. From what do we know what sin is and what is pleasing to God?
    From the Holy Law of God (Psalm 19:8).

5. What does God command us in His Law?
    To love Him above all and our neighbor as ourselves (Matthew 22:37-40).

6. What does it mean to love God above all?
    To acknowledge God only, to trust in Him alone, and to obey Him only.

7. What do we do when we love our neighbor as ourselves?
    Then we do no harm to our neighbor, but only good.

8. Can we do this of ourselves?
    No; God gives desire and strength thereto, unto those who love Him (Philippians 2:13).

9. Can these, who are turned unto God, keep the Law perfectly?
    By no means; for James says: "For in many things we offend all" (James 3:2).

10. To what must this urge them?
    To faith and humble prayer (Psalm 119:4,5). — *Donner's Catechism: Lesson XV*

CHECKING YOUR READING

1. Answer the following questions concerning the large debt which we all owe to God by nature:

   a. Why do we have such a large debt? _____

   _____

   _____

   b. Why can we not pay for some or all of this debt? _____

   _____

   _____

   c. What is the only way in which we can be freed from this debt? _____

   _____

   _____

2. What are the two parts of justification?

   a. _____

   _____

   b. _____

   _____

3. If Jesus Christ has earned a rich salvation for sinners, and a person has learned that he is a poor and needy sinner, why does faith become so important and necessary for him? _____

   _____

   _____

4. List the types of justification which take place:

   a. Before faith?   1. _____

                           2. _____

   b. By faith?   3. _____

                           4. _____

   c. In public?   5. _____

5. What is the only basis or ground upon which a person can be justified? _____

   _____

   _____

6. What does the word "sanctify" mean? _____

   _____

   _____

CHECKING YOUR READING

7. Name the two parts of sanctification:

   a. _____

   b. _____

8. Describe three differences between justification and sanctification:

   a. _____
   _____

   b. _____
   _____

   c. _____
   _____

9. From what motive or desire do God's people do good works? _____
   _____

10. a. Why is sanctification never perfect in the lives of God's children on earth?_____
   _____

   b. Will God's children ever live perfectly without sin? Explain. _____
   _____
   _____

━━━━━━ EXTRA CHALLENGE QUESTIONS ━━━━━━

1. a. From the story **From Orphan to Prince,** describe two benefits which this orphan boy
   received which are similar to the two benefits God's people receive in their justification:

   1. _____

   2. _____

   b. Why are the benefits God's people receive much greater than this orphan boy's? _____
   _____

2. From the story **An Enemy in Disguise,** what lesson can be learned about the necessity to strictly
   obey God's command to kill **all** sin and temptation in our lives?_____
   _____
   _____

3. Why is it correct to say ''God's children are saved **by** faith'', but wrong to say ''God's children are
   saved **because** of their faith?'' _____
   _____

4. If God's children always remain saved after they are regenerated, does it make any difference
   how they live after their regeneration? Why or why not?
   _____
   _____

TESTING YOUR KNOWLEDGE

1. Name the type of faith which is pictured in the following Bible verses:

    a. I Corinthians 13:2b _____

    b. Matthew 13:5-6; 20-21 _____

    c. Acts 8:37 _____

    d. Acts 26:27-28 _____

2. How is true saving faith different from all other types of faith?

    _____

    _____

3. Read the story in Matthew 15:21-28 of the Canaanitish woman who came to the Lord Jesus. Which words show:

    a. The *knowledge* of faith within her? _____

    _____

    b. The *agreement* of faith within her? _____

    _____

    c. The *trusting* of faith within her? _____

    _____

4. a. Name the three parts of true religious experience in their proper order.

    1. _____

    2. _____

    3. _____

    b. Why must these three parts be experienced in this order? _____

    _____

    _____

5. In the story, **The Highland Kitchen Maid,** what is meant by the maid's prayer:

    a. "Show me myself?" _____

    _____

    b. "Show me Thyself?" _____

    _____

6. a. How can God's children be spoken free from the guilt of their sin and be given a right to eternal life? _____

    _____

    b. What do we call the receiving of these two gifts? _____

TESTING YOUR KNOWLEDGE

7. Explain from the story **A Living Pipeline**, how true saving faith in Jesus Christ can be compared to a "living pipeline." _____

_____

_____

8. Name the five types of justification found in a five-fold justification. Circle the ones which happen during a person's lifetime, put a ✓ by those which happened before a person was born and underline that which is yet to take place in the future.

    a. _____

    b. _____

    c. _____

    d. _____

    e. _____

9. a. Is it possible for a person to be a child of God and not to know this assuredly?

        Explain. _____

        _____

    b. What do Hebrews 6:11-12 and II Peter 1:10 teach about this?

        _____

        _____

10. Sanctification is a daily turning from _____, _____, _____, and _____ and a turning toward _____ and _____.

11. a. What must God's people strive to avoid and what must they actively use in their lives of sanctification?

        Avoid — _____

        Use — _____

    b. Can God's people do this in their own power? _____ Who do they need to work this in them? _____

12. When their love is active, God's children obey God's law because they _____ to and not only because they are _____ to. God's children desire to serve God _____.

WORD SEARCH

```
K N O I T A C I F I T S U J I H M O K H
S N A F J C H E S U B S T I T U T E U T
A D O P T I O N G P R L A I N M V B F I
N S D W E C N A R U S S A E M I O R L A
C C H N L I S T P D J F B P E S K U F F
T V A L B E J K C U F D E C N E T N E S
I M P F O T D L A O R I G T H R H A I U
F A N H B E A G T S D I T F F Y G D I O
I G A B H U C N E I J M F O K O N E L L
C S T U D T E M P O R A R Y F A I T H U
A R I A U M B S I E F S A T V U N A T C
T T R U E S A V I N G F A I T H E C A A
I G O E G O R L A I D U A E U A V I B R
O T R U S T I N G O F F A I T H I D C I
N G T H A N K F U L N E S S T D L E E M
A H T I A F L A C I R O T S I H N D G O
F A T U W O D E L I V E R A N C E L A H
```

Find and circle each of the twenty Vocabulary Words found in Chapters Thirteen and Fourteen. Then write the word next to its proper definition below:

Salvation from the greatest evil through Jesus Christ _____

The assent or consent of faith _____

Forgiveness of the guilt of sin and the right to eternal life for Christ's sake _____

A belief of the truth for a time with mind and emotions _____

To wash; to cleanse from pollution of sin _____

To know something of Christ and God's way of salvation through Him _____

Confidence; a resting in Jesus Christ and a placing of full hope and expectation in Him _____

A judge's pronouncement of a guilty person's punishment _____

Set apart for a religous or special purpose _____

A belief that a miracle will be done by or for us _____

One who takes the place of another _____

The state of having full confidence _____

A belief in and confession of the truths of the Bible with the mind only _____

Giving life to; making more active _____

The extremely lost condition sinners are in because of their sin and separation from God _____

The legal act of bringing a child into one's family as his own _____

Changing by steps or degrees _____

A belief and trust in God from a renewed heart _____

Gratitude; a sincere desire to know, honor, and serve God from a spirit of love to Him _____

The washing away of the pollution of sin and the dedication unto God _____

BIBLE STUDY QUESTIONS

Read the following chapters and write out the verse or verses which most clearly teach the following doctrinal truths:

1. Knowledge, agreement, and confidence of true saving faith —

    Knowledge — Matthew 15:_____ — _____

    _____

    _____

    Agreement — Matthew 15:_____ — _____

    _____

    _____

    Confidence — Matthew 15:_____ — _____

    _____

    _____

2. Misery, deliverance, and thankfulness —

    Romans 7:_____ (2 verses) — _____

    _____

    _____

    _____

3. Justification is **by** faith and not **because** of faith —

    Ephesians 2:_____ (2 verses) — _____

    _____

    _____

    _____

4. The struggle between the old and new natures —

    Romans 7:_____ — _____

    _____

    _____

PROJECT IDEAS

1. Write a report and make a poster on the four types of faith. Use several biblical examples.
2. Design a chart which teaches the five parts of a five-fold justification.
3. Draw a large picture of the tabernacle. Explain how the Brazen Altar is a picture of justification and the Brazen Laver is a picture of sanctification. Draw an arrow from your explanations to the Brazen Altar and Laver.

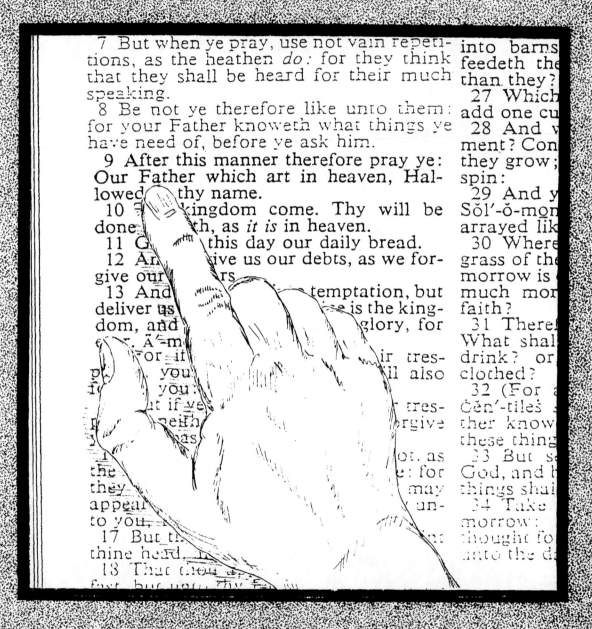

CHAPTER 15

7 But when ye pray, use not vain repetitions, as the heathen *do:* for they think that they shall be heard for their much speaking.

8 Be not ye therefore like unto them: for your Father knoweth what things ye have need of, before ye ask him.

9 After this manner therefore pray ye: Our Father which art in heaven, Hallowed ☐ thy name.

10 ☐ kingdom come. Thy will be done ☐ th, as *it is* in heaven.

11 G ☐ this day our daily bread.

12 An ☐ ive us our debts, as we forgive our ☐ rs

13 And ☐ temptation, but deliver us ☐ e is the kingdom, and ☐ glory, for ☐ Ā-m ☐

☐ For if ☐ ir tres-
☐ you ☐ ll also
☐ you: ☐
☐ t if ye ☐ tres-
☐ neith ☐ rgive
☐ as ☐
☐ ot as
the ☐ e: for
they ☐ may
appear ☐ un-
to you, ☐

17 But th ☐
thine head. ☐

18 That thou ☐
fast, but unto thy F ☐

into barns
feedeth the
than they?

27 Which
add one cu

28 And v
ment? Con
they grow;
spin:

29 And y
Sŏl'-ŏ-mon
arrayed lik

30 Where
grass of the
morrow is
much mor
faith?

31 There
What shall
drink? or
clothed?

32 (For a
Çĕn'-tiles
ther know
these thing

33 But s
God, and h
things shal

34 Take
morrow:
thought fo
unto the d

PRAYER

VOCABULARY

1. **Prayer** — Communion with God; the act of earnestly asking God for our needs, confessing our sins, and thanking Him for His blessings

2. **Communion** — The act of having spiritual friendship and fellowship

3. **Acknowledge** — To confess; to express thanks or appreciation for

4. **Reverence** — An attitude of deep respect; a worshipping of and bowing humbly before God

5. **Submission** — Obedience; the act of surrendering to, agreeing with, or placing oneself under

6. **Sincerity** — Honesty; truthfulness; free from deceit

7. **Urgency** — The state of being important and necessary; that which cannot be delayed

8. **Public** — That which is known to many; not private

9. **Humility** — Meekness; humbleness; having low thoughts of oneself

10. **Ceasing** — Stopping; coming to an end

PRAYER

What is **prayer**? The *Shorter Catechism* answers this question in the following manner:

> What is prayer? Prayer is an offering up of our desires unto God, for things agreeable to His will, in the Name of Christ, with confession of our sins, and thankful acknowledgement of His mercies.

Prayer is:

1. *Asking* God to care for our needs according to His will
2. *Thanking* God for all of His blessings
3. *Acknowledging* that all this is for Christ's sake and not for our sakes, because we are unworthy sinners

Prayer is **communion** or speaking with God. If you love someone, you wish to be with that person. You love to be in his presence and to speak with him. Likewise, God's people love being

WHAT DO YOU THINK?

MAN BROKE HIS FRIENDSHIP WITH GOD

After Adam and Eve fell into sin, did they continue to love God's presence or did they try to flee from God? We read in:

Genesis 3:8

And they heard the voice of the LORD God walking in the garden in the cool of the day: and Adam and his wife hid themselves from the presence of the LORD God amongst the trees of the garden.

Will a natural, unregenerated person love God and desire to seek His presence in prayer? Why not? What must take place first?

in the presence of God and speaking with Him. They do this in prayer.

In Paradise, before Adam fell, true prayer was natural. God walked with Adam in the cool of the day. As Creator and man, they loved one another and communed with each other as true friends.

Our deep fall into sin changed this beautiful relationship. God, who is perfectly holy, cannot have fellowship with sin. Fallen man now wanted to love and serve himself, sin, world, and Satan instead of God. True prayer and desiring to be in the presence of God is no longer the natural love of our hearts.

True prayer is now the result, the fruit of the Holy Spirit's saving work in a sinner's heart. After new spiritual life is planted in a person's soul, he truly loves God and desires His presence. Only then does he truly pray and truthfully ask, thank, and **acknowledge** God. True prayer must be offered from a principle of true saving faith.

Likewise the Spirit also helpeth our infirmities: for *we know not what we should pray for as we ought: but the Spirit itself maketh intercession* for us with groanings which cannot be uttered.
— Romans 8:26

But *without faith it is impossible to please Him:* for he that cometh to God must believe that He is, and that He is a rewarder of them that diligently seek Him.
— Hebrews 11:6

But let him *ask in faith,* nothing wavering. For he that wavereth is like a wave of the sea driven with the wind and tossed.
For let not that man think that he shall receive any thing of the Lord.
— James 1:6-7

This **does not** mean that unconverted people should not pray. Everyone should cry out to God for mercy; everyone should pray for true prayer. It **does** mean, however, that only the Holy Spirit can work true saving faith and love in our hearts.

True prayer includes the following elements:

ELEMENTS OF TRUE PRAYER

1. FAITH A believing and trusting in God	**James 1:6** But let him ask *in faith*, nothing wavering. For he that wavereth is like a wave of the sea driven with the wind and tossed.
Revelation 15:4 Who shall not *fear Thee*, O Lord, and glorify Thy Name? for *Thou only art holy:* for all nations shall come and worship before Thee; for Thy judgments are made manifest.	**2. REVERENCE** A deep respect for and worshipping of God
3. SUBMISSION A surrendering to God's will	**Luke 22:42** Saying, Father, if thou be willing, remove this cup from Me: nevertheless *not My will, but Thine, be done.*
Daniel 9:5 *We have sinned*, and have committed iniquity, and have done wickedly, and have rebelled, even by departing from Thy precepts and from Thy judgments.	**4. REPENTANCE** A confession of and turning away from sin
5. SINCERITY A truthfulness from the heart	**Psalm 17:1** Hear the right, O LORD attend unto my cry, give ear unto my prayer, that goeth *not out of feigned lips*.
Luke 18:3-5 And there was a widow in that city; and she came unto him, saying, Avenge me of mine adversary. And he would not for a while: but afterward he said within himself, Though I fear not God, nor regard man; Yet because this widow troubleth me, I will avenge her, lest by her *continual coming* she weary me.	**6. URGENCY** A felt need and concern which cannot be delayed

WHAT DO YOU THINK?

SINNERS MUST PRAY!

When still quite young, Rev. C. Spurgeon, a famous minister in England in the 1800's, was attacked by a group of older men after preaching a sermon. In his sermon, Rev. Spurgeon had urged all his listeners to pray and cry for mercy. A group of older men came to him after the service and argued with him, stating that God hates sinners and will not hear their cries.

An older lady was also waiting to speak to Rev. Spurgeon. After listening to the continual arguing of these men, she finally became angry, stepped forward, and said firmly, "You men leave the poor, young minister alone. I read in the Bible that God even hears the ravens' cries for food. Won't He then hear a poor sinner who is crying for mercy?"

The men left silently.

How do the following texts teach us that all people must pray?

Seek ye the LORD while He may be found, call ye upon Him while He is near.
— Isaiah 55:6

Those that seek Me early shall find Me.
— Proverbs 8:17b

He giveth to the beast his food, and to the young ravens which cry.
— Psalm 147:9

An unconverted person cannot pray with these six elements, for he has not received them from God in his heart. Yet, he is commanded to pray. What then must he do? He must cry out unto God, "Lord, teach me to pray," "God be merciful unto me, a sinner," or "Lord, please convert me that I too may pray with faith, **reverence, submission**, repentance, **sincerity**, and **urgency**."

WHAT DO YOU THINK?

TOO ANGRY TO PRAY!

Twelve-year-old Sally rode her bike to a shopping mall with several of her friends. When they returned to their bikes, Sally's bike was missing! After searching the entire area and speaking to the mall manager, they had to report it to the police as a stolen bicycle.

Poor Sally! When she arrived home she just cried and cried. How could she continue through the summer without a bike? Her parents could not afford to buy her another one. What could she do? Sally became angry. Why did it have to be her bike? There were probably fifty bikes there. Why hers?

That night, her mother noticed that Sally kept putting off going to bed. Finally, Sally burst into tears and sobbed, "Mother, I dare not to go to bed for I cannot pray. I am so angry. I...I... can't!"

Why couldn't Sally pray? What good attitude toward prayer could be seen in Sally here? Why is this attitude important in prayer?

Later in the evening, Sally's father left. He felt so sorry for her that he went and purchased a new bicycle for her. It was nicer than the one she had before. How surprised Sally was when she walked into the living room the following morning! She ran and hugged her parents, thanking them over and over and jumping up and down with excitement!

Suddenly she remembered something. Her face changed; her lips began to quiver, and she ran back to her bedroom! She fell on her knees and almost could not pray again, but for a different reason this time. What feeling was she full of now, do you think? Why is this attitude also important in prayer?

WHAT DO YOU THINK?

A SEVENTY-YEAR-OLD PRAYER

A seventy-three-year-old man often spoke about a prayer which his mother had taught him when he was three years old. He was quite proud to tell people that for seventy years he had repeated this prayer every night.

However, when God converted this man in his old age, he was led to see that his former life was only an outward form of godliness and that his desires came from his sinful pride.

God led him to seek for his deliverance in Jesus Christ. After this, he told people, "I am an old man who said my prayer for seventy years, and yet all that time, I never prayed at all."

What did this man mean by his last statement? What distinction was he making between his former prayers and his prayers after conversion?

— Adapted from *The Shorter Catechism Illustrated*

Prayer must be directed to God alone. We are forbidden to bow before or pray to saints or angels. How do the following texts speak of this truth?

> And as Peter was coming in, Cornelius met him, and fell down at his feet, and worshipped him.
>
> But Peter took him up, saying, Stand up; I myself also am a man.
>
> — Acts 10:25-26

> And I fell at his feet to worship him. And he said unto me, See thou do it not: I am thy fellowservant, and of thy brethren that have the testimony of Jesus: worship God: for the testimony of Jesus is the spirit of prophecy.
>
> — Revelation 19:10

> Then saith Jesus unto him, Get thee hence, Satan: for it is written, Thou shalt worship the Lord thy God, and Him only shalt thou serve.
>
> — Matthew 4:10

Prayer to God is very important and powerful. We could see the importance and power of our requests if we could bring them to the king of a country. How much more important it is when we may bring our needs before the Almighty God, the King of kings.

WHAT DO YOU THINK?

MOTHER AT PRAYER

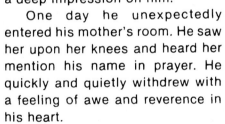

A well-known writer described a childhood experience which left a deep impression on him:

One day he unexpectedly entered his mother's room. He saw her upon her knees and heard her mention his name in prayer. He quickly and quietly withdrew with a feeling of awe and reverence in his heart.

As time went on, he completed his training at school and college, and entered his life's occupation. However, he never forgot that one glimpse of his mother at prayer, nor the one word, his own name, which he heard her speak. He realized that he had seen a glimpse of what went on every day in her sacred closet of prayer. This thought strengthened him often, especially in times of dangers and struggles in his daily life.

When his mother died, the sorest sense of loss he experienced was the knowledge that his mother was no longer praying for him.

Why was this mother of great value to her son? Why did her prayers have such an influence on him?

— Adapted from **The NRC Banner of Truth**

WHAT DO YOU THINK?

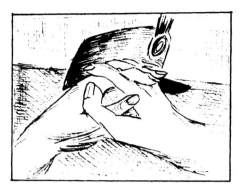

PRAYING SOLDIERS

Queen Wilhelmina of Holland once paid a visit to an army unit in 1914. The queen believed that the strongest army to defend their country would be a praying one. Therefore she asked some who paraded before her, "Who of you can pray?" She did not ask, "Who of you can fight well?" or "Who is very brave?" Her question was, "Who of you can pray?"

All eyes were on the queen, for they had not expected this question. They could fight, gamble, and swear; but pray? Most of them did not pray, and would have felt ashamed to be seen praying, and now their queen was asking who among them prayed.

The queen waited. At last, eight young men were found who acknowledged that they prayed. They had learned to pray at home, and had continued to pray in the army.

The queen spoke again. "Such soldiers are worth more than all the others," she said. "Such soldiers can defend our country." She then requested the soldiers to sing from Psalm 79:

Help us, God of our salvation,
For the glory of Thy Name;
For Thy Name's sake come and
    save us,
Take away our sin and shame.

Why were the most powerful soldiers praying ones?

— Adapted from **Young People's Magazine**

We are instructed by God to pray to Him for all things necessary for our soul and body, for ourselves, and for others. In more detail God directs us to pray for:

HUMAN NEEDS TO REMEMBER IN PRAYER	
1. *Our spiritual needs;* the forgiveness of our sin. Have mercy upon me, O God, according to Thy lovingkindness: according unto the multitude of Thy tender mercies blot out my transgressions. Wash me throughly from mine iniquity, and *cleanse me from my sin.* — Psalm 51:1-2	4. *Those in authority over us;* our parents, teachers, church office-bearers and government officials. I exhort therefore, that, first of all, supplications, prayers, intercessions, and giving of thanks, be made for all men: For *kings,* and for *all that are in authority;* that we may lead a quiet and peaceable life in all godliness and honesty. — I Timothy 2:1-2
2. *Our bodily needs;* our daily needs of food, shelter, and clothing. Give us this day our *daily bread.* — Matthew 6:11	5. *God's children and God's servants;* true believers and ministers of the Word. Praying always with all prayer and supplication in the Spirit, and watching thereunto with all perseverance and supplication *for all saints;* And for me, that utterance may be given unto me, that I may open my mouth boldly, to make known the mystery of the gospel. — Ephesians 6:18-19
3. *Our family;* those who are related to us. And it was so, when the days of their feasting were gone about, that Job sent and sanctified them, and rose up early in the morning, and *offered burnt offerings according to the number of them all:* for Job said, I may be that my sons have sinned, and cursed God in their hearts. Thus did Job continually. — Job 1:5	6. *All people;* even our enemies. But I say unto you, Love your enemies, bless them that curse you, do good to them *that hate you,* and *pray for them which despitefully use you,* and persecute you, — Matthew 5:44

Above all else, we must pray for God's Name to be honored, His will to be done, and His kingdom to be established. What well-known prayer in the Bible clearly teaches us to pray for these things?

We may not pray for people who have died, however, because their souls have been sent by God to heaven or hell and their destination is permanent.

WHAT DO YOU THINK?
THE RICH MAN AND LAZARUS

Read *Luke 16:22-26:*

And it came to pass, that the beggar died, and was carried by the angels into Abraham's bosom: the rich man also died, and was buried;

And in hell he lift up his eyes, being in torments, and seeth Abraham afar off, and Lazarus in his bosom.

And he cried and said, Father Abraham, have mercy on me, and send Lazarus, that he may dip the tip of his finger in water, and cool my tongue; for I am tormented in this flame.

But Abraham said, Son, remember that thou in thy lifetime receivedst thy good things, and likewise Lazarus evil things: but now he is comforted, and thou art tormented.

And beside all this, between us and you there is a great gulf fixed: so that they which would pass from hence to you cannot; neither can they pass to us, that would come from thence.

Were both the rich man's and the beggar's final destinations permanent immediately after they died? How do you know this?

God is not compelled or forced to hear or answer our prayers. He can justly ignore us for we have sinned away all our rights. However, God has freely and graciously promised in His Word to hear needy sinners when they cry. God is also completely free in how or when He answers prayer.

WHAT DO YOU THINK?

GOD ANSWERED ELIEZER'S PRAYER

Eliezer, Abraham's oldest servant, was sent back to Haran to find a wife for Isaac. He prayed that God would direct him to the right girl, and we read:

> And it came to pass, before he had done speaking, that, behold, Rebekah came out, who was born to Bethuel, son of Milcah, the wife of Nahor, Abraham's brother, with her pitcher upon her shoulder.
>
> — Genesis 24:15

GOD ANSWERED ABRAHAM'S PRAYER

Abraham often prayed for a son and God promised him, when he was seventy-five years old, that he would receive his desire. God kept His promise and answered Abraham's prayer twenty-five years later. We read:

> And Abraham was an hundred years old, when his son Isaac was born unto him.
>
> — Genesis 21:5

God is completely free in the manner and time in which He answers prayer. How can you see this in the answering of Eliezer's and Abraham's prayers? If we do not receive answers to our prayers immediately, does this necessarily mean that God has not heard or that He will not answer them? Can you give other biblical examples of prayers which are answered by God many years later?

God can give sudden or gradual answers to prayer. Often God's immediate answers to prayer result in remarkable stories to speak and read about because they show something of God's majesty and power so clearly. The following true story is an example of an immediate and remarkable answer to prayer.

WHAT DO YOU THINK?

A WONDERFUL DELIVERANCE

A godly widow, named Bertha Schmidt, lived with Karl, her only son, in a pleasant and neat cottage on the shore of the Baltic Sea.

However, some fearful news reached the people of this quiet village. A hostile army was rapidly approaching a nearby city, and would be passing through their area. Probably tomorrow these soldiers would arrive — plundering, stealing, and destroying whatever was in their path.

Poor Karl busied himself by barricading all the doors and windows and trying to make their little cottage as strong and hard to break into as possible. Out of fear, he worked at a feverish pace. Finally, unable to do anymore, he sank into his chair. His fear, however, was not decreased by all his efforts; instead his fear was increasing. To make matters worse, a terrible snowstorm was raging and the wind, as it howled around the little cottage, made all types of strange and terrifying noises.

Karl sat in gloomy silence, pale and trembling. His mother, however, was quietly busy. She was calmly reading her Bible and praying unto her God. At last she raised her eyes and her face broke into a bright smile as she repeated two lines of a well-known poem to Karl:

"Round us a wall our God shall rear,
And our proud foes shall quail with fear."

Karl stared in disbelief. "Mother, how can you believe that?" he cried out angrily, "How can God build a wall around our cottage strong enough to keep out an army?"

"Have you never read that not a sparrow falls to the ground without His will, Karl?" she answered quietly. Karl didn't answer but sank again into gloomy silence.

During the night, the storm ended. Soon after, the fearful sound of the approaching army could be heard. Screaming, crashing, and yelling could be heard from their neighbors' cottages. The sound of the uproar came closer and closer. Karl froze in terror.

At last, however, the awful sounds died away in the distance. The army had passed by. Karl still didn't dare to move, but after some hours, he removed the boards and tried to open the door but could not. After much pushing, he could force the door open just far enough to crawl out. He had to dig his way out and up for a snow drift had covered the entire front of the house.

After considerable effort he climbed over the drift and down onto the road in front of the house. He stopped there in his tracks. He could not believe what he saw! From the road, no house could be seen at all, only a large snowdrift!

Karl just stood there. "Round us a wall our God shall rear...," he thought. He ran over the drift back into the house. "Mother, you must come out! You must!" he called excitedly.

With much help, his mother was brought over the snowdrift. The two stood together in the street looking at "God's wall." They wept together for some time and finally the widow, looking up to heaven, said quietly, "Faithful is He who hath promised. His also hath done it."

What do you think? Can God provide remarkable and immediate answers to prayer in times of need? Are all of God's answers to prayer this sudden and remarkable? How can God answer prayer differently?

— Adapted from ***Religious Stories for Young and Old***

— Volume 1

The Bible mentions four different **kinds of prayer:**

1. **Public** prayer
2. Family prayer
3. Private prayer
4. Sudden prayer

When we pray, we must show **reverence, respect, and humility.** We close our eyes to show that we are not looking to the world or physical things for our help, but that we are communicating with God who is a spirit. When praying, we fold our hands to show that we do not seek our help from ourselves or our actions, but from God alone.

In the Bible we can find examples of praying in a position of: kneeling, lying with one's face to the ground, standing with a bowed head, and other postures, all of which show an attitude of respect, reverence, and humility. The **posture** we use in prayer can differ according to the place and circumstances we are in, but our position in prayer should always reflect an attitude of reverence, respect, and humility.

> Two men went up into the temple to pray; the one a Pharisee, and the other a publican.
> The Pharisee stood and prayed thus with himself, God, I thank Thee, that I am not as other men are, extortioners, unjust, adulterers, or even as this publican.
> I fast twice in the week, I give tithes of all that I possess.
> And the publican, standing afar off, would not lift up so much as his eyes unto heaven, but smote upon his breast, saying, God be merciful to me a sinner.
> I tell you, this man went down to his house justified rather than the other: for every one that exalteth himself shall be abased; and he that humbleth himself shall be exalted.
> — Luke 18:10-14

The Bible also speaks of some **set times** for prayer. These are pictured in the following chart.

WHAT DO YOU THINK?

TYPES OF PRAYER

Of which type of prayer would each of the following be an example?

1. **Matthew 6:6**

   But thou, when thou prayest, enter into thy closet, and when thou hast shut thy door, pray to thy Father which is in secret; and thy Father which seeth in secret shall reward thee openly.

2. **II Chronicles 6:12-14**

   And he stood before the altar of the LORD in the presence of all the congregation of Israel, and spread forth his hands:
   For Solomon had made a brasen scaffold, of five cubits long, and five cubits broad, and three cubits high, and had set it in the midst of the court: and upon it he stood, and kneeled down upon his knees before all the congregation of Israel, and spread forth his hands toward heaven.
   And said, O LORD God of Israel, there is no God like Thee in the heaven, nor in the earth; which keepest covenant, and shewest mercy unto Thy servants, that walk before Thee with all their hearts.

3. **Genesis 35:2-3**

   Then Jacob said unto his household, and to all that were with him, Put away the strange gods that are among you, and be clean, and change your garments:
   And let us arise, and go up to Bethel; and I will make there an altar unto God, who answered me in the day of my distress, and was with me in the way which I went.

4. **Matthew 14:29-30**

   And He said, Come. And when Peter was come down out of the ship, he walked on the water, to go to Jesus.
   But when he saw the wind boisterous, he was afraid; and beginning to sink, he cried, saying, Lord, save me.

SET TIMES FOR PRAYER

Time	Biblical Example	Biblical Text
1. Before a meal	Paul on the ship	And when he had thus spoken, he took bread, and *gave thanks to God* in presence of them all: and when he had broken it, *he began to eat.* — Acts 27:35
2. After a meal	Moses speaking to the children of Israel	When *thou hast eaten* and art full, then thou shalt *bless the LORD* thy God for the good land which He hath given thee. — Deuteronomy 8:10
3. Morning, noon, and evening	Life of Daniel	Now when Daniel knew that the writing was signed, he went into his house; and his windows being open in his chamber toward Jerusalem, he kneeled upon his knees *three times a day,* and *prayed,* and gave thanks before his God, as he did aforetime. — Daniel 6:10
4. Sudden emergencies	Peter, when sinking in the water	But when he saw the wind boisterous, he was afraid; and *beginning to sink, he cried, saying, Lord, save me.* — Matthew 14:30
5. Gatherings in homes	Friends gathering together to pray for Peter	And when he had considered the thing, he came to the house of Mary the mother of John, whose surname was Mark; where many *were gathered together praying.* — Acts 12:12
6. Church needs	The early New Testament church	These *all* continued with one accord *in prayer and supplication,* with the women, and Mary the mother of Jesus, and with his brethren. — Acts 1:14
7. Public and national needs	Jehoshaphat praying with all the people of Israel when the Moabites invaded their land	O our God, wilt Thou not judge them? for we have *no might against this great company* that cometh against us: neither know we what to do: but our eyes are upon Thee. — II Chronicles 20:12

WHAT DO YOU THINK?

UNCEASING PRAYER

Several ministers had gathered to discuss difficult questions, and it was asked how the command to "pray without ceasing" could be obeyed.

Various suggestions were offered, and at last one of the ministers was appointed to write an essay on the subject for the next meeting. A young maid servant, who was in the room serving, heard the discussion and exclaimed: "What! A whole month to tell the meaning of this text? Why, it's one of the easiest and best verses in the Bible."

"Well, well, Mary," said an old minister, "what do you know about it? Can you pray all the time?"

"Oh, yes Sir!"

"Really? How is that possible when you have so many things to do?"

"Why, Sir, the more I have to do, the more I pray."

"Indeed! Well, Mary, how do you do it? Most people wouldn't agree with you."

"Well, Sir," said the girl, "when I first open my eyes in the morning, I pray: 'Lord, open the eyes of my understanding'; and while I am dressing I pray that I may be clothed with the robe of righteousness; while I am washing, I ask to have my sins washed away; as I begin work, I pray that I may receive strength for all the work of the day; while I kindle the fire, I pray that revival may be kindled in me; while preparing and eating breakfast, I ask to be fed with the Bread of Life and the pure milk of the Word; as I sweep the house, I pray that my heart may be swept clean of all its impurities; as I am busy with the little children, I look up to God as my Father and pray that I may always have the trusting love of a little child; and as I ..."

"Enough, enough!" cried the minister. "These truths are often hid from the wise and prudent and revealed unto babes, as the Lord Himself said. Go on, Mary," he continued, "pray without ceasing. As for us, brothers, let us thank the Lord for this lesson."

Did this maid know the meaning of "to pray without ceasing" in her life's experience?

Do you know that you need God? Do you need to continually pray to Him?

— Adapted from *The NRC Banner of Truth*

While the Bible speaks of set times for prayer, it also commands us to pray **without ceasing,** or stopping. This means that we should never give up praying, but that we should continually be in a spirit of prayer, always asking God for our needs and thanking Him for His blessings in everything we do. How did the maid in the story, **Unceasing Prayer,** do this?

Form prayers are prayers which are memorized or written down and are often repeated. Form prayers are used in connection with baptism and the Lord's Supper in church. Some families use a form prayer at the table before or after a meal. Some children use a form prayer at night before going to bed or in the morning after awaking.

PRAYERS FOR CHURCH AND SCHOOL

A Prayer At The
Church Service

Lord Jesus, be Thou with us now,
As in Thy house of prayer we bow;
And when we sing, and when we
pray,
Help us to mean the words we
say.
Help us to listen to Thy Word,
And keep our thoughts from
wand'ring, Lord.

A Prayer For Our
Christian Schools

Great All in all, eternal Power,
On us Thy richest blessings
shower;
Inspire our hearts with ardent
zeal,
And let us now Thy presence
feel.

Shed on our school Thy heavenly
light,
And give it favor in Thy sight;
May each young learner early find
A Savior merciful and kind.

Direct their footsteps, God of
grace;
Teach them to seek their Maker's
face;
Let them Thy great salvation
know,
And be their portion here below.

And O may we, who teach them,
share
In the almighty Father's care;
In zeal and love may we be found,
And in each Christian grace
abound.

Thus, when the last great trump
shall sound,
To call us from beneath the
ground,
May we, with these dear children,
rise
To dwell forever in the skies.

— Adapted from *The NRC Banner of Truth*

Form prayers can be meaningful and valuable. They can provide us with a pattern for praying or can ensure that the proper requests are included in a public prayer for a special occasion.

Form prayers can be dangerous, however, if they are used only out of custom or habit. Then, form prayers can become words which are repeated without thoughts or feeling.

The most famous of all form prayers is the prayer of the Lord Jesus which He gave to the apostles when they asked Him to teach them to pray. This prayer is called the *Lord's Prayer*.

We may read this prayer in the following verses:

> After this manner therefore **pray** ye: Our Father which art in heaven, Hallowed be Thy Name.
>
> Thy kingdom come. Thy will be done in earth, as it is in heaven.
>
> Give us this day our daily bread.
>
> And forgive us our debts, as we forgive our debtors.
>
> And lead us not into temptation, but deliver us from evil: For Thine is the kingdom, and the power, and the glory, for ever. Amen.
>
> — Matthew 6:9-13

The Lord's Prayer may be divided into the following parts, which provide us with an example of what we should pray for and in what order we should present our requests.

THE LORD'S PRAYER

I.	**The Address**	**Our Father** which art in heaven
II.	**The Six Requests** A. **Requests for God's glory** 1. Honoring of God's Name	Hallowed be Thy **Name.**
	2. Establishing of God's rule	Thy **kingdom** come
	3. Doing of God's will	Thy **will** be done in earth as it is in heaven.
	B. **Requests for our needs** 1. To supply our daily needs	Give us this day our **daily bread**
	2. To forgive all our sins	And **forgive us our debts,** as we forgive our debtors
	3. To keep us from sin	And **lead us not into temptation,** but deliver us from evil
III.	**The Closing**	For Thine is the kingdom, and the power, and the glory, forever. Amen.

MEMORIZATION QUESTIONS

Prayer

1. For what must we pray to God?
    We must pray for all things needful for body and soul.

2. May we look and pray to God for all this?
    Yes; for Christ has said: "Whatsoever ye shall ask the Father in My Name, He will give it you" (John 16:23).

3. Whence do we know, how we are to pray to God?
    From the prayer which Christ Himself taught His disciples (Matthew 6:9-13; Luke 11:1-4).

4. How does that prayer read?
    Our Father which art in heaven, Hallowed be Thy Name. Thy kingdom come. Thy will be done in earth, as it is in heaven. Give us this day our daily bread. And forgive us our debts, as we forgive our debtors. And lead us not into temptation, but deliver us from evil: For Thine is the kingdom, and the power, and the glory, for ever. Amen.

5. May we address God in prayer as our Father?
    Yes; if we do so in the Name of Christ, and if we love and honor God as our Father (Malachi 1:6).

6. Why must we pray in the Name of Christ?
    Because He is the only Mediator and Advocate with the Father (I John 2:1).

7. Have we then nothing on account of which God can hear us?
    No; for we are guilty sinners, who have forfeited all claim upon God's mercy (Psalm 143:2).

8. How then ought our prayer to be?
    Humble, in childlike faith, and filled with love to God's honor, and our true welfare.

9. Should we not also give thanks to God?
    Yes; He also wants us to give Him thanks for His mercies (Philippians 4:6).

10. Can we of ourselves thus pray and give thanks?
    No; but we are to pray: "Lord, teach us to pray."

— Donner's Catechism: Lesson XVI

CHECKING YOUR READING

1. Name and explain the three parts included in prayer:

   a. _____ — _____

   _____

   b. _____ — _____

   _____

   c. _____ — _____

   _____

2. Why is true prayer no longer our natural desire as it was Adam's and Eve's in Paradise?

   _____

   _____

   _____

3. Name the six elements of true prayer:

   a. _____   d. _____

   b. _____   e. _____

   c. _____   f. _____

4. Should unconverted people pray? _____ For what should they

   especially pray? _____

   _____

5. Why is prayer very important and powerful?_____

   _____

   _____

6. a. For what must we pray? _____

   _____

   _____

   b. Name more specifically six things for which we must pray:

      1. _____   4. _____

      2. _____   5. _____

      3. _____   6. _____

7. Name four kinds of prayer:

   a. _____   c. _____

   b. _____   d. _____

CHECKING YOUR READING

8. What should our posture and behavior reflect when we pray?

_____

_____

9. Name seven set times for prayer mentioned in the Bible:

a. _____ e. _____

b. _____ f. _____

c. _____ g. _____

d. _____

10. How can form prayers be:

a. Valuable? _____

_____

b. Dangerous? _____

_____

━━━━ EXTRA CHALLENGE QUESTIONS ━━━━

1. How can we observe that God is completely free in how He answers prayer when we read the "What Do You Think" examples of Eliezer and Abraham?

_____

_____

2. From the story **Too Angry to Pray!**, why did Sally first feel that she could not pray? What proper attitude toward prayer did Sally reveal at this time?_____

_____

_____

3. What does it mean to pray "unceasingly"? _____

_____

_____

4. Explain two important lessons about prayer that can be learned from studying the six requests of the Lord's Prayer:

a. _____

_____

b. _____

_____

CHAPTER 16

THE CHURCH
CHURCH OFFICES
CHURCH GOVERNMENT
CHURCH DISCIPLINE

VOCABULARY

1. **Church Visible** — The outward body of Christian believers; all members who meet together to worship God under the preaching of His Word
2. **Church Invisible** — All God's elect; the body of all true believers in Christ
3. **Church Denomination** — A group of church people who meet under the same name and share the same beliefs
4. **Church Militant** — The Church Invisible on earth which is fighting a spiritual war against sin, Satan, the world, and sinful self
5. **Church Triumphant** — the true believers in heaven who rejoice in God who caused them to triumph over their enemies
6. **Church Discipline** — A loving correction which serves as a means to promote personal repentance and church purity
7. **Classis** — A meeting of church representatives from each congregation of a denomination located within a certain area
8. **Synod** — A meeting of church representatives from each classis within a certain country or countries
9. **Private Sin** — A sin of a church member which is not generally known; a sin which is known by only one or a few
10. **Public Sin** — A sin of a church member which is known to many or all of the people in a local congregation

THE CHURCH

The **Church** is not a building or man-made organization; the Church is the entire body of believers in Christ. Scripture speaks of God's children as the body of Christ because they are so closely united with Christ, their Savior. Jesus Christ is the Head of His Church and His children are the body.

For the husband is the head of the wife, as **Christ is the Head of the Church: and He is the Saviour of the body.**
— Ephesians 5:2

And **He is the Head of the body, the Church**: who is the beginning, the firstborn from the dead; that in all things He might have the preeminence.
— Colossians 1:18

Christ's **Church** is not found only in one place or country. Its members are gathered from all nations and languages.

After this I beheld, and, lo, a great multitude, which no man could number, **of all nations, and kindreds, and people, and tongues,** stood before the throne, and before the Lamb, clothed with white robes, and palms in their hands.
— Revelation 7:9

WHAT DO YOU THINK?
WHAT IS "THE CHURCH"?

What does the word "church" mean in each of the following verses? Does it refer to a building or to people?

And I say also unto thee, That thou art Peter, and upon this rock I will build My **Church**; and the gates of hell shall not prevail against it.
— Matthew 16:18

And hath put all things under His feet, and gave Him to be the Head over all things to the **Church.**
— Ephesians 1:22

To the intent that now unto the principalities and powers in heavenly places might be known by the **Church** the manifold wisdom of God.
— Ephesians 3:10

Concerning zeal, persecuting the **Church;** touching the righteousness which is in the law, blameless.
— Philippians 3:6

Now ye are the body of Christ, and members in particular.
And God hath set some in the **Church,** first apostles, secondarily prophets, thirdly teachers, after that miracles, then gifts of healings, helps, governments, diversities of tongues.
— I Corinthians 12:27-28

THE SHEEP AND THEIR SHEPHERD

A certain person made a journey through Syria, and told the following true story:

On my journey I saw three shepherds who let their sheep drink at the bank of a little river. It was a great mingling of sheep, and it seemed impossible to separate them into the three flocks.

When the animals were finished, one of the shepherds came to the front, and called in the Arabian language, "Follow me!" Immediately, movement came into the great flock and more than thirty sheep climbed behind the shepherd up a little hill.

Afterwards the second shepherd called, "Follow me!" and also the second flock separated itself and followed him.

Surprised, I turned to the third shepherd, who also made himself ready to depart.

I asked him, "Will the sheep also follow me when I call them?"

But the man shook his head and said, "Not under any circumstances, Sir."

I asked him then if he would allow me to put on his shepherd's mantle for a moment. The man permitted this and even put his turban on my head.

Then I also called in the Arabian language, "Follow me!" But in the whole flock there was not one sheep that moved. They scarcely looked at me with their dreamy eyes.

To whose call do we answer, to God's or to the world's? Are all Church Visible members sheep of Christ's fold? How can you know if you are one of Christ's sheep?

Jesus said:

> My sheep hear My voice, and I know them, and they follow Me.
> — John 10:27

What does it mean to follow Jesus? Why is this so important?

In its deepest meaning God's Church is *invisible* to man for it is spiritual. It is the body of all regenerated, saved, and eternal believers in Christ. But the church also has a visible appearance in this world. There is an outward form of the church which can be seen and heard by people. We speak of the visible body of outward believers and the invisible, spiritual body of inward believers, as the **Church Visible** and the **Church Invisible.**

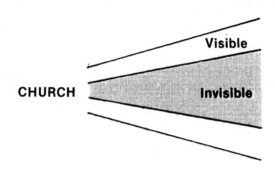

The Church Visible is the outward body or form of the church in this world. It refers to all church members who gather together under the preaching of God's Word throughout the world. We can *see* these gatherings of people. For this reason the outward appearance of the church in the world is called the *Church Visible.*

Due to wrong doctrines, sinful practices, human misunderstandings, and personal quarrels, the Church Visible has become divided. Parts of the Church Visible which are united and hold to the same doctrinal beliefs and practices are called **"church denominations."** Today, there are hundreds of different church denominations in the United States and Canada. It is not to our honor, as church members, but to our shame that sinful teachings, practices and quarrels have produced so many splits and different church denominations in the Church Visible. As church members, we are not called to fight for a certain denomination, but to strive to uphold the doctrines and practices taught in the Word of God.

The **Church Invisible** is the spiritual body of all true believers. All the elect, all those who have been converted from serving sin to serving God are members of the Church Invisible. Christ is their Head inwardly as well as outwardly. They are united eternally to Him by true saving faith. They are called Christ's "body." Christ is their Head and King. The chief desire of the Church Invisible is to love and serve the Lord totally.

The Church Invisible is **invisible** to us as human beings on earth because we cannot perfectly see or judge who are and who are not members of the Church Invisible. Its exact membership is invisible and unknown to us as human beings, but, it is clearly visible and known to God.

The Church Invisible, the body of all regenerated believers who have received true saving faith from God, will be gathered from all over the world and from various church denominations.

We must examine ourselves carefully, for the Bible tells us clearly that not all members of the Church Visible are members of the Church Invisible. How can you know if you are a saved member?

> They answered and said unto Him, Abraham is our father. Jesus saith unto them, **If ye were Abraham's children, ye would do the works of Abraham.**
> — John 8:39

> For he is not a Jew, which is one outwardly; neither is that circumcision, which is outward in the flesh;
> But he is a **Jew, which is one inwardly; and circumcision is that of the heart, in the spirit,** and not in the letter; whose praise is not of men, but of God.
> — Romans 2:28-29

WHAT DO YOU THINK?

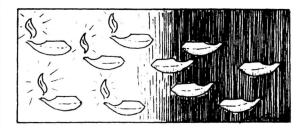

FIVE WISE AND FIVE FOOLISH VIRGINS

We can read the Lord Jesus' Parable of the Ten Virgins in:

Matthew 25:1-13

> Then shall the kingdom of heaven be likened unto ten virgins, which took their lamps, and went forth to meet the Bridegroom.
> And five of them were wise, and five were foolish.
> They that were foolish took their lamps, and took no oil with them:
> But the wise took oil in their vessels with their lamps.
> While the Bridegroom tarried, they all slumbered and slept.
> And at midnight there was a cry made, Behold, the Bridegroom cometh; go ye out to meet Him.
> Then all those virgins arose, and trimmed their lamps.
> And the foolish said unto the wise, Give us of your oil; for our lamps are gone out.
> But the wise answered, saying, Not so; lest there be not enough for us and you: but go ye rather to them that sell, and buy for yourselves.
> And while they went to buy, the Bridegroom came; and they that were ready went in with Him to the marriage: and the door was shut.
> Afterward came also the other virgins, saying, Lord, Lord, open to us.
> But He answered and said, Verily I say unto you, I know you not.
> Watch therefore, for ye know neither the day nor the hour wherein the Son of man cometh.

What is meant by:
— The virgins carrying lamps?
— The oil?
— Midnight?
— It being too late to buy oil after midnight?
— The marriage feast?
— The door being closed?
Could you see an outward difference in the ten virgins? Which virgins were only Church Visible members? Which were also members of the Church Invisible? When will the difference between these two groups be clearly seen by all?

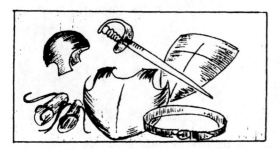
The Church Invisible is and will remain divided into two parts until the final judgment day. When Christ returns, the entire body of true believers will be united perfectly and eternally in heaven with Christ their Head. Until that time, however, the Church Invisible has two parts: the **Church Militant** on earth and the **Church Triumphant** in heaven. The church can be pictured in the following way:

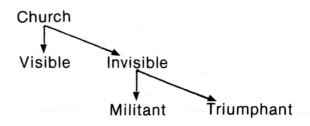

The *Church Militant* is the Church Invisible on earth. It is continually at war in this world. It is constantly fighting against its enemies: self, sin, world, and Satan. Its soldiers, God's true children, are daily fighting in this spiritual war. Their new spiritual nature, which desires to love God and their neighbor, is continually at war with their old nature which loves to serve self, sin, the world, and Satan.

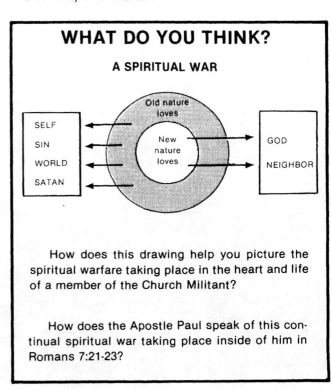

WHAT DO YOU THINK?

A CARELESS SOLDIER

Robert was a soldier in the infantry division of his army. He was placed on the front lines of battle for several hours each day. Robert was commanded and warned to remain very alert and on his guard at all times. But, Robert was often careless. "Oh, I'll hear the enemy when they attack," he thought, and would often doze and fall asleep.

One afternoon, as he was sleeping, Robert was shot in his right arm. He was severely wounded and had to be rushed to the army hospital. He was there for several weeks with severe pain.

Whose fault was this? Who would Robert have to blame for his weakness and suffering?

A true Christian is warned to remain alert and on his guard against sin, the world, Satan and his own sinful heart. If he takes it easy, spiritually sleeps, falls into sin, and is spiritually wounded, whose fault is it? What means should a Christian soldier use to stay spiritually awake and alert?

WHAT DO YOU THINK?

WHY GO TO CHURCH?

There is a good lesson to be learned regarding one answer to this question from the example of an old British chieftain in the following story:

The Romans had invaded Britain and the chiefs of the tribes were gathered in council. Each had a different plan, and each was determined to go his own way. At last the old chieftain arose. Picking up a bunch of sticks, he handed each man a stick. "Break them!" he directed. Each broke his stick with ease.

Then he took an equal number of sticks and tied them together into a bundle. "Now break them!" he commanded. Not even the strongest man could do it. "That," he pointed out, "is the difference between working separately and working together as one!"

How does this example illustrate one reason why we should gather together as a church? Against which enemies should we be unitedly fighting? Can you list some other reasons why we should always attend church?

— Adapted from *3,000 Illustrations for Christian Service*

95

While the enemies of the Church Militant are very powerful, all God's true children shall gain the complete victory in the end. This is not because of their strength or faithfulness, but because of the strength and faithfulness of their Captain and Head, Jesus Christ.

> Who shall separate us from the love of Christ? shall tribulation, or distress, or persecution, or famine, or nakedness, or peril, or sword?
>
> Nay, in all these things we are more than conquerors through Him that loved us.
> For I am persuaded, that neither death, nor life, nor angels, nor principalities, nor powers, nor things present, nor things to come,
> Nor height, nor depth, nor any other creature, shall be able to separate us from the love of God, which is in Christ Jesus our Lord.
>
> — Romans 8:35, 37-39

God shall uphold all of His children in their struggles and warfare here on earth. Jesus Christ will overthrow all of His children's enemies and cast them away forever. God shall bring all true believers into a wonderful heaven prepared for them, where there will be no more sin, Satan, world, or sinful self. There His children shall triumph over their enemies forever and rejoice in Christ their King. What a wonderful, glorious, and everlasting future awaits the true soldiers of God fighting against sin here on earth!

The church which is rejoicing in heaven is called the *Church Triumphant.* When a child of God dies on earth, his soul is immediately taken into heaven. After the final judgment day his body will be reunited with his soul to perfectly rejoice and praise God forever in heaven, with both body and soul. How wonderfully and wholeheartedly the Church Triumphant will sing to the praise and honor of their great King who saved and delivered them, cand caused them to triumph over all of their enemies!

Is this your present desire, prayer, and activity?

WHAT DO YOU THINK?

FROM SOLDIERS TO VICTORS

How do the following texts show us that those who are actively fighting in the Church Militant shall win this spiritual war through their Captain and Head, Jesus Christ, and be in the Church Triumphant eternally?

> Blessed are the poor in spirit: for theirs is the kingdom of heaven.
> Blessed are they that mourn: for they shall be comforted.
> — Matthew 5:3-4

> He that hath an ear, let him hear what the Spirit saith unto the churches; To him that overcometh will I give to eat of the tree of life, which is in the midst of the paradise of God.
> — Revelation 2:7

> And one of the elders answered, saying unto me, What are these which are arrayed in white robes? and whence came they?
> And I said unto him, Sir, thou knowest. And he said to me, These are they which came out of the great tribulation, and have washed their robes, and made them white in the blood of the Lamb.
> Therefore are they before the throne of God, and serve Him day and night in His temple: and He that sitteth on the throne shall dwell among them.
> They shall hunger no more, neither thirst any more; neither shall the sun light on them, nor any heat.
> For the Lamb which is in the midst of the throne shall feed them, and shall lead them unto living fountains of waters: and God shall wipe away all tears from their eyes.
> — Revelation 7:13-17

Why are the following statements true?

If we desire to die as God's people, then we must live as God's people. If we wish to rejoice with the Church Triumphant, we must be fighting with the Church Militant.

With so many different church denominations in our country today, how can we distinquish the true church from the false?

We may not judge a church denomination by some of its members. All church members should be members like the peddlar in the story on this page. However, every church denomination also has members who do not live according to its teachings. If a person tries to judge a church denomination by some of its members, his judgment will vary according to which member or members of that denomination he meets or knows. This can result in wrong judgments.

We must judge a church denomination by its confession, what it teaches in word and practice. Our forefathers gave us three important marks to clearly distinquish the true church from the false. These marks are as follows:

1. The pure **preaching** of God's Word

2. The proper administration of the **sacraments**

3. The proper exercise of **church discipline**

The **Belgic Confession of Faith** states in Article XXIX:

The marks, by which the **true Church** is known, are these: if the **pure doctrine of the gospel is preached** therein; if she maintains **the pure administration of the sacraments** as instituted by Christ; if **church discipline is exercised** in punishing of sin: in short, if all things are managed according to the pure Word of God, all things contrary thereto rejected, and Jesus Christ acknowledged as the only Head of the Church.

WHAT DO YOU THINK?

AN ACTIVE CHURCH MEMBER

There once was a quiet peddlar of fruits and vegetables who passed a minister's house each day. One day the peddlar dropped a little black notebook that he always carried with him. The minister happened to find this notebook and looking through it to find to whom it belonged, he was amazed at what was written in it. Throughout the book were comments like: "Visit the following who have been missing church"..."Ask about the sick baby"..."Leave fruit for the blind lady" . . . "Speak a word with the old discouraged man on the corner"... "Invite the young man and his wife to church and Bible Class," etc.

The next day the minister asked the peddlar if the notebook belonged to him. "Oh, yes," answered the peddlar, "That's my book of reminders. I thank you very much!"

"I am pleased with your reminders," replied the minister.

"Well, Sir," replied the peddlar, "it helps to keep my soul out of the dust, and I do it," he said turning to a quotation on the first page of his notebook, "for His body's sake, which is the church."

Was this peddlar an active church member? What benefits did he also receive personally through this daily activity?

— Adapted from **3,000 Illustrations for Christian Service**

The pure **preaching** of God's Word is the first and central mark of a true church denomination. The Word of God must be the center of all preaching and stand above all human thoughts or teachings. The Word of God, which exalts God to the highest and places fallen man in the lowest, must be preached in purity. No church denomination is perfect, but the true Church strives for this.

The proper administration of the **sacraments** refers to the practice of the Lord's Supper and Holy Baptism. A true church denomination will only observe the sacraments which were given by Jesus Christ, the Head of the Church, and only administer them in the manner taught in God's Word.

The proper exercise of **church discipline** is also an important mark of the true Church. A true church denomination is concerned about purity in the daily life and walk of its members as well as purity in doctrinal teaching. When its members become involved in public sins, they must be disciplined by the church. We hope to study this in more detail later in this chapter.

It is a great blessing to be living in a country which does not outlaw Christian churches. It is an even greater blessing to be a member of a church denomination which observes the marks of the true Church. It is the greatest blessing of all to be a living member, through God's regenerating work, of the eternal Church Invisible.

WHAT DO YOU THINK?

THE POWER OF GOD'S CHURCH

Years ago, Captain Cook was sailing among the South Sea Islands. Anchoring near an island, he permitted his men to go ashore. Suddenly the natives rushed down upon them, and before they could regain their boats, one of the number had been captured. Being unarmed, the men had to helplessly sit in their boats while the natives killed and ate their comrade before their eyes.

Twenty years later Captain Cook was again cruising in this same part of the sea when he was overtaken by a storm and his vessel damaged. For days they drifted upon the waves until they were driven upon this same shore. When Captain Cook recognized the same island where his comrade had been eaten twenty years before, he urged his men to use all their strength to keep the boat out to sea, but in spite of all their efforts, they were driven upon the rocks.

Crouching for fear in the bushes and keeping a sharp watch for the savages, they sent one of the men up to the top of a little hill to spy. Cautiously he went higher until he reached the top and looked around. Down in the valley, amid a clump of trees, he saw the white steeple of a church. With great joy, he turned and began waving his arm and shouting to his companions: "Come on, come on; it's safe; there's a church here now!"

How can the blessed influence of God's church through the power of His Word be seen in this story? How are God's Word and church an outward blessing to a country? What will happen to a country which departs from God's Word and church?

— Adapted from *3,000 Illustrations for Christian Service*

WHAT DO YOU THINK?

A STRANGE CHURCH SERVICE

All the members were seated in a church building for a Sunday morning worship service, and the minister had just begun his sermon when the interruptions started.

First, Sally started playing with her pet kitten, Puff. Then George ran and jumped to catch a baseball. Patricia was soon pedalling her new bike at quite a speed and was just a flash as she went by. Mr. Rodgers started cutting the wood he needed for the garage he was building. What a noise his sawing made! Mrs. Smith started cutting out her new dress, as Sandra saddled her horse and rode off at a full gallop. Jack gradually began working on his car engine.

What distractions! At times, the voice of the minister could not even be heard. This certainly was a strange church service, don't you think?

Sadly, the church service just described is not that strange. All these things took place without an actual sound in the church building . . . for they all happened in the minds of the "listeners." However, these poor "listeners" never heard most of the sermon.

What do these things tell us about the spiritual life of these members? Some people sin by not attending church; others sin by not "attending" church when they are in church. What does this mean? How do *you* listen?

To be able to freely attend a true church denomination and to hear the pure preaching of God's Word is a great and valuable privilege. All people in the world have not received this blessing. The preaching of God's Word is an important means of grace. God has promised to bless the preaching of His Word for the conversion of spiritually-dead sinners and the strengthening and comforting of His true children.

Therefore, we must never go to church thoughtlessly or carelessly. Ask God to earnestly bless the Word spoken to your heart. Listen attentively and strive to think deeply about what you have heard. We cannot apply God's Word to our own hearts; that is the gracious work of the Holy Spirit alone.

But, we may and must carefully use the means of grace that God has given and plead with the Lord to bless it in our hearts and lives.

How then shall they call on Him in whom they have not believed? and how shall they believe in Him of whom they have not heard? and *how shall they hear without a preacher?*

— Romans 10:14

For after that in the wisdom of God the world by wisdom knew not God, it pleased God *by the foolishness of preaching* to save them that believe.

I Corinthians 1:21

So shall *My Word* be that goeth forth out of My mouth: *it shall not return unto Me void,* but it shall accomplish that which I please, and it shall prosper in the thing whereto I sent it.

— Isaiah 55:11

WHAT DO YOU THINK?

CHURCH OFFICES

As Head of His church, the Lord Jesus Christ has given various **offices** to rule and guide His church according to His Word. He has called and placed **officebearers** to serve His church in these offices.

Christ has given **ordinary** and **extraordinary** offices in His New Testament church. The **extraordinary** offices mentioned in the Bible are: **prophets, apostles,** and **evangelists.**

> And He gave some, **apostles;** and some, **prophets;** and some, **evangelists.**
> — Ephesians 4:11a

Prophets were persons who were specially instructed by God to bring a new message or revelation of God to the people. This form of special revelation ended when God's written Word, our Bible, was completed.

A SERMON TO ONE HEARER

Dr. Branner once promised to preach for a country minister in England. When the Sabbath came, it was terribly stormy, cold, and uncomfortable. It was in the middle of the winter and the snow was piled high along the roads, so that traveling was difficult. Still, the minister urged his horse through the drifts. He put his animal in the shed, and went into the church. No hearers had arrived as yet. After looking around, Dr. Branner took his seat in the pulpit. Soon the door opened, and one man walked up the aisle, looked about, and took a seat. The hour came for the service to begin, but there was only one hearer.

The minister wondered whether he should preach for such a small audience, but decided he had a duty to do, and had no right to refuse to do it because only one man would hear it. So he went through the whole service: praying, singing, preaching, and the benediction, with only ONE hearer. When he had finished, he came down from the pulpit to speak to his hearer, but he had gone away.

Such an unusual event was spoken of occasionally, but twenty years later it was brought to the minister's mind in the following way:

The minister, being on a journey, stepped down from his coach one day in a pleasant village. A gentleman walked up and said, "Good morning, Dr. Branner."

"I do not remember you," said the minister.

"I suppose not," said the stranger, "but we once spent two hours together in a church alone in a storm."

"I do not recall it, Sir," added the old man. "Tell me when it was."

"Do you remember preaching twenty years ago in such a place to only one person?"

"Yes, yes," said the minister, grasping his hand. "I do, indeed; and if you are the man, I have been wishing to see you ever since."

"I am the man, Sir, and that sermon was used of God for my salvation. I have become a minister of the gospel, and over there is my church. The converts from that sermon, Sir, are many."

How does this story illustrate the truth of God's promise in a remarkable manner as it is found in:

Matthew 18:20?

> For where two or three are gathered together in My Name, there am I in the midst of them.

Are you aware of the importance of the preaching of God's Word when you attend a church service?

— Adapted from **Religious Stories for Young and Old**

Apostles were men who had seen Jesus physically after His resurrection and had received special gifts of miraculous healing, speaking in tongues, and prophesying as visible evidences of their ministry.

Evangelists were special assistants to the apostles.

These extraordinary offices were necessary during the special time of the birth and establishment of the New Testament church.

The **ordinary** officebearers in the New Testament church are:

1. Ministers
2. Elders
3. Deacons

These three offices are separate and distinct offices.

The work of a **minister** is to:

1. Preach the Word of God

2. Perform baptism and the Lord's Supper

3. Pray for the congregation

4. Help govern the church with the elders

5. Visit, teach, warn, and comfort the families in the congregation

> **MINISTERS**
>
> Who then is Paul, and who is Apollos, but **ministers** by whom ye believed, even as the Lord gave to every man?
> — I Corinthians 3:5
>
> **ELDERS**
>
> Let the **elders** that rule well be counted worthy of double honour, especially they who labour in Word and doctrine.
> — I Timothy 5:17
>
> **DEACONS**
>
> And let these also first be proved; then let them use the office of a **deacon,** being found blameless.
> — I Timothy 3:10

The work of an **elder** is to:

1. Rule and govern the church with the minister

2. Uphold and guard the true doctrines of God's Word in the teachings of the church and in the lives of its members

3. Help the minister in giving instruction, advice, and comfort in the families of the congregation

4. Read sermons in church worship services when ministers are absent or there are ministerial vacancies

The work of a **deacon** is to:

1. Collect and care for the proper distribution of the money donated to the church

2. Visit and care for the poor, both materially and spiritually

These three New Testament church offices compare with the three offices in the Old Testament for which people were anointed, namely: prophets, priests, and kings. This comparison is clearly pictured on a later chart in this chapter. As Head Officebearer of His Church, the Lord Jesus Christ is the only Person who has served in all three offices.

WHAT DO YOU THINK?

CAUGHT IN THE NET!

Several years ago, a certain minister was sent by God to a fishing village. Most of the villagers went out daily with their boats to fish, except on Sunday when they attended the preaching of God's Word in church.

However, in this village there lived an old fisherman who was, and always had been, very rough and ungodly. He broke the Sabbath, never attended church, cursed those who tried to speak with him about spiritual matters, and swore loudly on numerous occasions.

After arriving in this small village, the new minister began visiting all the people. He usually visited the various families with one of his elders. When coming to this old fisherman's house, his elder warned, "Reverend, if you do not want to hear God's Name misused and His Word mocked, do not go there. To speak with this man about religion is hopeless."

The minister, however, did not agree. He said to his elder, "God opened the eyes of a blind man with clay from the ground. Possibly I am the clay which God plans to use for this old sinner. If he remains hardened, then at least I have done my duty as a minister of the Lord. Let us go; maybe God will bless it."

They both entered the house and saw the gray-haired man sitting on a rough stool, tying a fishing net. He received the men with a stern, cold look and angry face, but did not say a word. The minister, being quite a friendly person, asked him several questions about fishing—about his nets, the wind, his boats, methods of fishing, and so on.

Such talk surprised the old fisherman and soon his frown changed into a smile. He liked nothing better than to tell stories about his fishing days and to have people ask him about his experiences at sea. The minister continued this conversation for a full hour and then stood up to leave, much to the surprise and disapproval of the elder who was with him.

"Come back again—I liked our talk," the old fisherman told the minister. "There's nothing I like better than talking about fishing."

"I can understand your love for your work," replied the minister. "I also love my work. Will you come and listen to me talk about my work next Sunday in church?"

"Never!" the old fisherman responded, "I am not interested in that. I'm a fisherman with body and soul."

"I will promise to speak about fishing, then, if you promise to be in church Sunday morning," the minister replied.

The old man thought for awhile and finally agreed, for the minister did seem to have a love for fishing. "But if you start talking about other things—I'll walk out right away!" he threatened.

Sunday morning the rough, old fisherman was in church—to the amazement of the entire village! The minister preached from Mark 1:16-18: "Now as He walked by the sea of Galilee, He saw Simon and Andrew his brother casting a net into the sea: for they were fishers. And Jesus said unto them, Come ye after Me, and I will make you to become fishers of men. And straightway they forsook their nets, and followed Him."

With open eyes and ears the old fisherman listened. He never missed a single word. In the application, the minister earnestly warned all sinners to flee to the great Fisher of men. God blessed this sermon to the soul of the old fisherman. God's Word completely broke the hardened heart of this old man. He could not contain himself anymore but cried aloud in the church, "You have caught me in the net!"

The minister paused . . . then spoke, "Have I caught you in the net as I desired? May God in His mercy help you out and bring you to liberty!" After that, the old fisherman often went to visit the minister—not to speak anymore about fishing, but about his need for deliverance from sin. God blessed the visits and talks, and Jesus Christ became the hope and salvation of this formerly hardened sinner.

Can you observe the love, warmth, and concern of this minister for the souls of men? Why is this a necessary quality for a minister? Do you listen to your minister's sermons as this man listened? Do you value God's messenger and message?

THE OLD AND NEW TESTAMENT OFFICES		
OLD TESTAMENT OFFICE	*MAIN DUTY*	*NEW TESTAMENT OFFICE*
Prophet	To teach and preach God' Word	Minister
Priest	To collect and offer the gifts of the people	Deacon
King	To rule and govern	Elder

Those placed by God in a church office are placed there to serve and rule according to God's will and Word and not according to their own thoughts or desires. It is our duty to respect the officebearers God has placed in the church. We must listen carefully to their teaching and advice. Never mock or think lightly about the offices or officebearers in God's church.

WHAT DO YOU THINK?

Which biblical story powerfully shows that: 1) we are to respect God's officebearers; and 2) we are to serve according to God's will if placed in a church office?

STRANGE FIRE PUNISHED

God had carefully instructed the priests as to how they were to serve in their office in the Tabernacle. Nadab and Abihu were sons of Aaron who were ordained as priests. They decided that they could bring their own fire to burn incense in the Holy Place instead of using the fire from off the Brazen Altar as God had commanded.

What punishment did these two men receive? What does this story teach us about being a church officebearer? How must a church officebearer serve in his office?

MOCKING A PROPHET PUNISHED

After Elijah was taken up into heaven, Elisha served in his place as God's prophet to Israel. As he was walking to Bethel, children from that city started to mock him by following him and yelling, "Go up, thou bald head, go up thou bald head!"

They mocked with the fact that God had taken Elijah into heaven and with Elisha's appearance.

What happened to forty-two of these children? What warning does this story provide for us?

CHURCH ORDER
Drawn up in the National Synod of Dordrecht held in 1618 and 1619

Our church order is divided into four main parts which speak about the following:

First Head — The Offices
Articles 1-28

— Ministers and Professors of Theology
— Elders
— Deacons
— Christian School Teachers

Second Head — The Ecclesiastical Assemblies
Articles 29-52

— Consistory Meetings
— Classical Meetings
— Particular Synod Meetings
— Synodical Meetings

Third Head — Doctrine, Sacraments, and Ceremonies
Articles 53-70

— Doctrinal Standards
— Baptism
— Lord's Supper
— Funeral Services
— Church Holidays
— Songs for Church Worship Services
— Marriage Services

Fourth Head — Censure and Ecclesiastical Admonition
Articles 71-86

— Secret Sin Procedure
— Public Sin Procedure
— Censure Steps
— Excommunication
— Suspension and Deposition of Church Office-bearers
— Transfer of Church Membership

Why are both church government and a written church order necessary in church life?

CHURCH GOVERNMENT

The **form** of church government used in all Reformed denominations is the **Presbyterian** form of church govenment.

In this form of government each local congregation is led by an elected **consistory**, which includes the:

1. Minister

2. Elders

3. Deacons

All the congregations from one denomination within a certain locality form a **classis.** This classis meets a few times a year. Each congregation sends two representatives to this classis meeting.

Once every two years each classis sends representatives to a **synod** meeting. At this meeting, officebearers from the entire church denomination within a country or continent meet together to discuss matters which concern the church denomination.

The Reformed churches follow a list of rules for governing the church which is called the **Church Order of Dordt.** This church order was written and approved by the Synod of Dordrecht which met in 1618 and 1619 in the Netherlands. You can find this church order printed on the last pages in your Psalter.

CHURCH DISCIPLINE

As King, the Lord Jesus has given two "keys" to His Church. These "keys" open or close the kingdom of heaven. They include or exclude us from the true Church. These two "keys" are the:

1. Pure *preaching* of God's Word
2. Proper exercise of *church discipline*

HEIDELBERG CATECHISM

Q. 83. What are the keys of the kingdom of heaven?

A. The preaching of the holy gospel, and Christian discipline, or excommunication out of the Christian church; by these two, the kingdom of heaven is opened to believers, and shut against unbelievers.

How do these *"keys"* open or close the kingdom of heaven? They do so in the following ways:

1. **The pure preaching** of God's Word clearly distinguishes those who are: lost, missing the marks and fruits of grace, unconverted, and unbelieving. Such persons, in their present condition, are yet **excluded** from the kingdom of heaven. The pure preaching also clearly defines those who are: saved, have believingly experienced the marks of grace, are converted to God, and are bringing forth the necessary fruits of regeneration. These are **included** in the kingdom of heaven.

2. **Church discipline** declares members to be outside of the kingdom of heaven who stubbornly continue in their own sinful ways after being warned by the church officebearers time and again. Church discipline excludes us from the true Church if we continue to live unrepentantly in public sin.

Church discipline is a loving attempt to correct and turn a church member from a publicly sinful practice in his life. This must be done out of a spirit of wisdom, love, and concern. Each member of church should have a true love and concern for all other church members. This deep concern should cause him to speak in love to anyone he sees going in a wrong and sinful way. If a person truly loves his neighbor and desires his welfare, he will speak with and warn him in a loving manner when he observes him going in a sinful and wrong way.

And let us consider one another *to provoke unto love* and to good works.
— Hebrews 10:24

We can witness two types of sin in the lives of our fellow church members; these are the:

1. Teaching of false doctrines, and

2. Committing of sins in words or actions

In order to properly exercise church discipline, we must make a distinction between *private* and *public* sin.

A **private sin** is a sin which was heard or seen by only one or a few. When this happens, the following must be done:

1. Speak privately with the person about his sin; this must be done both wisely and with sincere love and concern.

2. If he will not listen but continues in the same sin, take one or two trustworthy and confidential witnesses with you to speak with him again in love.

3. If he still does not listen and stubbornly refuses to break with his sin, then you must bring this matter, out of true concern for his well-being, to the attention of the consistory.

The Lord Jesus has clearly instructed us on how we must deal with a fellow church member who we privately witness sinning. He explains this in:

Matthew 18:15-17

Moreover if thy brother shall trespass against thee, go and tell him his fault *between thee and him alone:* if he shall hear thee, thou hast gained thy brother.

But if he will not hear thee, *then take with thee one or two more,* that in the mouth of two or three witnesses every word may be established.

And if he shall neglect to hear them, *tell it unto the church:* but if he neglect to hear the church, let him be unto thee as an heathen man and a publican.

WHAT DO YOU THINK?

WOULD YOU WARN YOUR FRIEND OF DANGER?

Imagine having a very leaky rowboat tied to your pier waiting for repair. If you saw some of your friends untie and jump into this rowboat, what would you do?

What type of friend would you be if you looked the other way and said, "Well, that's none of my business"?

If we see a friend sin and do not warn him about the danger of his sin, what type of friend are we? If we truly love and care for someone, what would we do, if we saw him begin upon a wrong and dangerous way?

Public sin is different from private sin. Public sin is a sin which is or has become known to many or all of the church members. A sin can become public in the following two ways:

1. When a sin is committed publicly or becomes public knowledge due to its nature
2. When a person stubbornly refuses to listen to correction and to turn from his private sin after the three steps previously mentioned have been tried

The consistory must deal with all cases of public sin in the lives of its members. The consistory must speak seriously and lovingly to the person, warning him and urging him to repent and turn from his sinful practice. If the person does not listen to these warnings, but continues in his sinful practice, then the consistory must begin with steps of *censure*.

The church *steps of censure* are as follows:

1. The member is placed under *silent censure*. No public mention is made of this to the congregation, but the person is notified by the consistory that he may not use *the sacraments* until he repents and turns from his sin.

2. *Announcement is made* to the congregation that a member *(his name is not mentioned)* has been placed under censure for breaking a certain commandment of God's law. The congregation is urged to pray for this person's repentance.

3. *Announcement is made* to the congregation *with the name* of the person and the commandment broken. Again, the congregation is urged to pray for him. This step may only be taken by a consistory after approval of the classis is obtained.

4. *Excommunication* takes place. The member is cut off from membership in the church of God.

WHAT DO YOU THINK?

A POORLY-TIMED WARNING

Bob, Scott, and some other boys were hired by a farmer to clean his barns. Poor Scott; nothing seemed to go right for him that day! He had one problem after another and became more and more angry. But the angrier he became, the more it seemed that things went wrong.

As the boys were finishing their work that afternoon, the others watched Scott sweep the last of the dirt into his dustpan. He then jumped up to yell, "We're done!", never realizing that he was bending under a heavy iron railing. As he jumped up, he hit his head so hard on the bar that it knocked him over and the dust pan flew out of his hand. The other boys roared with laughter, but Scott exploded with anger and swore at the others.

Bob immediately called out to him that he should not do that, for swearing was wrong. This, however, made Scott angrier yet and he swore again and again.

It was good that Bob wanted to warn his friend, but how could he have warned him in a wiser manner? Why is the time and manner in which we warn someone very important?

WHAT DO YOU THINK?
A LOVING FATHER DISCIPLINES HIS CHILDREN

Imagine a certain father claiming to love his children, but when his children do wrong and sinful things, he never punishes them. If you ask him why he never punishes his children, he tells you that he loves them too much and does not want to hurt their feelings or cause them to dislike him.

What do you think of this father's love? Although it is difficult to discipline, what would this father do if he really loved his children? What is going to happen to these children if their father continues with this thought and practice?

The officebearers in church are the "fathers" of the congregational "family." If they truly love their church members, and one needs disciplining, what must they do? What will happen to the church "family" if they do not?

When advancing from one step of censure to the next, the consistory must be patient and provide time for repentance. They must act carefully and wisely, out of a spirit of true love and concern. The consistory's efforts must be to wholeheartedly try to bring the person to repentance rather than to cut him off from the church.

The reasons for exercising church discipline in the church are to:

1. Uphold the honor and glory of God's Name.

2. Uphold the purity and spiritual health of the congregation

3. Use discipline as a medicine to try to bring the person to repentance

> But if he neglect to hear the church, *let him be unto thee as an heathen man and a publican.*
>
> Verily I say unto you, Whatsoever ye shall bind on earth shall be bound in heaven: and whatsoever ye shall loose on earth shall be loosed in heaven.
>
> — Matthew 18:17b-18

> Now we command you, brethren, in the name of our Lord Jesus Christ, that *ye withdraw yourselves* from every brother that walketh disorderly, and not after the tradition which he received of us.
>
> And if any man obey not our word by this epistle, note that man, and *have no company with him,* that he may be ashamed.
>
> Yet count him not as an enemy, but admonish him as a brother.
>
> — II Thessalonians 3:6, 14-15

> A man that is an heretic after the first and second admonition *reject.*
>
> — Titus 3:10

To be excommunicated from the church of God is a very terrible and frightful thing. Each confessing member has answered "yes" when he made confession of faith in the church, to the question:

"Do you promise that you will submit to admonition, correction, and church discipline in the event (which God forbid) that you may become delinquent either in doctrine or life?"

May God graciously prevent us from ever being placed under church censure.

However, if a person who has been excommunicated later repents, confesses his guilt, and turns from his sin, the church may and must receive him back in love.

No repenting sinner was ever turned away by the Lord Jesus Christ; in like manner, no repenting sinner may ever be turned away by His church.

WHAT DO YOU THINK?

LOVE IN READMISSION

Read the closing sentences and prayer in the:

Form for Readmitting Excommunicated Persons

And you, beloved Christians, receive this your brother, with hearty affection; be glad that he was dead and is alive, he was lost and is found; rejoice with the angels of heaven, over this sinner who repenteth: count him no longer as a stranger, but as a fellow-citizen with the saints, and of the household of God.

And whereas we can have no good of ourselves, let us, praising and magnifying the Lord Almighty, implore His mercy, saying:

Gracious God and Father, we thank Thee through Jesus Christ, that Thou hast been pleased to give this our fellow-brother repentance unto life, and us cause to rejoice in his conversion. We beseech Thee, show him Thy mercy, that he may become more and more assured in his mind of the remission of his sins, and that he may receive from thence inexpressible joy and delight, to serve Thee. And whereas he hath heretofore by his sins offended many, grant that he may, by his conversion, edify many. Grant also that he may steadfastly walk in Thy ways to the end; and may we learn from this example, that with Thee is mercy, that Thou mayest be feared; and that we, counting him for our brother and co-heir of life eternal, may jointly serve Thee with filial fear and obedience all the days of our life, through Jesus Christ, our Lord, in whose Name we thus conclude our prayer: Our Father, etc.

From this form, can you see and feel something of the love and joy with which a repenting excommunicated person should be received back into the church?

MEMORIZATION QUESTIONS

THE CHURCH

1. How is the gathering of all the true believers called?
   The Congregation or The Church of Christ.

2. Why is this gathering called the Congregation or the Church of Christ?
   Because Christ is the only Head and King of the Church (Colossians 1:18).

3. For what else?
   Because He has loved the Church, and gave Himself for it (Ephesians 5:25).

4. For what other reason?
   Because He gathers the Church, rules it, and preserves it forever.

5. By what means does Christ gather and rule His Church?
   By His Word and Spirit (Psalm 43:3).

6. Does Christ gather His Church out of the whole human race?
   Yes; out of every kindred and tongue, and people and nation (Revelation 5:9).

7. Against whom does Christ defend His Church?
   Against all her spiritual and corporal enemies (John 16:33).

8. Does Christ also use men to serve in His Church?
   Yes; He uses ministers, elders, and deacons.

9. When will the Church of Christ be complete?
   In the day when Christ has taken all His people up unto Himself in glory (John 17:24).

— *Donner's Catechism: Lesson XVII*

CHECKING YOUR READING

1. Define the Church:
   a. Visible — _____
      _____

   b. Invisible — _____
      _____

2. Give two examples from the Bible of a person who was a member of the Church Visible, but not of the Church Invisible:

   a. _____

   b. _____

3. Name and define the two parts of the Church Invisible:

   a. _____ — _____
      _____
      _____

   b. _____ — _____
      _____
      _____

4. Name three clear marks for distinguishing the true church from the false:

   a. _____

   b. _____

   c. _____

5. Why is attending a church service very serious and important?
   _____
   _____
   _____

6. Name the three ordinary New Testament offices and the main duties of each:

   a. _____ — _____

   b. _____ — _____

   c. _____ — _____

7. Who are the members of a:

   a. Consistory? _____

   b. Classis? _____

   c. Synod? _____

CHECKING YOUR READING

8. What is a Church Order? _____

_____

9. Name the two "keys" given by Christ to His church:

a. _____ b. _____

10. What procedure must be followed when we witness a private sin of one of our fellow
church members?

a. _____

b. _____

c. _____

11. What procedure must be followed by a consistory when dealing with public sin in the
life of a church member:

a. _____

b. _____

c. _____

d. _____

12. Why is church excommunication a tremendously serious event? _____

_____

━━━━━ EXTRA CHALLENGE QUESTIONS ━━━━━

1. In the Parable of the Ten Virgins, what is pictured by:

a. The virgins' lamps? _____

b. The oil? _____

c. Midnight? _____

d. The marriage feast? _____

e. The door being closed? _____

2. In the story, **A Poorly-Timed Warning**, how could Bob have warned and spoken to Scott in a wiser manner?

_____

_____

3. Some day the Church Invisible will become clearly visible. When will this be? Explain. _____

_____

4. Church discipline and censure are used as both "medicine" and "surgery." How are they used as:

a. "Medicine"? — _____

b. "Surgery"? — _____

TESTING YOUR KNOWLEDGE

1. If we truly love God, why will we also love to pray? _____

   _____

   _____

   _____

2. Name six elements found in true prayer:

   a. _____   d. _____

   b. _____   e. _____

   c. _____   f. _____

3. Name six things for which we should pray:

   a. _____   d. _____

   b. _____   e. _____

   c. _____   f. _____

4. Name four kinds of prayer:

   a. _____   c. _____

   b. _____   d. _____

5. What does it mean to pray without ceasing? How can a person do this?

   _____

   _____

   _____

6. List the six requests found in the Lord's Prayer:

   a. The three requests for God's glory:

      1. _____

      2. _____

      3. _____

   b. The three requests for our needs:

      1. _____

      2. _____

      3. _____

TESTING YOUR KNOWLEDGE

7. How can a person be a member of the Church Visible and not of the Church Invisible?

   Explain: _____

   _____

   _____

8. Against which enemies are the members of the Church Militant fighting?

   a. _____   c. _____

   b. _____   d. _____

9. Why will the Church Militant become the Church Triumphant in the end?

   _____

   _____

10. Name the three:

    Extraordinary New Testament   *Ordinary New Testament*

    Church Offices   *Church Offices*

    a. _____   a. _____

    b. _____   b. _____

    c. _____   c. _____

11. What is a church order and why is it necessary for church life?

    _____

    _____

    _____

12. Name the four steps which a consistory takes in matters of church censure:

    a. _____

    b. _____

    c. _____

    d. _____

13. List three important reasons for exercising church discipline:

    a. _____

    b. _____

    c. _____

WORD SCRAMBLE

Unscramble the following Vocabulary Words from Chapters Fifteen and Sixteen and write them on the blanks provided. Then place the letter of the best matching definition in front of the proper word.

_____ 1. everrecen

_____ 2. ruiihelvbcshc

_____ 3. sbsismiuno

_____ 4. aiscssl

_____ 5. necriysti

_____ 6. ydnos

_____ 7. csihieilcnbuvrh

_____ 8. mnoocnium

_____ 9. biuspclni

_____ 10. engyucr

_____ 11. ocerhdncmnohiautin

_____ 12. geelcdkanwo

_____ 13. taevnipsri

_____ 14. bcuipl

_____ 15. lcriuhmcinhtat

_____ 16. imiyhlut

_____ 17. aerypr

_____ 18. cnhruhcthimuprat

_____ 19. agencis

_____ 20. ehrduipicsclhcin

A. Spiritual friendship and fellowship
B. All God's elect; the body of all true believers
C. Not private; that which is known to many
D. The Church Invisible on earth which is fighting against its spiritual enemies
E. Deep respect; a worshipping of God
F. A loving correction which serves as a means to work personal repentance and maintain church purity
G. The state of being important and necessary
H. The outward body of Christian believers
I. A meeting of church representatives from each classis
J. An earnest request and sincere thanking of God for His blessings, for Christ's sake
K. A sin which becomes known to many or all of the people in a local congregation
L. Meekness; a thinking of low thoughts of self
M. The true believers in heaven who rejoice in God who saved them from their enemies
N. A surrendering to; a placing oneself under
O. A group of church people who meet under the same name and share the same beliefs
P. A sin known only to one or a few church members
Q. Honesty; truthfulness
R. A meeting of church representatives from each consistory within a certain area
S. Stopping
T. An expressing of thanks or appreciation for

BIBLE STUDY QUESTIONS

Read the following chapters and write out the verse or verses which most clearly teach the following doctrinal truths:

1. God's command that all people should pray —

   Isaiah 55: _____ — _____

   _____

   _____

2. We must only pray to God —

   Matthew 4: _____ — _____

   _____

   _____

3. An outward (visible) church member is different from an inward (invisible) church member —

   Romans 2: _____ (2 verses) — _____

   _____

   _____

   _____

   _____

4. The great importance of the preaching of God's Word —

   Romans 10:_____ — _____

   _____

   _____

   _____

PROJECT IDEAS

1. Write a report on our Church Order which was approved by the Synod of Dordt in 1618 and 1619. List what is taught in each of its four main parts. Explain some interesting things you learned in each part.

2. Construct a large chart showing the elements, kinds, and times of prayer and the needs which are to be remembered in prayer.

3. Make a poster which shows the parts and requests of the Lord's Prayer. Explain what each part means.

4. Design a chart which shows and defines the Church Visible, Invisible, Militant, and Triumphant.

5. Draw a chart and write a report which explains the Old Testament and New Testament church offices and their respective duties.

CHAPTER 17

VOCABULARY

1. **Means** — Something which is used to help accomplish a certain purpose

2. **Means of Grace** — The Bible and the sacraments which God the Holy Spirit uses to work and strengthen true saving faith

3. **Offer** — Something presented to be accepted or rejected

4. **Reject** — To refuse; to cast away

5. **Slander** — A lie which is intended to purposely hurt the reputation of another person

6. **Law** — A rule which informs us of that which we must or may not do, the breaking of which will result in punishment

7. **Institution** — An organization established for a certain public purpose

8. **Civil Laws** — Laws for everyday matters in society

9. **Ceremonial Laws** — Israel's Old Testament religious laws which pointed to and were fulfilled by Jesus Christ

10. **Moral Law** — God's Ten Commandments; God's law for all people and times

THE MEANS OF GRACE

And now, brethren, I commend you to God, and to the **Word of His grace,** which is able to build you up, and to give you an inheritance among all them which are sanctified.

— Acts 20:32

Go ye therefore, and teach all nations, **baptizing** them in the Name of the Father, and of the Son, and of the Holy Ghost.

— Matthew 28:19

And when He had given thanks, He brake it, and said, Take, eat: this is My body, which is broken for you: this do in remembrance of Me.

After the same manner also He took the cup, when He had supped, saying, This cup is the New Testament in My blood: this do ye, as oft as ye drink it, in remembrance of Me.

For as often as ye **eat this bread,** and **drink this cup,** ye do shew the Lord's death till He come.

— I Corinthians 11:24-26

God the Holy Spirit is the author and worker of true saving faith in a person's heart. However, the Holy Spirit uses **means of grace** as tools to work and to strengthen faith. His two means of grace are:

1. **God's Word,** The Bible

2. **God's sacraments,** Holy Baptism and the Lord's Supper

The means of grace do not have the power of themselves to work or strengthen faith. Only God the Holy Spirit has this power. He uses **His Word** as an instrument or tool to both plant and strengthen faith. The Holy Spirit uses the **sacraments** as a **means** to only strengthen faith.

117

WHAT DO YOU THINK?

FORGETTING THE CRAFTSMAN!

Mr. Booker visited Mt. Rushmore in South Dakota and became very interested in how four large Presidents' heads could be carved out of a mountain so exactly.

He spent several years studying how these heads had been carved. However, he spent the entire time searching into and admiring the type of scaffolding used, the dynamite required, the size and make of the air hammers employed, the type of chisels which were most helpful, etc.

The various tools which were used to complete this great task are important. A true craftsman values good tools. But, if Mr. Booker were only interested in the tools being used, why would this be a strange way to study how the Mt. Rushmore monument was formed? Why would he be missing the most important element in his study? What could the best of tools do of themselves?

God's Word is the most valuable tool or means of salvation. It was made and given by God Himself. However, to be saving, who must use the Word and be the "power" which works through the Word?

For our gospel came not unto you in Word only, but also in power, and in the Holy Ghost.

— I Thessalonians 1:5a

God the Holy Spirit works with an irresistible power when regenerating sinners and turning them from loving and serving themselves, the world, and sin, to God. We all need this converting work of the Holy Spirit in our hearts.

For *it is God which worketh in you* both to will and to do of His good pleasure.

— Philippians 2:13

For *as many as are led by the Spirit of God,* they are the sons of God.

— Romans 8:14

And a certain woman named Lydia, a seller of purple, of the city of Thyatira, which worshipped God, heard us: *whose heart the Lord opened,* that she attended unto the things which were spoken by Paul.

— Acts 16:14

The means through which the Holy Spirit works and strengthens faith are also very important. Why? God has chosen to work His saving work through means. He has given us these means of grace and commanded us to use them. Read the story of the sick man on the next page. How did this man **undervalue** the means which God had given?

We can err in undervaluing God's means as the sick man in this story did. However, we can also be guilty of **overvaluing** the means. When we do this, we trust in the means, rather than in God who must apply and bless the means. Read the story of the sick woman on page 120. How was she guilty of overvaluing the means?

WHAT DO YOU THINK?

A SICK MAN

Imagine going to visit a man who is very ill. He can no longer walk nor breathe properly because of his serious sickness.

"Are your medicines helping at all?" you ask him.

"My medicines?" he answers, "I am not taking any medicines."

"You're not!" you reply, quite shocked. "Why, who is your doctor?"

"My doctor?" the man gasps between breaths, "Why, I am not seeing a doctor."

"You're not!" you exclaim, even more shocked. "Why not?"

"Well," the man slowly answers, "the doctors and medicines cannot help me if God does not bless them. I pray that God will heal me and I am waiting to see what will happen."

What is wrong with this man's reasoning? How is he **undervaluing** the means which God has given? How is he separating God from the means through which God works? When the man said, "The doctors and medicines cannot do anything if God does not bless them," was this true? How is this only half of the truth, however? What also needs to be said?

By nature, we too are sick with a deadly disease — a deadly disease of sin. It is certainly true that God must convert us and that our use of the means of grace will do

nothing without God's blessing. But if we sit back to see what will happen and do not actively use the means of grace that God has given, how are we mistaken in our reasoning? How is our reasoning wrong just as this sick man's?

God commands us to actively seek Him through the use of His means of grace. We must pray to God to bless His means, for without His blessing, all is in vain. However, we must actively use God's means. We must attend and listen carefully to the preaching of God's Word in church; and read, think about, and try to understand the truths of God's Word at home and in school. We must continually ask God in prayer to bless His Word in our lives.

God has never said in His Word, "Seek Me for nothing." God has commanded sinners to prayerfully use His means of grace and has promised to bless them, not because they seek Him so well, but because He is so gracious.

I have not spoken in secret, in a dark place of the earth: *I said not* unto the seed of Jacob, *Seek ye Me in vain.*

— Isaiah 45:19a

WHAT DO YOU THINK?

A SICK WOMAN

Imagine visiting an older woman who is very ill. "How are you feeling?" you ask her with concern, noticing that she looks very weak and pale.

"Not too well yet," she says, "but I trust that I will get better. I am seeing the best doctor in the city who is a specialist in my disease and he has put me on a new medicine which he thinks will help. This medicine should make me better in a short time."

It is good that this lady is using the means God has provided for curing bodily disease. However, where is this woman's trust? Without God's blessing, can these means cure her? She has faith in the means and not in God who needs to work through the means. Why is this wrong?

A person can also *overvalue* the means of grace. A person might think, "I believe I will become better and enter heaven because I go to church twice every Sunday, pray before and after my meals as well as each morning and evening, read the Bible every day, and listen carefully to God's Word at home, school, and church. Because I use these means faithfully, I believe that I will be saved."

What is wrong with this person's reasoning? Of themselves, can the means of grace save us? Who must bless and work through the means of grace to save a person?

GOD'S WORD

God will use His inspired and infallible Word, **the Bible,** to both work and strengthen faith. God has promised to bless the reading, teaching, studying, and especially, the preaching of His Word.

When God converts a sinner from a loving and serving of sin to God, He uses His Word as the means. God will either bring this person to the Word or the Word to this person. Sometimes this takes place in remarkable ways. Read the next two stories as examples of this.

So then *faith* cometh by hearing, and hearing *by the Word of God.*
— Romans 10:17

For after that in the wisdom of God the world by wisdom knew not God, it pleased God by the foolishness of *preaching* to save them that believe.
— I Corinthians 1:21

How then shall they call on Him in whom they have not believed? and how shall they believe·in Him of whom they have not heard? and *how shall they hear without a preacher?*
And how shall they preach, except they be sent? as it is written, How beautiful are the feet of them that *preach the gospel of peace,* and bring glad tidings of good things!
— Romans 10:14-15

WHAT DO YOU THINK?

THE OLD COLONEL

One cold winter evening, a tall, ragged man wandered into the Water Street Chapel in the heart of New York City to warm himself. This man was known as "the old colonel."

He was over sixty years old, but looked older. He had a long, dirty, gray beard. His gray hair was filthy and uncut, hanging way down his back. His eyes were bleary. His face was rugged and dirty. His ragged overcoat was fastened with a nail. His trousers were filled with holes. Instead of shoes, he had rags tied with strings on his feet.

Sin and whiskey had brought "the old colonel" to this pitiable condition. One would never have thought that he was a college graduate; that he had studied law in the office of President Lincoln's great Secretary of War, Stanton!

Seeing the lights on in the small chapel, "the old colonel" stepped inside to warm himself for a few minutes.

A visiting minister was preaching that evening and the truth of God's Word struck "the old colonel." His sin became real — his entire life of sin. In the middle of the service he cried out, "O God, if it is not too late, forgive this old sinner!"

Everytime the church was open "the old colonel" was now there. No one paid closer attention to the Word being preached than he. From that moment on he was a changed man — both inwardly and outwardly. Later, when the Lord

revealed Himself as a complete Savior for completely lost sinners then there was not a more joyous and thankful person in the church than "the old colonel." He told everyone — his previous slum-area friends and his new church friends that Jesus came to save sinners of whom he was the chief.

He often looked back in amazement upon the time that he was directed to step into the little chapel on Water Street. He often testified that God's grace in saving such an old, established, back-slidden sinner as he was, was too great for him to understand and yet he knew that it was true.

Did God bring this person to His Word or did He bring His Word to this person? Can you see the power of the Holy Spirit working through the means of God's Word in this story?

— Adapted from *1001 Stories for Children*

WHAT DO YOU THINK?

SAVED ON HER DEATHBED

Rev. Guthrie, a well-known minister in Scotland from 1650-1665, was once traveling home on horseback very late at night. It being very dark, he lost his way entirely and soon did not even know in which direction he should travel. He asked the Lord for guidance and laid the reins on the neck of the horse.

The horse traveled over ditches and fields for some time and finally came to a poor farmhouse. Rev. Guthrie knocked on the door and asked permission to stay there until morning.

In the farmhouse he met a woman who was dying. As he earnestly spoke to her from the Word of God about her lost condition and need for Jesus Christ, God blessed His Word to the heart of this woman. When she died, Rev. Guthrie believed that she was taken into heaven.

When the minister returned home the following day, he said to his wife, "I came to a farmhouse where I found a woman in a state of nature, I saw her in a state of grace, and I left her in a state of glory."

Did God bring this person to the Word, or the Word to this person? Can you see the power of the Holy Spirit working through the means of His Word in this remarkable story?

— Adapted from *3,000 Illustrations for Christian Service*

It is very important to prayerfully use the means of grace which God has provided and promised to bless to work saving conversion in the lives of sinners. Do you find time for Bible reading and prayer? Do you listen carefully to religious instruction at home, church, and school? Do you place yourself in the way of God's means of grace by reading from, listening to, and thinking about God's Word?

WHAT DO YOU THINK?

WHERE JESUS PASSES BY

Read the story of Zacchaeus in:

Luke 19:1-10

And Jesus entered and passed through Jericho.

And, behold, there was a man named Zacchaeus, which was the chief among the publicans, and he was rich.

And he sought to see Jesus who He was; and could not for the press, because he was little of stature.

And he ran before, and climbed up into a sycomore tree to see Him: for He was to pass that way.

And when Jesus came to the place, He looked up, and saw him, and said unto him, Zacchaeus, make haste, and come down; for to day I must abide at thy house.

And he made haste, and came down, and received Him joyfully.

And when they saw it, they all murmured, saying, That He was gone to be guest with a man that is a sinner.

And Zacchaeus stood, and said unto the Lord: Behold, Lord, the half of my goods I give to the poor; and if I have taken any thing from any man by false accusation, I restore him fourfold.

And Jesus said unto him, This day is salvation come to this house, forsomuch as he also is a son of Abraham.

For the Son of man is come to seek and to save that which was lost.

Zacchaeus placed himself where Jesus would pass by and God blessed this to his salvation. Where does Jesus "pass by" today? Where must we place ourselves? How should verse ten encourage lost sinners to do this?

It is a great blessing to be brought up with the Word of God. It is a wonderful privilege to have the Bible in our home, school, and church. The Bible is the means the Holy Spirit uses to convert sinners from sin to God.

Sometimes the experience of conversion takes place very instantly and dramatically as in the life of the Apostle Paul; at other times it takes place more gently as with Lydia; and with others, it takes place more gradually as in the life of Timothy. Yet each person who is converted to God will experience something of total sinfulness and *misery;* his need for *deliverance* through a complete Savior, and the desires of his heart being won over to love, serve, and walk in the ways of God out of true *thankfulness.*

Being brought up under God's Word is not only a precious blessing, but it is also a *great responsibility.* God is speaking to us in His Word and one day He will ask each of us what we have done with His Word and invitations.

By nature, however, we are dead to God's callings and alive to sin. We are interested in ourselves, sin,

WHAT DO YOU THINK?

ALL IN ONE

A man was once packing his suitcase, preparing for a trip. A friend was watching him. The man said, "Well I have a little corner left in the suitcase. In it, I am going to pack a map, a lamp, a mirror, a telescope, a book of poems, some biographies, a bundle of letters, a psalm book, and a sharp sword — all in a space of about five by three inches!"

"How are you going to do that?" asked the friend.

"Very easily," replied the man, "for my Bible is all of these things!"

Do you value your Bible as this man did his? Is your Bible your map, light, mirror, and telescope? What is meant by these four terms?

EXPERIENCE OF CONVERSION IN THE LIFE OF:

Paul

And as he journeyed, he came near Damascus: and suddenly there shined round about him a light from heaven:

And he fell to the earth, and heard a voice saying unto him, Saul, Saul, why persecutest thou Me?

And he said, Who art Thou, Lord? And the Lord said, I am Jesus whom thou persecutest: it is hard for thee to kick against the pricks.

And he trembling and astonished said, Lord, what wilt Thou have me to do?

— Acts 9:3-6a

Lydia

And a certain woman named Lydia, a seller of purple, of the city of Thyatira, which worshipped God, heard us: whose heart the Lord opened, that she attended unto the things which were spoken by Paul.

— Acts 16:14

Timothy

When I call to remembrance the unfeigned faith that is in thee, which dwelt first in thy grandmother Lois, and thy mother Eunice; and I am persuaded that in thee also. And that from a child thou hast known the Holy Scriptures, which are able to make thee wise unto salvation through faith which is in Christ Jesus.

— II Timothy 1:5 and 3:15

and the evil desires of this world. We turn away from God and do not desire to love or serve Him. Therefore, we need God the Holy Spirit to plant new spiritual life in us and turn us from sin and death to God. We must continually pray for this and actively use the means of grace God has given for this purpose. We cannot regenerate or convert ourselves, but we may and must seriously use God's Word, pleading with the Lord to apply its truths in our hearts by the power and work of the Holy Ghost.

WHAT DO YOU THINK?

GOD'S OFFER OF SALVATION

Read the Canons of Dordt: III—IV Head, Articles 8,9, & 10:

Article 8. As many as are called by the gospel, are unfeignedly called. For God hath most earnestly and truly declared in His Word, what will be acceptable to Him; namely, that all who are called, should comply with the invitation. He, moreover, seriously promises eternal life, and rest, to as many as shall come to Him, and believe on Him.

Article 9. It is not the fault of the gospel, nor of Christ, offered therein, nor of God, who calls men by the gospel, and confers upon them various gifts, that those who are called by the ministry of the Word, refuse to come, and be converted: the fault lies in themselves; some of whom when called, regardless of their danger, reject the Word of life; others, though they receive it, suffer it not to make a lasting impression on their heart; therefore, their joy, arising only from a temporary faith, soon vanishes, and they fall away; while others choke the seed of the Word by perplexing cares, and the pleasures of this world, and produce no fruit. — This our Savior teaches in the parable of the sower. Matt. 13.

Article 10. But that others who are called by the gospel, obey the call, and are converted, is not to be ascribed to the proper exercise of free will, whereby one distinguishes himself above others, equally furnished with grace sufficient for faith and conversions, as the proud heresy of Pelagius maintains; but it must be wholly ascribed to God, who as He has chosen His own from eternity in Christ, so He confers upon them faith and repentance, rescues them from the power of darkness, and translates them into the kingdom of His own Son, that they may show forth the praises of Him, who hath called them out of darkness into His marvelous light: and may glory not in themselves, but in the Lord according to the testimony of the apostles in various places.

Does God sincerely offer salvation to all who come under His Word? Who is at fault if sinners reject this offer? Who is to receive all the credit if sinners are converted and respond to this call?

WHAT DO YOU THINK?

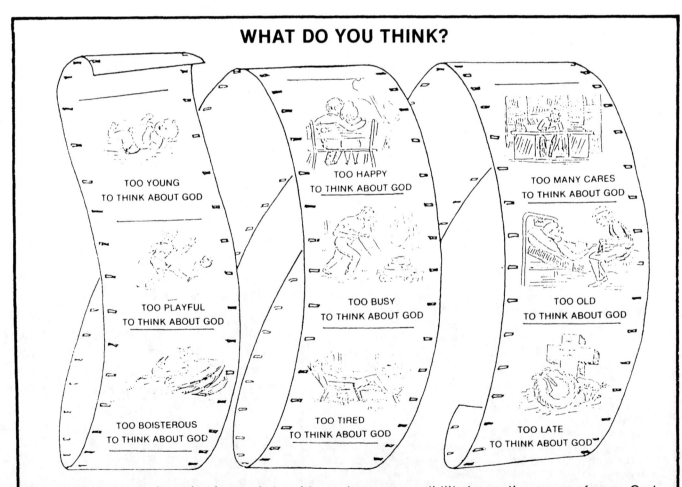

TOO YOUNG TO THINK ABOUT GOD

TOO HAPPY TO THINK ABOUT GOD

TOO MANY CARES TO THINK ABOUT GOD

TOO PLAYFUL TO THINK ABOUT GOD

TOO BUSY TO THINK ABOUT GOD

TOO OLD TO THINK ABOUT GOD

TOO BOISTEROUS TO THINK ABOUT GOD

TOO TIRED TO THINK ABOUT GOD

TOO LATE TO THINK ABOUT GOD

In these examples, what lesson is taught about our responsibility to use the means of grace God has given us? What will happen to us if we continually ignore these means?

— Adapted from *The NRC Banner of Truth Tract Committee*

WHAT DO YOU THINK?

"MARY, I LOVE YOU STILL"

At last Mary was allowed to move from her cottage home in the country to a large city nearby. Her father was dead, and her mother had not wanted to part with her. How could she let her daughter live among strangers in a place where there were so many temptations, but no one to give her advice?

The poor widow finally agreed, however, and Mary left the home of her childhood. At first, the weekly letters exchanged were warm and loving. The loving mother eagerly anticipated each letter. She cherished every word, even the little things about clothes and friends, for she was deeply concerned about her daughter.

As time went on, however, she noticed that Mary's letters were changing. Mary no longer asked for advice, and was not sharing much about her life. The letters gradually became shorter and less loving, and finally stopped arriving altogether.

The poor widow's heart sank, and in her trouble she cast her burden upon her "Burden-Bearer," the Lord Jesus Christ. Day after day she prayed that He would guide and protect her daughter.

Then sad news reached the mother's ears from the distant city—news which nearly broke her heart. She heard that her daughter had forgotten her loving words of warning and advice, had forgotten her mother's God, and had so far forgotten herself that she was leading a life of sin and shame. When the mother heard this, she decided to find her lost child. She at once set out for the city and upon arriving there, began to look for the place where her daughter was living. This was difficult, for she had moved from

the address where the mother had sent her letters. Day and night, into every likely place, the poor heartbroken mother went in search of her wandering child.

After a number of days of searching without success, she decided to return home, but a new thought flashed across her mind. She went to the photographer's and had her picture taken. She had a number of copies made and then went to the various places of sin, asking permission to hang them on the walls. It was a strange request, indeed; but seeing the type of person she was, no one turned her away.

Some time after that, the daughter and her friend walked into one of these places. Her attention was immediately drawn to the picture on the wall. She said, "That looks like my mother!" She went to look at it more closely, and exclaimed in amazement, "IT *IS* MY MOTHER!" Then she noticed something written at the bottom of it, and recognized the familiar handwriting at once. But she was not prepared for what those words expressed: "Mary, I love you still!"

This was too much for her.

She was prepared for scoldings and hard words, and expected nothing else; but to think that her mother had actually been searching for her in places of sin and folly, and was willing to receive her back home just as she was, she could not understand. As she thought about the words, "Mary, I love you still!" the days of her childhood came back before her and all memories of her godly home — her mother's prayers, tears, and loving advice; and as she thought about the difference between what she was then and what she was now, she completely broke down. Tears flowed from her eyes as her heart broke. The awfulness of her evil ways was clearly brought into her mind, and she at once decided to leave her sinful friends and go back to her mother. Great was the joy of the widowed mother at the unexpected arrival of her long-lost daughter.

How is this story a picture of God's sincere call and invitation extended to sinners, calling them to repent and return to Him? How can this story be compared to the prodigal son who returned to his father?

— Adapted from *The NRC Banner of Truth*

GOD'S LAW AND GOSPEL

God's Word includes both **law** *and gospel.* A law is a rule which is to be obeyed. It informs us of that which we must or may not do. God has given us His law. It tells us what is right and wrong.

God's law requires true love toward God and our neighbor.

The law of the LORD is perfect, converting the soul: the testimony of the LORD is sure, making wise the simple.

*The **statues of the LORD** are right, **rejoicing the heart:** the commandment of the LORD is pure, enlightening the eyes.*

The fear of the LORD is clean, enduring for ever: the judgments of the LORD are true and righteous altogether.

*More to be desired are they than gold, yea, than much fine gold: **sweeter also than honey and the honeycomb.***
— Psalm 19:7-10

And thou shalt **love the Lord** thy God with all thy heart, and with all thy soul, and with all thy mind, and with all thy strength: this is the first commandment.

And the second is like, namely this, Thou shalt **love thy neighbor** as thy self. There is none other commandment greater than these.
— Mark 12:30-31

We must obey God from a spirit of love; not only because God requires it, but because we love and desire to do that which is pleasing in God's sight. We must serve and obey God, not only because we **have** to, but also because we **want** to. Our obedience must be a willful obedience.

WHAT DO YOU THINK?

WILLING OR UNWILLING OBEDIENCE?

"Annette, would you come and vacuum the kitchen, please?" Annette's mother calls from the kitchen.

"Oh . . . do I **have** to? How come I always have to help? Janice hardly ever has to help. Why always me? I just started reading my book again. I was just at such a good part, of course. Why does the floor need to be vacuumed anyway?"

With stomping feet and a scowling face, Annette arrives in the kitchen, and disgustedly attacks the vacuum cleaner.

Did Annette obey her mother or not? She did as she was told, didn't she? Even though outwardly Annette was vacuuming the kitchen as she was asked, what was wrong? Do you think Annette's mother was pleased with her obedience? Did Annette's behavior show a loving thankfulness to her mother who has done so much for her? Was Annette obeying because she **wanted** to or because she **had** to? Is this an example of willing or unwilling obedience?

God's law requires obedience. However, God is not pleased if we obey only because we **have** to. The obedience which is pleasing to God is an obedience because we **want** to obey out of a thankful and loving spirit to God. God delights in willful obedience.

Do you know something in your life of wanting and loving to walk in a manner which is pleasing to God?

God uses His law as a means in converting a soul from sin to God. God opens a person's spiritual eyes to see that which God is requiring in His law. When this happens, the sinner begins to see how sinful he actually is; how all his thoughts, words, and actions come from a love for himself, the world, and sin. He begins to see how even the things in his life which he thought were good are actually sinful in the sight of God. He begins to realize that he does not do anything from a true love for God, but only out of a desire for his own honor.

The more God the Holy Spirit shines His light through the law into a sinner's heart, the more this person feels his totally sinful and lost condition.

Therefore by the deeds of the law there shall no flesh be justified in His sight: for **by the law is the knowledge of sin.**
— Romans 3:20

But we are all as an unclean thing, and **all our righteousnesses are as filthy rags;** and we do all fade as a leaf; and our iniquities, like the wind, have taken us away.
— Isaiah 64:6

This learning of personal sinfulness and misery works a true need and desire for the only Savior, the Lord Jesus Christ. This person comes to see that he needs the Lord Jesus, the one who kept God's law perfectly. He sees that he can only be saved through the work of Jesus, who gave His perfect life for sinners.

WHAT DO YOU THINK?

THE RICH YOUNG RULER'S OBEDIENCE

Read the story of the rich young ruler in:

Matthew 19:16-22:

And, behold, one came and said unto Him, Good Master, what good thing shall I do, that I may have eternal life?

And He said unto him, Why callest thou Me good? there is none good but One, that is, God: but if thou wilt enter into life, keep the commandments.

He saith unto Him, Which? Jesus said, Thou shalt do no murder, Thou shalt not commit adultery, Thou shalt not steal, Thou shalt not bear false witness,

Honour thy father and thy mother: and, Thou shalt love thy neighbour as thyself.

The young man saith unto Him, All these things have I kept from my youth up: what lack I yet?

Jesus said unto him, If thou wilt be perfect, go and sell that thou hast, and give to the poor, and thou shalt have treasure in heaven: and come and follow Me.

But when the young man heard that saying, he went away sorrowful: for he had great possessions.

The rich young ruler told Jesus that he had obeyed all of God's commandments from his youth until that moment. But, what did Jesus point out to him about the manner in which he had kept God's commandments? What was missing in the way he was trying to fulfill God's law? Why had he actually never kept any of God's commandments? In one word, what does the law of God require that this young man was missing?

WHAT DO YOU THINK?

DIRTIER INSTEAD OF CLEANER

Christian, in John Bunyan's **Pilgrim's Progress,** was taken by Mr. Interpreter into a room full of dust. A man came into the room and started to sweep. The harder he swept, the more the dust filled the room until poor Christian almost choked to death.

The dust in this story pictures our sinfulness. The man sweeping is a picture of a person trying to clean his own sinful heart by working with God's law. He is trying to make himself clean through his own obedience.

What is meant by the room becoming more and more difficult to live in, and by Christian nearly choking to death?

What does Paul mean in:

Romans 7:9-10

For I was alive without the law once: but when the commandment came, sin revived, and I died.
And the commandment, which was ordained to life, I found to be unto death.

When the Holy Spirit reveals to this person something of his salvation in Jesus Christ by free grace, then his heart will overflow with love in return unto God for the wonderful mercy shown to him.

He will then wish to love and serve God with all his heart, mind, and strength. How can this person know what is pleasing to God? The Holy Spirit again uses the law to teach him. The law informs us of that which is pleasing and displeasing to the Lord. His deepest love is now to obey God's law and he is truly sorrowful when he breaks it.

True faith and love must be revealed in works of thankful obedience. The deepest love of those who are truly regenerated is to walk in a way which is pleasing to God. This way is clearly taught in God's law.

Is this your deepest longing and desire? Do you love to live according to God's law? Can the fruits of a loving obedience be seen in your life?

If ye **love** Me, **keep My commandments.**
— John 14:15

Even so **faith,** if it hath not works, **is dead, being alone.**
Yea, a man may say, Thou hast faith, and I have works: shew me thy faith without thy works, and I will shew thee my faith by my works.
Thou believest that there is one God: thou doest well: the devils also believe, and tremble.
But wilt thou know, O vain man, that **faith without works is dead?**
— James 2:17-20

Ye are My friends, if **ye do whatsoever I command you.**
— John 15:14

But **be ye doers of the Word,** and not hearers only, deceiving your own selves.
— James 1:22

To summarize, God uses His law as a means in the conversion of a sinner in two ways:

1. *In misery;* to convince and convict the person of his totally sinful and lost condition and of his need for the only complete Savior, Jesus Christ.

2. In *thankfulness;* to show the person how to thankfully serve and love God by walking in a manner which is pleasing in God's sight.

God's law stands above all of man's laws. God's laws are absolute. They tell us that which is right and wrong. To break any of God's laws is sin. People may fight against God and believe or teach that something is right which God has said is wrong, but this is only sin, rebellion, and foolishness. On the final judgment day we shall not be judged by what we or other people thought or said was right or wrong, but by God's law.

> And it is easier for heaven and earth to pass, than **one tittle of the law to fail.**
> — Luke 16:17

> Whosoever committeth sin transgresseth also the law: for **sin is the transgression of the law.**
> — I John 3:4

> For this is the love of God, that we **keep His commandments:** and His commandments are not grievous.
> — I John 5:3

God is King over all creation. He has created all things and rules over all. God has given authority to some people to rule according to His law in certain areas. This can be pictured as follows:

WHAT DO YOU THINK?

THE THREE PARTS OF TRUE CONVERSION

Can you find misery, deliverance and thankfulness in the experience of:

David?

I waited patiently for the LORD; and He inclined unto me, and heard my cry.

He brought me up also out of an horrible pit, out of the miry clay, and set my feet upon a rock, and established my goings.

And He hath put a new song in my mouth, even praise unto our God: many shall see it, and fear, and shall trust in the LORD.

— Psalm 40:1-3

Paul?

O wretched man that I am! who shall deliver me from the body of this death?

I thank God through Jesus Christ our Lord. So then with the mind I myself serve the law of God; but with the flesh the law of sin.

— Romans 7:24-25

Ethiopian Eunuch?

And Philip ran thither to him, and heard him read the prophet Esaias, and said, Understandest thou what thou readest?

And he said, How can I, except some man should guide me? and he desired Philip that he would come up and sit with him.

And Philip said, If thou believest with all thine heart, thou mayest. And he answered and said, I believe that Jesus Christ is the Son of God.

And when they were come up out of the water, the Spirit of the LORD caught away Philip, that the eunuch saw him no more: and he went on his way rejoicing.

— Acts 8:30-31, 37, 39

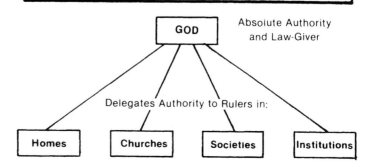

129

God has appointed ruler in our homes, churches, civil government, and **institutions** such as your school and father's place of business. Each person placed in authority must be respected and obeyed, for God has chosen to govern us through this means. God has given rulers in each area of human life. Obedience must begin at home and be followed in all areas of

> Let every soul be **subject unto the higher powers.** For there is no power but of God: **the powers that be are ordained of God.**
>
> Whosoever therefore resisteth the power, resisteth the ordinance of God: and they that resist shall receive to themselves damnation.
>
> — Romans 13:1-2

> Children, **obey your parents** in all things: for this is well pleasing unto the Lord.
>
> — Colossians 3:20

WHAT DO YOU THINK?

OBEDIENCE OR DISOBEDIENCE?

The Sanhedrin, the Jewish Council, commanded Peter and John not to speak or teach in the Name of Jesus.

> And they called them, and commanded them not to speak at all nor teach in the Name of Jesus.
>
> — Acts 4:18

But Peter and John disobeyed their rulers. We read:

> But Peter and John answered and said unto them, Whether it be right in the sight of God to hearken unto you more than unto God, judge ye.
>
> And they spake the word of God with boldness.
>
> — Acts 4:19, 31b

Were Peter and John right or wrong in disobeying their rulers in this case? Why? Were they obeying or disobeying God?

Those who are placed in positions of authority may not rule and govern as they desire and please, but they must rule according to God's law. God will judge them according to how they have ruled in the positions where God has placed them. Your parents may not rule your home or bring you up in whatever way they want. They must bring you up according to God's law and expectations. Therefore, you must honor and obey them, for God has placed them in your home to rule according to His will.

> And he said unto them, Set your hearts unto all the words which I testify among you this day, which ye shall **command your children to observe to do, all the words of this law.**
>
> — Deuteronomy 32:46

> **Train up a child in the way he should go:** and when he is old, he will not depart from it.
>
> — Proverbs 22:6

> And, ye fathers, provoke not your children to wrath: but **bring them up in the nurture and admonition of the Lord.**
>
> — Ephesians 6:4

If a person in authority would command us to do something which is against God's law, we must obey God rather than man. In all other cases, we are commanded by God to obey those whom God has placed to rule over us.

> Put them in mind **to be subject to** principalities and powers, **to obey magistrates,** to be ready to every good work.
>
> — Titus 3:1

> **Submit yourselves to every ordinance of man for the Lord's sake:** whether it be to the king, as supreme;
>
> Or unto governors, as unto them that are sent by him for the punishment of evildoers, and for the praise of them that do well.
>
> — I Peter 2:13-14

God has given three types of law in His Word. These are:

1. Civil Law
2. Ceremonial Law
3. Moral Law

Civil laws are the rules for *everyday matters in society.* Today's civil laws would include rules for limiting speed, stopping for red lights, not walking on another's private property, and thousands of other things. Can you imagine what our lives would be like without civil laws? The nation of Israel received their civil laws directly from God in the Old Testament. Many of these civil laws do not apply directly to us anymore today, for our type of lifestyle and its needs have changed. But, we should study the thoughts and teachings in these laws and try to pattern our civil laws after them.

Ceremonial laws were the rules for *Israel's Old Testament religious worship.* These laws included rules regarding: Priests, High Priest, Tabernacle, Holy Place, Holy of Holies, special feast days, altars, sacrifices, bloodshedding, and washings. All of these things pointed to the Lord Jesus who would come in the future. When Christ died on the cross, the ceremonial law ended. It is wrong for us to have priests or altars in church or to sacrifice today, because the full price has been paid in the sacrifice of the Great High Priest, Jesus Christ. While we may not practice the ceremonial laws anymore today, we should study them for they give us an instructive picture of Jesus Christ and His work.

The **Moral law** is *God's ten commandments.* These rules were written for all people and times. To show their lasting value, they were engraved in two stone tables. The first table contained the first four commandments which concern our love to God. The last six commandments, which speak about our love to other people, were written on the second table.

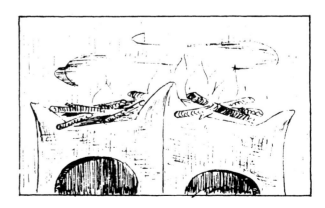

Jesus said unto him, Thou shalt *love the Lord* thy God with all thy heart, and with all thy soul, and with all thy mind.

This is the first and great commandment.

And the second is like unto it, Thou shalt *love thy neighbour* as thyself.

On these two commandments hang all the law and the prophets.

— Matthew 22:37-40

Each of God's ten commandments teaches us what we *may not* do, but also what we *must* do in our thoughts, words, and actions. God's ten commandments, our rules for life, are as follows:

THE TEN COMMANDMENTS

FIRST TABLE

Commandment I
Exodus 20:3

Thou shalt have *no other gods* before Me.

We may not: Serve idols or other gods.
We must: Love and serve the true God above all else in our lives.

Commandment II
Exodus 20:4-6

Thou shalt *not make unto thee any graven image,* or any likeness of any thing that is in heaven above, or that is in the earth beneath, or that is in the water under the earth:

Thou shalt *not bow down thyself to them,* nor serve them: for I the LORD thy God am a jealous God, visiting the iniquity of the fathers upon the children unto the third and fourth generation of them that hate Me;

And shewing mercy unto thousands of them that love Me, and keep My commandments.

We may not: Try to serve and worship God by using images or pictures of God. We may not add things to our worship service which God has not commanded.
We must: Worship God in spirit and in truth as He has commanded in His Word.

Commandment III
Exodus 20:7

Thou shalt *not take the Name of the LORD thy God in vain;* for the LORD will not hold him guiltless that taketh His, Name in vain.

We may not: Misuse or lightly use God's Name.
We must: Use God's Name with deep love and respect.

Commandment IV
Exodus 20:8-11

Remember the Sabbath Day, to keep it holy.
Six days shalt thou labour, and do all thy work:
But the seventh day is the Sabbath of the LORD thy God: in it thou shalt not do any work, thou, nor thy son, nor thy daughter, thy manservant, nor thy maidservant, nor thy cattle, nor thy stranger that is within thy gates:
For in six days the LORD made heaven and earth, the sea, and all that in them is, and rested the seventh day: wherefore the LORD blessed the Sabbath Day, and hallowed it.

We may not: Use Sunday for unnecessary work or for our purposes.
We must: Keep Sunday holy by seeking and worshipping God.

SECOND TABLE

Commandment V
Exodus 20:12

Honour thy father and thy mother: that thy days may be long upon the land which the LORD thy God giveth thee.

We may not: Disobey or disrespect those in authority over us.
We must: Obey, respect, and honor those in authority over us.

Commandment VI
Exodus 20:13

Thou shalt not kill.

We may not: Hate, wound, or kill others.
We must: Forgive, love, and live in peace with others.

Commandment VII
Exodus 20:14

Thou shalt not commit adultery.

We may not: Have or use unclean thoughts, desires, words, or actions.
We must: Live a clean and pure life.

Commandment VIII
Exodus 20:15

Thou shalt not steal.

We may not: Steal from or cheat others.
We must: Seek the good of others and care for their possessions.

Commandment IX
Exodus 20:16

Thou shalt not bear false witness against thy neighbour.

We may not: Lie, exaggerate, gossip or slander.
We must: Love to speak the exact truth for the good name of others.

Commandment X
Exodus 20:17

Thou shalt not covet thy neighbour's house, thou shalt not covet thy neighbour's wife, nor his manservant, nor his maidservant, nor his ox, nor his ass, nor any thing that is thy neighbour's.

We may not: Covet or envy other people or their possessions.
We must: Be content and thankful for that which God has given us.

WHAT DO YOU THINK?

DAVE'S IDOLS

Dave is sitting in church and his minister has just begun his sermon. "If only I can trade these two players for the one I need from Chicago, I would then have the complete team. I wonder if I will ever get him — he's an All-Star, of course. I bet they purposely don't make many cards of him. I will have to count my cards when I get home — I'm sure I've got close to 300."

These are Dave's thoughts during the sermon. What is of more value to Dave at the moment: God or his hockey cards?

What is an idol? Which commandment is Dave breaking? Why? Are poor, ignorant, heathen people the only persons who have idols?

NO ONE SWEARS BEFORE I DO!

"Men," said the new captain to his rough crew of sailors, "I would like to ask each of you a favor, and that is that you allow me to swear the first oath on my new ship."

"Fine! Good!" laughed all the sailors.

"All right, we will make that a command," answered the captain, "No man on board is allowed to swear before I do. Agreed?"

"Certainly!" the sailors laughed again at this strange request of the new captain.

However, after several days, they understood why their captain had said this. Their new captain conducted himself very carefully and spoke very thoughtfully. No one had ever heard him swear, and they had agreed not to swear either until he had!

Which commandment was this captain trying to enforce on his new ship?

— Adapted from *The Shorter Catechism Illustrated*

I'LL WORK ON SUNDAY INSTEAD

Shirley had put off working on her Social Studies report for several days. She knew that it was due on Monday, February 7, but that sounded so far away.

However, on the final Saturday afternoon before the due date, she still had a lot to do to finish her report. Her best friend, Frances, had just phoned and asked her to go iceskating.

Shirley thought, "What shall I do? I really cannot pass up this opportunity. It will be so much fun. I'll just have to finish my report Sunday afternoon."

"Sure, I'll be ready. It sounds like fun," she told Frances.

Which commandment has Shirley just decided to break? Why?

HONOR THY FATHER

A young man, who appeared well-behaved and honest, ran up to an enlisting officer for the British army.

"I want to sell myself and enlist in the army," he told the officer, "but I will need ten pounds for it immediately."

The officer looked into the honest eyes of the young man. "Ten pounds is a high price," he said, "but for you I will do it. Here you are."

"Please excuse me now, for I must pay a debt with this, but I will be right back."

The officer agreed, but followed the boy. He saw him run to the village jail, pay the debt and joyfully release his father, sadly kiss him good-bye, and prepare to run back to begin his service in the army.

The officer was overcome by what he had seen. "No, my boy," he said, "one who loves his father so greatly must stay with his father. The ten pounds are yours!"

Which commandment was this young man honoring? Why?

— Adapted from *The Shorter Catechism Illustrated*

133

WHAT DO YOU THINK?

"MURDERER!"

Carrying her one-year-old child, a mother once entered a doctor's office to ask for an abortion. "Doctor," she said, "I need your help. I am expecting a child again and I cannot take care of two children so close in age."

"If you want one of the children to be killed," answered the doctor calmly, picking up a sharp knife, "why don't we kill the one on your lap? That will be much easier and safer for you."

Seeing the doctor approach her child with a knife in his hand, the woman almost fainted. Then, jumping up, she screamed one word, "Murderer!"

The doctor then calmed her and explained that she had asked him to murder the child growing inside her. He could no more murder the unborn child than the child on her lap.

Which commandment was the woman planning to break by asking for an abortion? Why?

— Adapted from *The NRC Banner of Truth*

JUST PICTURES?

"Say, Peter," his friend whispered, "see if you can come over to Rick's place tonight."

"Why?" Peter asked.

"Well, Rick has a bunch of . . . well, you know, . . . some magazines . . . with lots of pictures of girls . . .

and he'll be home alone. His parents are going away for the night."

"You mean dirty magazines, don't you?" asked Peter, looking his friend in the eye.

"Well . . . I suppose you could call them that if you want to . . . but I don't see anything so wrong with just looking at pictures . . . Are you going to be there or not?"

Which commandment was Peter's friend tempting him to break? Why?

A CHEATER!

Linda wanted to earn a good grade on her Science report. She had a poor grade on her last Science test and a higher grade on this report would surely help.

She asked Laura if she could see her report.

"Laura always gets A's on her work," Linda thought. "Maybe I'll just copy a few parts that I don't understand so well."

Later, Linda was reading in the encyclopedia. "I need more pages in my report to get a good grade," she thought. "I'll quickly copy some pages out of here."

Linda did this, then put **her** name on the report and handed it in to her teacher.

Can you name two commandments which Linda broke by doing this?

"I'D BE HAPPY IF ONLY I HAD . . ."

When Allan was five years old, he had a tricycle, but he didn't like it anymore. He wanted a two-wheeler. "If I had a two-wheel bike, I'd be happy," he told himself.

After he received a two-wheel bike, he seemed happy for a few weeks, but

then he started wishing for a ten-speed bike. "If only I had a ten-speed like Jeff's," he kept thinking, "then I'd be happy."

Later, he received a new ten-speed bike and seemed happy for a time. But, soon he started wishing for a motorcycle. "If only I had a motorcycle," he thought.

Now Allan has had a motorcycle for a few months, and is he happy? "Boy, if I only had a neat car like Bob has. Wouldn't that be something?" he thinks.

Poor Allan! What lesson can we learn from this story? Which commandment is Allan continually breaking? Why?

If God's Word only contained His law, all of us, as fallen sinners, would remain in our lost condition forever. By nature, we are in a state worthy of eternal destruction for breaking all of God's commandments. However, God has also revealed His *gospel* in His Word.

The word "gospel" means "good news" or "glad tidings." The most wonderful news ever heard on earth was the announcement that God would provide a Savior to deliver lost sinners from death and restore them to life!

This Savior is the Lord Jesus Christ. The first four books in the New Testament speak about the life and death of this Savior. They are called the four "Gospels."

Do you need, value, and love this Savior in your life? His Name was called "Jesus" or "Savior" because He saves His people from their sins.

> And thou shalt **call His Name JESUS:**
> **for He shall save His people from their**
> **sins.**
>
> — Matthew 1:21b

WHAT DO YOU THINK?

THE GOSPEL MESSAGE

Read the message of the angels to the shepherds in the fields of Bethlehem when they announced the birth of Jesus:

> And, lo, the angel of the Lord came upon them, and the glory of the Lord shone round about them: and they were sore afraid.
> And the angel said unto them, Fear not: for, behold, I bring you good tidings of great joy, which shall be to all people.
> For unto you is born this day in the city of David a Saviour, Which is Christ the Lord.
> And suddenly there was with the angel a multitude of the heavenly host praising God, and saying,
> Glory to God in the highest, and on earth peace, good will toward men.
> — Luke 2:9-11, 13-14

Why is the word "gospel" a good name for the books in the New Testament which speak about the life and death of Christ?

MEMORIZATION QUESTIONS

Exodus 20:1-11

And God spake all these words, saying,

I am the LORD thy God, which have brought thee out of the land of Egypt, out of the house of bondage.

Thou shalt have no other gods before Me.

Thou shalt not make unto thee any graven image, or any likeness of any thing that is in heaven above, or that is in the earth beneath, or that is in the water under the earth:

Thou shalt not bow down thyself to them, nor serve them: for I the LORD thy God am a jealous God, visiting the iniquity of the fathers upon the children unto the third and fourth generation of them that hate Me:

And shewing mercy unto thousands of them that love Me, and keep My commandments.

Thou shalt not take the Name of the LORD thy God in vain; for the LORD will not hold him guiltless that taketh His Name in vain.

Remember the Sabbath Day, to keep it holy.

Six days shalt thou labour, and do all thy work:

But the seventh day is the Sabbath of the LORD thy God: in it thou shalt not do any work, thou, nor thy son, nor thy daughter, thy manservant, nor thy maidservant, nor thy cattle, nor thy stranger that is within thy gates:

For in six days the LORD made heaven and earth, the sea, and all that in them is, and rested the seventh day: wherefore the LORD blessed the Sabbath Day, and hallowed it.

Honour thy father and thy mother: that thy days may be long upon the land which the LORD thy God giveth thee.

Thou shalt not kill.

Thou shalt not commit adultery.

Thou shalt not steal.

Thou shalt not bear false witness against thy neighbour.

Thou shalt not covet thy neighbour's house, thou shalt not covet thy neighbour's wife, nor his manservant, nor his maidservant, nor his ox, nor his ass, nor any thing that is thy neighbour's.

CHECKING YOUR READING

1. a. Name the two means of grace that God the Holy Spirit uses to strengthen faith:

    1. _____

    2. _____

    b. Name the means of grace which the Holy Ghost uses to work faith:

    _____

2. a. How did the "sick man" undervalue the means that God has given?

    _____

    _____

    b. How did the "sick woman" overvalue the means that God has given?

    _____

    _____

3. Why is it so important to bring the Word of God to people who have not yet received it?

    _____

    _____

4. Why is it very important to place myself under God's Word, and to carefully and prayerfully use this means? _____

    _____

5. Why is being brought up under God's Word a:

    a. Great blessing? — _____

    _____

    b. Great responsibility?— _____

    _____

6. a. Whose fault is it when we do not respond to God's callings and invitations? _____

    _____

    b. Whose credit or work is it if we do repent and turn to God? _____

7. With what spirit must God's law be obeyed? _____

    _____

8. How does God the Holy Spirit use the law when teaching a person:

    a. Misery? — _____

    _____

    b. Thankfulness? — _____

    _____

CHECKING YOUR READING

9. a. Whose law has absolute authority? _____

    b. How must a person rule after being placed in a position of authority? _____

    _____

    c. Why must we obey those placed in authority over us? _____

    _____

    d. When and only when must we disobey a person placed in authority over us? _____

    _____

10. Name which type of law the following texts are examples of:

a. And thou shalt take the garments, and put upon Aaron the coat, and the robe of the ephod, and the ephod, and the breastplate, and gird him with the curious girdle of the ephod:

And thou shalt put the mitre upon his head, and put the holy crown upon the mitre.

Then shalt thou take the anointing oil, and pour it upon his head, and anoint him.

— Exodus 29:5-7

b. Honour thy father and thy mother: that thy days may be long upon the land which the LORD thy God giveth thee.

Thou shalt not kill.

Thou shalt not commit adultery.

Thou shalt not steal.

Thou shalt not bear false witness against thy neighbour.

— Exodus 20:12-16

c. When thou buildest a new house, then thou shalt make a battlement for thy roof, that thou bring not blood upon thine house, if any man fall from thence.

Thou shalt not sow thy vineyard with divers seeds: lest the fruit of thy seed which thou hast sown, and the fruit of thy vineyard, be defiled.

Thou shalt not plow with an ox and an ass together.

— Deuteronomy 22:8-10

_____ Law _____ Law _____ Law

11. a. What does the word "gospel" mean? _____

    b. Why is this a fitting name for the first four books in the New Testament?

    _____

■■■■■■■■ EXTRA CHALLENGE QUESTIONS ■■■■■■■■

1. From the story **A Sick Man,** explain why this person was mistaken in his reasoning: _____

    _____

2. From the story **A Cheater!,** explain which two commandments Linda broke when cheating:

    _____

    _____

3. Name which of the ten commandments has been broken in the following examples. In some cases more than one commandment is involved.

Example	*Number(s) of the Commandments That Have Been Broken*
a. A man writing down five hours on his time card when he actually worked 3½ hours.	_____
b. A girl disliking another girl because she always wears such nice clothes.	_____
c. A boy not doing his best on his school homework.	_____
d. A person using very strong and rough language to impress others.	_____
e. A girl not dressing modestly or decently to draw attention to herself.	_____

CHAPTER 18

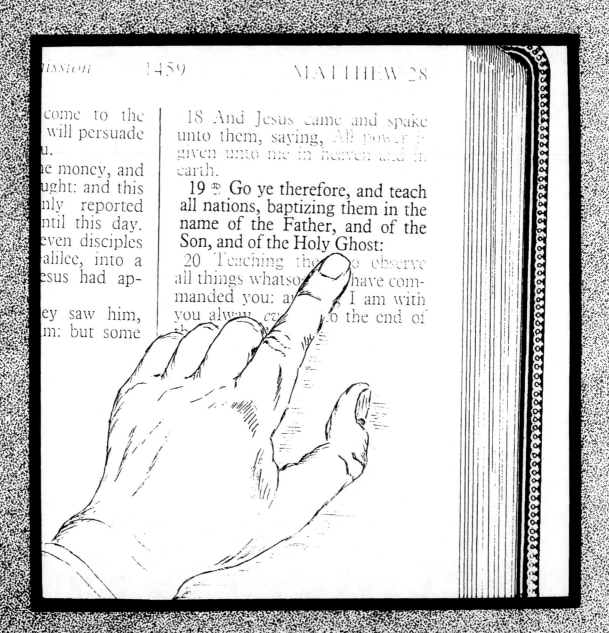

GOD'S SACRAMENTS
HOLY BAPTISM

GOD'S SACRAMENTS

God has graciously given us two means of grace: His **Word** and **sacraments.** The two New Testament sacraments are **Holy Baptism** and **the Lord's Supper.** These distinctions are pictured as follows:

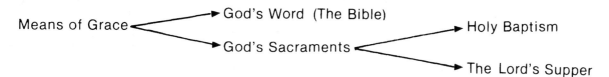

God the Holy Spirit works through both of these means of grace. He uses His Word, the Bible, to both **work** and **strengthen** faith. He uses His sacraments only to **strengthen** faith.

THE HEIDELBERG CATECHISM

Q.65. Since then we are made partakers of Christ and all His benefits by faith only, whence doth this faith proceed?

A. From the Holy Ghost, who works faith in our hearts by the preaching of the gospel, and confirms it by the use of the sacraments.

Q.67. Are both Word and sacraments, then, ordained and appointed for this end, that they may direct our faith to the sacrifice of Jesus Christ on the cross, as the only ground of our salvation?

A. Yes, indeed: for the Holy Ghost teaches us in the gospel, and assures us by the sacraments, that the whole of our salvation depends upon that one sacrifice of Christ which He offered for us on the cross.

And now, brethren, I commend you to God, and to the **Word of His grace,** which is able to build you up, and to give you an inheritance among all them which are sanctified.

— Acts 20:32

So then faith cometh by hearing, and hearing by the **Word of God.**

— Romans 10:17

Not by works of righteousness which we have done, but according to His mercy He saved us, **by the washing of regeneration, and renewing of the Holy Ghost;** which He shed on us abundantly through Jesus Christ our Saviour.

— Titus 3:5-6

The cup of blessing which we bless, is it not the **communion of the blood of Christ?** The bread which we break, is it not **communion of the body of Christ?**

— I Corinthians 10:16

God's sacraments are based upon His Word; they are a means to strengthen faith in God's Word and promises.

The sacraments are both: **signs** and **seals** of God's grace.

THE HEIDELBERG CATECHISM

Q.66. What are the sacraments?

A. The sacraments are holy visible signs and seals, appointed of God for this end, that by the use thereof, He may the more fully declare and seal to us the promise of the gospel, viz., that He grants us freely the remission of sin, and life eternal, for the sake of that one sacrifice of Christ, accomplished on the cross.

And ye shall circumcise the flesh of your foreskin; and it shall be a *token of the covenant* betwixt Me and you.

— Genesis 17:11

And he received the *sign* of circumcision, a *seal* of the righteousness of the faith which he had yet being uncircumcised:

— Romans 4:11a

Then Peter said unto them, Repent, and be *baptized* every one of you in the Name of Jesus Christ *for the remission of sins,* and ye shall receive the gift of the Holy Ghost.

— Acts 2:38

For as often as ye eat this bread, and drink this cup, ye *do show the Lord's death* till He come.

— I Corinthians 11:26

A **sign** is something we can see that speaks to us of a deeper meaning. A **seal** is an **official** stamp of approval that **confirms** and guarantees something to be true.

WHAT DO YOU THINK?

A SIGN

As Susan was driving, she approached a yellow sign displaying two large black "R" letters.

These two "R's" immediately had a deeper meaning to her. What did this sign mean?

How are the broken bread and the poured wine in the Lord's supper signs? What is the deeper meaning of these signs? Why are these signs valued so highly by God's true children?

WHAT DO YOU THINK?

A SEAL

Mr. Goodwin purchased a sixty-acre dairy farm for a large sum of money.

As he paid his down payment on this property and signed various papers at a lawyer's office, Mr. Goodwin carefully observed that each of the documents were properly sealed with the official seal of his state.

Why was this very important? What did the seal on these papers prove and guarantee?

What is sealed to God's people in His sacraments? Why is this very important to them?

The signs used in the New Testament sacraments are:

1. **Water** in baptism
2. **Bread and wine** in the Lord's Supper

These signs speak to us of a deeper meaning; they refer to the forgiveness of the sins of God's people through the broken body and shed blood of Christ. They seal to God's children the truth of God's Word. They confirm Christ's promises to them, that their sins are washed away and that they are and will continue to be fed and nourished through the death and shed blood of Christ. The sacraments are God-given means to strengthen the faith of His people, assuring them that through Christ's death they have received the forgiveness of all their sins and the gift of eternal life.

New Testament sacraments must be signs and seals of God's grace which Jesus Christ commanded His Church to begin and continue to practice. There are two New Testament sacraments which meet these requirements:

1. Holy Baptism
2. The Lord's Supper

Then Peter said unto them, Repent, and be **baptized** every one of you in the Name of Jesus Christ **for the remission of sins,** and ye shall receive the gift of the Holy Ghost.
— Acts 2:38

And as they were eating, Jesus took **bread,** and blessed it, and brake it, and gave it to the disciples, and said, Take, eat; **this is My body.**
And He took the **cup,** and gave thanks, and gave it to them, saying, Drink ye all of it;
For **this is My blood** of the New Testament, **which is shed for many for the remission of sins.**
— Matthew 26:26-28

Go ye therefore, and teach all nations, **baptizing** them in the Name of the Father, and of the Son, and of the Holy Ghost.
— Matthew 28:19

And He **took bread,** and gave thanks, and **brake it,** and gave unto them, saying, This is My body which is given for you: **this do in remembrance of Me.**
— Luke 22:19

WHAT DO YOU THINK?

A WONDERFUL SIGN AND SEAL!

A child of God named Joseph Williams wrote in his diary the following description of his feelings after partaking in the sacrament of the Lord's Supper:

"How my heart burned within me! How tenderly it throbbed! What streams of tears, tears of joy, joy unspeakable and full of glory, flowed from my eyes, while the minister was speaking! 'As often as ye eat this bread, and drink this cup, ye do show forth the Lord's death till He come.'

With what humble boldness did I appeal to the all-knowing God, who knew the sincerity of my heart, despite all my imperfections and sins. With what holy freedom and confidence I could desire of God to search and try me! How my heart glowed with thankfulness and admiration, at the amazing love of God in Christ Jesus, to a creature so low, and sinful! Had the tide of joy swelled a few degrees higher, I could hardly have restrained myself from crying out in the congregation, 'O He is come! He is come!' "

Can you see how this man experienced a deep joy in the wonderful sign and seal provided in the Lord's Supper through the applying power of the Holy Spirit?

God had given two sacraments to the Old Testament church which He replaced with two sacraments in the New Testament church. These sacraments are:

SACRAMENTS	
Old Testament	*New Testament*
CIRCUMCISION This is My covenant, which ye shall keep, between Me and you and thy seed after thee; *Every man child among you shall be circumcised.* — Genesis 17:10	BAPTISM Go ye therefore, and teach all nations, *baptizing* them in the Name of the Father, and of the Son, and of the Holy Ghost: — Matthew 28:19
PASSOVER And it shall come to pass, when ye shall come to the land which the LORD will give you, according as He hath promised, that ye shall keep His service. And it shall come to pass, when your children shall say unto you, What mean ye by this service? That ye shall say, It is *the sacrifice of the LORD's Passover,* who passed over the houses of the children of Israel in Egypt, when He smote the Egyptians, and delivered our houses. And the people bowed the head and worshipped. — Exodus 12:25-27	LORD'S SUPPER And when He had given thanks, He brake it, and said, *Take, eat:* this is My body, which is broken for you: this do in remembrance of Me. After the same manner also He took the cup, when He had supped, saying, This cup is the New Testament in My blood: this do ye, as oft as ye *drink* it, in remembrance of Me. For as often as ye eat this bread, and drink this cup, ye do show the Lord's death till He come. — I Corinthians 11:24-26

The Old Testament sacraments included the shedding of blood. This bloodshedding was necessary for it pointed to Christ's death which was to come in the future; it testified that bloodshedding was yet necessary to cleanse from sin. However, after Christ died and His blood was shed, the full price for sin had been paid. It would now be unnecessary and wrong to shed more blood, for that would deny the truth that the full blood payment has been made. Therefore, new, non-bloody forms of the sacraments were needed in the New Testament, even though they pointed to the same truths.

By the which will we are sanctified through the *offering* of the body of Jesus Christ *once* for all.

For by *one offering* He hath perfected for ever them that are sanctified.
— Hebrews 10:10,14

Both circumcision and baptism point to spiritual *birth;* being cleansed through Christ's blood and passing from spiritual death into spiritual life. Therefore, they must be performed only *once* in a person's life.

Both the Passover and Lord's Supper point to spiritual *life, strength,* and *nourishment* through Christ's death. Therefore, they must be used *repeatedly.*

HOLY BAPTISM

Holy Baptism was commanded by the Lord Jesus Christ. As King of His Church, Christ changed the signs of the sacraments from bloody to non-bloody ones after His death. The New Testament church was commanded to baptize with water.

Being baptized with water pictures the washing away of sin through the blood of Jesus Christ. It speaks of entering into God's church.

> And now why tarriest thou? arise, and **be baptized, and wash away thy sins,** calling on the Name of the Lord.
> — Acts 22:16

> Then Peter said unto them, Repent, and **be baptized every one of you in the Name of Jesus Christ for the remission of sins,** and ye shall receive the gift of the Holy Ghost.
> — Acts 2:38

The water used in baptism is not "special" or "holy" water. It is plain, **ordinary** water. Water is used as the sign in baptism because it pictures washing or **cleansing.** We normally wash our bodies with water; therefore, water is used to picture the spiritual washing away of sin.

Baptism must be done:

1. In the **Name of the Triune God;** in the Name of the Father, the Son, and the Holy Ghost

2. By an **ordained minister**

> And Jesus came and spake unto them, saying, All power is given unto Me in heaven and in earth.
> Go **ye** therefore, and teach all nations, baptizing them in the **Name of the Father, and of the Son, and of the Holy Ghost.**
> — Matthew 28:18-19

WHAT DO YOU THINK?

SPECIAL OR ORDINARY WATER?

Read the following three descriptions of baptisms in the New Testament:

JESUS

> Then cometh Jesus from Galilee to Jordan unto John, to be baptized of him.
> — Matthew 3:13

THE EUNUCH

> And as they went on their way, they came unto a certain water: and the eunuch said, See here is water: what doth hinder me to be baptized?
> — Acts 8:36

CORNELIUS

> Can any man forbid water, that these should not be baptized, which have received the Holy Ghost as well as we?
> — Acts 10:47

Is any mention made in these verses of "special" or "blessed" water? How can we see from these examples that ordinary water was used?

Baptism is important for all Christians. It is important because Christ has commanded it and because the Holy Spirit will use it as a means to strengthen faith. Baptism does not, however, actually give faith or wash away sin. A person who has received true saving faith and yet was never baptized, can be saved but

He that **believeth** and is **baptized** shall be saved; but he that believeth not shall be damned.

— Mark 16:16

For in Jesus Christ **neither circumcision availeth any thing, nor uncircumcision,** but faith which worketh by love.

— Galatians 5:6

without true saving faith, no one will be saved. A baptized person will be lost if he dies without true saving faith. It is a great blessing to be baptized, but we need the saving power of the Holy Spirit to work through and apply it in our lives; otherwise baptism will remain only an outward form.

WHAT DO YOU THINK?

CIRCUMCISED OR BAPTIZED . . . BUT LOST

How do the following verses of Scripture testify of circumcised or baptized persons being lost?

ISHMAEL

Nevertheless what saith the Scripture? Cast out the bondwoman and her son: for the son of the bondwoman shall not be heir with the son of the freewoman.

— Galatians 4:30

JUDAS

The Son of man goeth as it is written of Him: but woe unto that man by whom the Son of man is betrayed! it had been good for that man if he had not been born.

— Matthew 26:24

ESAU

As it is written, Jacob have I loved, but Esau have I hated.

— Romans 9:13

SIMON THE SORCERER

Thou hast neither part nor lot in this matter: for thy heart is not right in the sight of God.

For I perceive that thou art in the gall of bitterness, and in the bond of iniquity.

— Acts 8:21,23

UNCIRCUMCISED OR UNBAPTIZED . . . BUT SAVED

RAHAB

By faith the harlot Rahab perished not with them that believed not, when she had received the spies with peace.

— Hebrews 11:31

THE THIEF ON THE CROSS

And Jesus said unto him, Verily I say unto thee, To day shalt thou be with Me in paradise.

— Luke 23:43

RUTH

And Ruth said, Entreat me not to leave thee, or to return from following after thee: for whither thou goest, I will go; and where thou lodgest, I will lodge: thy people shall be my people, and thy God my God:

— Ruth 1:16

THE SYROPHOENICIAN WOMAN

Then Jesus answered and said unto her, O woman, great is thy faith: be it unto thee even as thou wilt. And her daughter was made whole from that very hour.

— Matthew 15:28

The Thief on the Cross

The church has practiced baptism in the following three different manners:

1. *Sprinkling* — Sprinkling water on the person, usually on the forehead

2. *Pouring* — Pouring water over the person

3. *Immersing* — Placing the person entirely under the water

All three of these methods of baptizing are acceptable in the church because they all picture the same truth: the cleansing from sin through the blood of Jesus Christ. Some church denominations teach that only **immersion** is an acceptable form and that baptism by sprinkling or pouring is not a true baptism. They teach that the New Testament only gives examples of baptism by immersion. Read the following New Testament examples of baptism, and observe that the Bible does not say in which manner these people were baptized. Why would these baptism examples be very hard to imagine taking place by immersion?

WHAT DO YOU THINK?

IMMERSING, POURING, OR SPRINKLING?

In the New Testament times most homes did not have pools or bathtubs. Water was usually kept in pots or pitchers in the house. Bathing was generally done by hand washing or in a river, lake, pool, or a public Roman bath. With this in mind, read the following New Testament examples of baptism.

The Baptism of Paul
And immediately there fell from his eyes as it had been scales: and he received sight forthwith, and arose, and was baptized.
— Acts 9:18

Does the Bible tell us how Paul was baptized? Do we read that he left the house of Judas, where he lodged, to be baptized by Ananias? What does the word "forthwith" mean? Why would it be hard to picture Paul's baptism as baptism by immersion?

The Baptism of the Jailer

And he took them the same hour of the night, and washed their stripes; and was baptized, he and all his, straightway.
— Acts 16:33

Do the Scriptures explain how the jailer and his household were baptized? What does the word "straightway" mean? Why would it be hard to picture this verse as meaning that they traveled to a place where they could be immersed in the middle of the night?

The Baptism of Cornelius
Can any man forbid water, that these should not be baptized, which have received the Holy Ghost as well as we?
And he commanded them to be baptized in the Name of the Lord. Then prayed they him to tarry certain days.
— Acts 10:47-48

Does the Bible inform us of how Cornelius, his family, and close friends were baptized? What does "Can any man forbid water" mean? Why would it be difficult to picture the bringing of enough water to immerse all these people in the home of Cornelius?

The Baptism of 3,000 on Pentecost Day

Then they that gladly received his word were baptized: and the same day there were added unto them about three thousand souls.
— Acts 2:41

Do the Scriptures tell us how the three thousand were baptized on Pentecost Day? Do we read of this crowd being led to a pool or river? Why would it be difficult to picture these 3,000 people all being immersed in one day?

WHAT DO YOU THINK?

HOW WAS THE EUNUCH BAPTIZED?

The baptism of the Ethiopian eunuch is often spoken of as a clear scriptural example of baptism by immersion. Read this history carefully.

Acts 8:38-39:

> And he commanded the chariot to stand still. and *they* went down **both** into the water, **both Philip and the eunuch;** and he baptized him.
> And when *they* were come up out of the water, the Spirit of the Lord caught away Philip, that the eunuch saw him no more: and he went on his way rejoicing.

Those who believe in baptism only by immersion teach that the going "down into the water" referred to in these verses means the person's being "put under the water", and that the coming "up out of the water" means the person's being "lifted back up above the water."

But, read these verses very carefully. Who went "down into the water"? Only the eunuch or both Philip and the eunuch? If this expression meant immersion, then both Philip and the eunuch were immersed, which is impossible. Who "came up out of the water"—only the eunuch, or both?

In these verses, Scripture tells us that both Philip and the eunuch walked into the water. There Philip baptized him. After baptism, both walked out of the water. Does the Bible say how Philip baptized the eunuch when they both were in the water? How could this have been by sprinkling, pouring, or immersing?

WHAT DO YOU THINK?

The water used in baptism pictures washing or cleansing. What does sprinkling picture in the following Scriptural texts?

Leviticus 14:7
And he shall sprinkle upon him that is to be cleansed from the leprosy seven times, and shall pronounce him clean, and shall let the living bird loose into the open field.

Numbers 8:7
And thus shalt thou do unto them, to cleanse them: Sprinkle water of purifying upon them, and let them shave all their flesh, and let them wash their clothes, and so make themselves clean.

Hebrews 12:24
And to Jesus the Mediator of the new covenant, and to the blood of sprinkling, that speaketh better things than that of Abel.

Hebrews 10:22
Let us draw near with a true heart in full assurance of faith, having our hearts sprinkled from an evil conscience, and our bodies washed with pure water.

Ezekiel 36:25
Then will I sprinkle clean water upon you, and ye shall be clean: from all your filthiness, and from all your idols, will I cleanse you.

1 Peter 1:2
Elect according to the foreknowledge of God the Father, through sanctification of the Spirit, unto obedience and sprinkling of the blood of Jesus Christ: Grace unto you, and peace, be multiplied.

Why are sprinkling, pouring, or immersing all acceptable methods of baptizing? What do they all picture?

The Bible teaches us that baptism is only for believing adults and their children. When a missionary minister enters a new area where the people have not heard God's Word, he may not begin by baptizing. He must first preach and adults must understand, believe, and confess their belief. Only after this takes place, may he baptize the believing adults with their households or families.

This was true with circumcision in the Old Testament and remains true with baptism in the New Testament. Adults from outside the church who became believers and joined the church had to first confess their belief and were then circumcised or baptized. After they were circumcised or baptized, their entire household or family was also.

CHRIST'S MISSION COMMAND

And He said unto them, 'Go ye into all the world, and **preach the gospel to every creature.**

He that believeth and is baptized shall be saved: but he that believeth not shall be damned.

— Mark 16:15-16

WHAT DO YOU THINK?

BELIEVING ADULTS AND THEIR CHILDREN

How do the following scriptural examples show that children were included with their parents in receiving the mark of circumcision or baptism?

CIRCUMCISION

And God said unto Abraham, Thou shalt keep My covenant therefore, thou, and thy seed after thee in their generations.

This is My covenant, which ye shall keep, between Me and you and thy seed after thee; Every man child among you shall be circumcised.

And he that is eight days old shall be circumcised among you, every man child in your generations.

In the selfsame day was Abraham circumcised, and Ishmael his son.

And all the men of his house, born in the house, and bought with money of the stranger, were circumcised with him.

— Genesis 17:9,10,12a,26,27

BAPTISM

And a certain woman named Lydia, a seller of purple, of the city of Thyatira, which worshipped God, heard us: whose heart the Lord opened, that she attended unto the things which were spoken of Paul.

And when she was baptized, and her household, she besought us, saying, If ye have judged me to be faithful to the Lord, come into my house, and abide there. And she constrained us.

— Acts 16:14-15

And they spake unto him the Word of the Lord, and to all that were in his house.

And he took them the same hour of the night, and washed their stripes; and was baptized, he and all his, straightway.

— Acts 16:32-33

WHAT DO YOU THINK?

CITIZENSHIP

To be a Roman citizen at the time of Paul was a great privilege. Once Paul spoke about this with a Roman chief captain in:

Acts 22:27-28:

Then the chief captain came, and said unto him, Tell me, art thou a Roman? He said, Yea.

And the chief captain answered, With a great sum obtained I this freedom. And Paul said, But I was free born.

How did the chief captain become a Roman citizen, as a child or as an adult? How did Paul become a Roman citizen, as a child or as an adult? Was one more of a Roman citizen than the other? Why not? How can this be compared to church citizenship and baptism? Name two ways in which we can become church members and be baptized.

We must include children of believing parents in baptism for the following biblical reasons:

1. It is **God's command** that believing parents place the mark of the Covenant of Grace upon their children.

And he that is eight days old **shall be circumcised** among you, every man child in your generations, he that is born in the house, or bought with money of any stranger, which is not of thy seed.

He that is born in thy house, and he that is bought with thy money, **must needs be circumcised:** and My **covenant** shall be in your flesh for an everlasting covenant.

And the uncircumcised man child whose flesh of his foreskin is **not circumcised,** that soul shall be cut off from his people; he **hath broken My covenant.**

— Genesis 17:12-14

And I will establish My **covenant** between Me and thee and **thy seed** after thee in their generations for an everlasting covenant, to be a God unto thee, and to thy seed after thee.

— Genesis 17:7

2. **God's Covenant of Grace** includes children of believers.

For the unbelieving husband is sanctified by the wife, and the unbelieving wife is sanctified by the husband: else were your children unclean; but **now are they holy.**

— I Corinthians 7:14

And he that is eight days old shall be circumcised among you, **every man child** in your generations, he that is born in the house, or bought with money of any stranger, which is not of thy seed.

— Genesis 17:12

3. **God's promises** include children of believers.

And I will establish My covenant between Me and thee and **thy seed after thee in their generations** for an everlasting covenant, to be a God unto thee, and to thy seed after thee.

— Genesis 17:7

For the promise is unto you, **and to your children,** and to all that are afar off, even as many as the Lord our God shall call.

— Acts 2:39

4. Baptism is the New Testament sacrament which **replaces** the Old Testament sacrament of **circumcision.** Circumcision included all the children of the church.

In whom also ye are circumcised with the circumcision made without hands, in putting off the body of the sins of the flesh by the circumcision of Christ:

Buried with Him in baptism, wherein ye are risen with Him through the faith of the operation of God, who hath raised Him from the dead.

— Colossians 2:11-12

And he that is eight days old **shall be circumcised among you,** every man child in your generations.

— Genesis 17:12a

For **we are the circumcision,** which worship God in the spirit, and rejoice in Christ Jesus, and have no confidence in the flesh.

— Philippians 3:3

5. Baptism is a sign of **entrance into God's church** which includes children.

And God said unto Abraham, Thou shalt keep My covenant therefore, thou, and thy seed after thee in their generations.

This is My covenant, which ye shall keep, between Me and you and thy seed after thee; Every man child among you shall be circumcised.

— Genesis 17:9-10

And they brought young children to Him, that He should touch them: and His disciples rebuked those that brought them.

But when Jesus saw it, He was much displeased, and said unto them, Suffer the **little children** to come unto Me, and forbid them not: **for of such is the kingdom of God.**

— Mark 10:13-14

6. Baptism is a mark of **separation from the world** which God requires from all church members.

> And the uncircumcised man child whose flesh of his foreskin is **not circumcised,** that soul shall be cut off from his people; **he hath broken My covenant.**
> — Genesis 17:14

> For he is not a Jew, which is one outwardly; neither is that circumcision, which is outward in the flesh:
> But he is a Jew, which is one inwardly, and **circumcision is that of the heart,** in the spirit, and not in the letter; whose praise is not of men, but of God.

> What advantage then hath the Jew? or what profit is there of circumcision?
> Much every way: chiefly, because that **unto them were committed the oracles of God.**
> — Romans 2:28-3:2

7. The **New Testament examples** of baptism, which follow the Old Testament practice, **include the children with their believing parents** in receiving the mark of God's covenant. There is no special command in the Bible to stop this practice.

> And a certain woman named Lydia, a seller of purple, of the city of Thyatira, which worshipped God, heard us: whose heart the Lord opened, that she attended unto the things which were spoken of Paul.
> And when she was baptized, **and her household,** she besought us, saying, If ye have judged me to be faithful to the Lord, come into my house, and abide there. And she constrained us.
> — Acts 16: 14-15

> And I baptized also **the household of Stephanas:** besides, I know not whether I baptized any other.
> — I Corinthians 1:16

Our baptism places us in a covenant relationship with God; it makes us **members** of God's church. This makes our baptism very important. However, as you learned in Chapter Eight, this can be in an **outward** or in an **inward** manner.

Our baptism places us in an **outward relationship** to God's Covenant of Grace, which is a **breakable relationship.** It includes us as **outward church members** or members of the Church Visible.

BAPTIZED AND UNREGENERATED — AN OUTWARD RELATIONSHIP

An Outward and Breakable Relationship to the Covenant of Grace

> Not according to the covenant that I made with their fathers in the day that I took them by the hand to bring them out of the land of Egypt; which **My covenant they brake,** although I was an Husband unto them, saith the LORD.
> — Jeremiah 31:32

> But the **children of the kingdom shall be cast out** into outer darkness: there shall be weeping and gnashing of teeth.
> — Matthew 8:12

> I know that ye are **Abraham's seed;** but ye seek to kill Me, because **My Word hath no place in you.**
> They answered and said unto Him, Abraham is our father. Jesus saith unto them, If ye were Abraham's children, ye would do the works of Abraham. — John 8:37, 39

> That is, They which are the children of the flesh, **these are not the children of God:** but the children of the promise are counted for the seed.
> As it is written, **Jacob have I loved, but Esau have I hated.**
> — Romans 9:8, 13

Outward, but not Inward Church Members

> **For he is not a Jew, which is one outwardly;** neither is that circumcision, which is outward in the flesh:
> But he is a Jew, which is one **inwardly**; and circumcision is that of the heart, in the spirit, and not in the letter; whose praise is not of men, but of God.
> — Romans 2:28-29

> For they are not all Israel, which are of Israel:
> **Neither, because they are the seed of Abraham, are they all children:** but, In Isaac shall thy seed be called.
> — Romans 9:6b-7a

Being an *outward* member of God's church by baptism is a great blessing. This is a **privilege** that is not given to everyone. Millions of children in the world are not baptized. Our baptism gives us the following blessings and privileges:

1. Our baptism confirms us as members of God's church (the Church Visible)

2. Our baptism places us under God's Word which God has promised to bless to the salvation of many. Baptism places us under the callings and invitations of the gospel.

3. Our baptism includes us continually in the prayers of the church.

4. Our baptism places God's mark upon us. Baptism separates us from the world and places us in an outward relationship to God's Covenant of Grace.

I may and should plead with my baptism in prayer to God, saying, "Lord, please remember me in Thy mercy. I am baptized in Thy Name. Bless Thy Word and all the benefits of my baptism to me in a saving way. Please give me the deepest meaning of baptism; please wash me clean from all my sin!"

For he is a not a Jew, which is one outwardly; neither is that circumcision, which is outward in the flesh:

But **he is a Jew, which is one inwardly;** and **circumcision is that of the heart,** in the spirit, and not in the letter; whose praise is not of men, but of God.

What advantage then hath the Jew? or what profit is there of circumcision?

Much every way: chiefly, because that **unto them were committed the oracles of God.**

— Romans 2:28-3:2

Baptism is such a great privilege because it places us near to the way of salvation; it places us under the means of grace which God has promised to bless to save sinners.

WHAT DO YOU THINK?
THE IMPORTANCE OF BAPTISM

What do you think these ministers meant when they wrote the following statements about baptism?

Martin Luther

Martin Luther wrote on the walls of Wartburg Castle, "O God, I am baptized in Thy Triune Name!"

Rev. J. Fraanje

Rev. Fraanje often said to young people, "Be not afraid to show the Lord your baptized forehead."

John Bunyan

John Bunyan wrote, "Baptism places us before the gates of heaven."

Can you see how these men saw the great value of baptism? Do you value your baptism?

The great benefits received in our baptism make us more responsible before God. God will ask each of us what we have done with all the blessings and privileges He has given us. The more the Lord gives us, the more He expects from us. If we were baptized, have lived under God's Word, were brought up in the church and were related outwardly to God's Covenant of Grace, and still go lost, our judgment will be far more severe than that of those who never knew God's Word and were never baptized.

And that servant, which knew his lord's will, and prepared not himself, neither did according to his will, shall be beaten with many stripes.

But he that knew not, and did commit things worthy of stripes, shall be beaten with few stripes. *For unto whomsoever much is given, of him shall be much required:* and to whom men have committed much, of him they will ask the more.
— Luke 12:47-48

Therefore we need to urgently use the means of grace God has given us and plead with Him to bless His Word in our hearts to savingly turn us from our sinful love of self, world, and Satan, to loving Him. Our outward baptism with its precious blessings is **not** sufficient to save us. To be saved, we need the almighty, regenerating, and converting work of God the Holy Spirit in our hearts.

WHAT DO YOU THINK?

BLESSINGS AND RESPONSIBILITIES

How do the following verses of Scripture clearly testify that the misuse of God's blessings will add to our judgment and condemnation?

Matthew 11:20-24

Then began He to upbraid the cities wherein most of His mighty works were done, because they repented not;

Woe unto thee, Chorazin! woe unto thee, Bethsaida! for if the mighty works, which were done in you, had been done in Tyre and Sidon, they would have repented long ago in sackcloth and ashes.

But I say unto you, It shall be more tolerable for Tyre and Sidon at the day of judgment, than for you.

And thou, Capernaum, which art exalted unto heaven, shalt be brought down to hell: for if the mighty works, which have been done in thee, had been done in Sodom, it would have remained until this day.

But I say unto you, That it shall be more tolerable for the land of Sodom in the day of judgment, than for thee.

Luke 12:47-48

And that servant, which knew his lord's will, and prepared not himself, neither did according to his will, shall be beaten with many stripes.

But he that knew not, and did commit things worthy of stripes, shall be beaten with few stripes. For unto whomsoever much is given, of him shall be much required: and to whom men have committed much, of him they will ask the more.

Matthew 23:37-38

O Jerusalem, Jerusalem, thou that killest the prophets, and stonest them which are sent unto thee, how often would I have gathered thy children together, even as a hen gathereth her chickens under her wings, and ye would not!

Behold, your house is left unto you desolate.

NICODEMUS

Nicodemus was born in the generations of Abraham. He was a Jew and was circumcised. He was a member of the church and was a chief ruler in the church.

Yet, in reply to Nicodemus's question:

> Jesus answered and said unto him, Verily, verily, I say unto thee, Except a man be born again, he cannot see the kingdom of God.
> Nicodemus saith unto Him, How can a man be born when he is old? can he enter the second time into his mother's womb, and be born?
> Jesus answerd, Verily, verily, I say unto you, Except a man be born of water and of the Spirit, he cannot enter into the kingdom of God.
> That which is born of the flesh is flesh; and that which is born of the Spirit is spirit.
> Marvel not that I said unto thee, Ye must be born again.
> The wind bloweth where it listeth, and thou hearest the sound thereof, but canst not tell whence it cometh and whither it goeth: so is every one that is born of the Spirit.
>
> — John 3:3-8

Was Nicodemus related to the Covenant of Grace in an outward or in an inward way? What did Jesus say was necessary in order to enter the kingdom of God, to become a true child of God inwardly?

Do church people need to be personally regenerated? to personally experience conversion? Why?

Baptism can be compared with the Word of God. It is a great blessing to have them outwardly, but to be saving, we need the truths of them to be applied and sealed in our hearts. This saving and converting work is the work of God. When the Holy Spirit converts a person from his deepest love of sin to God, He places him in an *inward and unbreakable relationship* to God's Covenant of Grace. This person then becomes a *spiritual child of God; an inward, living, and spiritual church member.* Study the textual references concerning this in the chart on the next page and contrast these verses with the chart on page 149.

This inward and saving relationship to Jesus Christ is that which we all need. This is the *deepest meaning of baptism.* Only by being spiritually born again can we be brought into this wonderful, saving, and eternal relationship with God.

God is an almighty God. He is able and delights to save sinners! Do you earnestly and continually pray and plead with God to bless the means of grace and the privilege He has given you? Do you also plead with your baptism? Jacob would not let the Lord go until He blessed him. Is this the same with you?

> And He said, Let Me go, for the day breaketh. And he said, *I will not let Thee go, except Thou bless me.*
> — Genesis 32:26

The Form for Holy Baptism which we use in church was written from the deepest view and meaning of baptism. It was written for the true, living, spiritual church members. Why did our forefathers write this form in this manner? They wrote it in this way to teach us that:

1. Only those who are truly converted to God (those who are brought into an inward and unbreakable covenant relationship with God) receive the deepest, saving meaning of baptism, the washing away of their sins through the blood of Jesus Christ.

2. No one should rest, be **content,** nor stop short with only the outward benefits of baptism, but each person should seek the deepest, saving value of baptism for his own soul and life.

Study the chart on the following page to clearly understand the differences between the outward and inward: blessings of baptism, relationship to the Covenant of Grace, and church membership.

WHAT DO YOU THINK?

THE FORM FOR HOLY BAPTISM

When you read the beginning and closing paragraphs of our Form for Holy Baptism, how can you see that it is written for the saved, spiritual, inward church members?

The principal parts of the doctrine of Holy Baptism are these three:

First. That we with our children are conceived and born in sin, and therefore are children of wrath, in so much that we cannot enter into the kingdom of God, except we are born again.

Almighty God and merciful Father, we thank and praise Thee that Thou hast forgiven us, and our children, all our sins, through the blood of Thy beloved Son Jesus Christ, and received us through Thy Holy Spirit as members of Thine only begotten Son, and adopted us to be Thy children, and sealed and confirmed the same unto us by Holy Baptism; we beseech Thee, through the same Son of Thy love, that Thou wilt be pleased always to govern these baptized children by the Holy Spirit, that they may be piously and religiously educated, increase and grow up in the Lord Jesus Christ, that they then may acknowledge Thy fatherly goodness and mercy, which Thou hast shown to them and us, and live in all righteousness, under our only Teacher, King, and High Priest, Jesus Christ; and manfully fight against, and overcome sin, the devil and his whole dominion, to the end that they may eternally praise and magnify Thee, and Thy Son Jesus Christ, together with the Holy Ghost, the one only true God. Amen.

— Psalter   p. 55-57

COVENANT OF GRACE

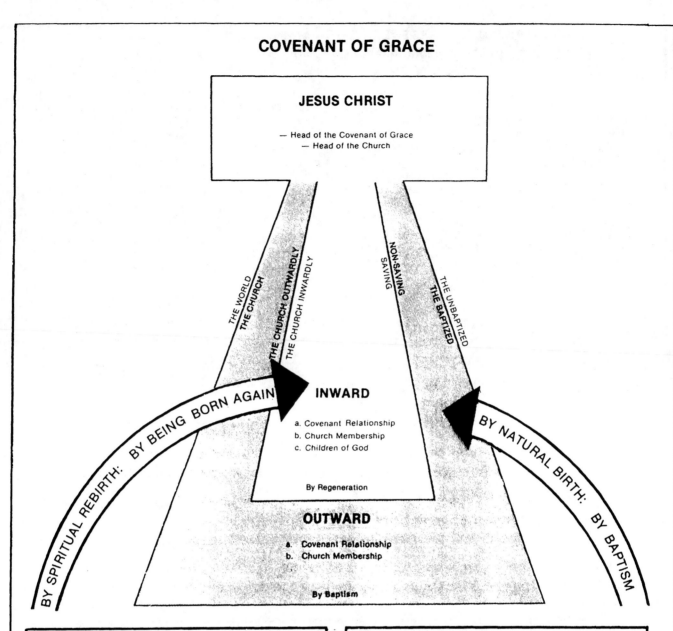

JESUS CHRIST

— Head of the Covenant of Grace
— Head of the Church

THE WORLD
THE CHURCH
THE CHURCH OUTWARDLY
THE CHURCH INWARDLY

NON-SAVING
SAVING

THE BAPTIZED
THE UNBAPTIZED

BY SPIRITUAL REBIRTH: BY BEING BORN AGAIN

BY NATURAL BIRTH: BY BAPTISM

INWARD

a. Covenant Relationship
b. Church Membership
c. Children of God

By Regeneration

OUTWARD

a. Covenant Relationship
b. Church Membership

By Baptism

INWARD COVENANT RELATIONSHIP	OUTWARD COVENANT RELATIONSHIP
(Baptism applied *Inwardly*)	(Baptism applied *Outwardly*)
An *inward* relationship to the Covenant of Grace includes:	An *outward* relationship to the Covenant of Grace by baptism includes:
Inward and eternal spiritual blessings	*Outward* blessings of separation from the world
An *unbreakable* relationship to God's Covenant of Grace	A *breakable* relationship to God's Covenant of Grace
Coming under God's *inward call:* the regenerating and converting work of the Holy Spirit	Coming under God's *outward call:* His Word, the invitation of the gospel, and the teachings, prayers, and warnings of the church, which God often blesses to work salvation.
These are the *greatest* blessings: true conversion and salvation	These are *great* blessings, but not enough to be saved.

WHAT DO YOU THINK?

TWO PARABLES — ONE LESSON

What similar lesson is being taught by the following two parables? How does this lesson apply to baptism and church membership?

THE PARABLE OF THE TWO SONS

But what think ye? A certain man had two sons; and he came to the first, and said, Son, go work today in my vineyard.

He answered and said, I will not: but afterward he repented, and went.

And he came to the second, and said likewise. And he answered and said, I go, Sir: and went not.

Whether of them twain did the will of his father? They say unto him, The first. Jesus saith unto them, Verily I say unto you, That the publicans and the harlots go into the kingdom of God before you.

For John came unto you in the way of righteousness, and ye believed him not: but the publicans and the harlots believed him: and ye, when ye had seen it, repented not afterward, that ye might believe him.

— Matthew 21:28-32

What is meant by the two **sons?**
What is referrred to by the second son saying, "I go, Sir"?
What does his not going mean?
How is this a special warning to baptized persons? to church members?

THE PARABLE OF THE WICKED HUSBANDMEN

Hear another parable: There was a certain householder, which planted a vineyard, and hedged it round about, and digged a winepress in it, and built a tower, and let it out to husbandmen, and went into a far country:

And when the time of the fruit drew near, he sent his servants to the husbandmen, that they might receive the fruits of it.

And the husbandmen took his servants, and beat one, and killed another, and stoned another.

Again, he sent other servants more than the first: and they did unto them likewise.

But last of all he sent unto them his son, saying, They will reverence my son.

But when the husbandmen saw the son, they said among themselves, This is the heir; come, let us kill him, and let us seize on his inheritance.

And they caught him, and cast him out of the vineyard, and slew him.

When the lord therefore of the vineyard cometh, what will he do unto those husbandmen?
* They say unto him, He will miserably destroy those wicked men, and will let out his vineyard unto other husbandmen, which shall render him the fruits in their seasons.

Jesus saith unto them, Did ye never read in the Scriptures, The stone which the builders rejected, the same is become the head of the corner: this is the Lord's doing, and it is marvellous in our eyes?

Therefore say I unto you, The kingdom of God shall be taken from you, and given to a nation bringing forth the fruits thereof.

And whosoever shall fall on this stone shall be broken: but on whomsoever it shall fall, it will grind him to powder.

And when the chief priests and Pharisees had heard His parables, they perceived that He spake of them.

But when they sought to lay hands on Him, they feared the multitude, because they took Him for a prophet.

— Matthew 21:33-46

What does the vineyard with a hedge, winepress, and tower represent?
Who do the husbandmen in the vineyard represent?
Of what are the expected fruits a picture?
Of what is the killing of the owner's servants and son a type?
How is the verse marked with an * a clear warning to baptized persons? to church members?

WHAT DO YOU THINK?

THE BIBLE IN HIS TRUNK

When Charles was eighteen, he worked as a clerk in Boston. He stayed at a boarding house where fifteen other clerks about his own age also lived. When Charles got up on Sunday morning, he had three or four hours before it was time for church. He had been brought up to spend extra time reading his Bible each Sunday, and now felt a strong desire to get his Bible from his trunk. However, his two roommates were reading other types of books and this made Charles afraid to take out his Bible.

As the voice of his conscience became louder, however, he decided to get his Bible. But when the trunk lid was half raised, he suddenly thought that the others might think he was trying to be pious, so he let the lid fall shut again. For twenty minutes Charles gazed out the window. He felt very miserable for he knew he was doing wrong. He started a second time to open his trunk, and this time had his hands on the Bible. But again he became afraid of being laughed at and dropped the trunk lid.

"I say!" laughed Henry who had observed his nervousness. "What is the matter with you? You are as restless as a weather vane!"

At first, Charles just laughed with him, but then decided that it would be better to be honest, and told both his roommates the whole story.

To his surprise, they did not laugh but agreed with him! "Well!" said Henry, "I have a Bible in my trunk, too. I have secretly been wishing that I could read it."

"So do I," spoke John, the other roommate, "but I was afraid you would laugh if I used it."

Charles was overjoyed and quickly replied, "Then let's all agree to read our Bibles every Sunday." Soon the three boys were busily reading their formerly-hidden Bibles.

The following Sunday, while they were each reading their Bibles, two of the boarders from another room entered. When they saw what was happening, they stared, and then exclaimed, "What is this, a conventicle?"

Smiling, Charles told them exactly what had happened; how he had struggled to get his Bible from his trunk, and how all three, having found they had all been afraid of each other for no reason, had now agreed to read every Sunday.

"Not a bad idea," answered one of them. "You have more courage than I. I have a Bible, too, but have not looked in it since I came to Boston. But I'll read after this, since you've broken the ice."

The other then asked one of them to read aloud, and both sat quietly listening until the bell rang for church.

That evening, the three boys in the same room agreed that one of them would read every night at ten o'clock, and they strictly followed this plan. A few evenings later, four or five other boarders happened to be in Charles' room talking when the ten o'clock bell rang. One of his roommates, looking at him, opened the Bible. The others looked up questioningly, so Charles explained their new custom.

"We'll all stay and listen," they said.

The final result of this was that, without exception, every one of the sixteen clerks spent Sunday morning reading the Bible, and the moral effect upon the entire household was very beneficial.

In later years, when Charles became a minister, he told this experience to show how much good influence even a young person can have. No one should ever be afraid to do that which is right.

Baptism is a mark of separation from the world. Could this mark of separation be clearly seen in this story? Can your mark of baptism be clearly seen by your friends in the way you talk and act?

— Adapted from *Religious Stories for Young and Old: Vol. I*

WHAT DO YOU THINK?

AN UNSEEN BAPTISM!

Sally was invited to the birthday party of a girl who lived a few houses away on her street. After she was there for some time, with several other girls who were invited, the girl's mother drove them to a nearby restaurant for dinner.

After the meals were served, Sally looked around. None of the other girls were praying; they all just started to eat. None of the girls attended or belonged to a church, except Sally.

Sally attended church and was a baptized member. She knew what she should do; her conscience clearly told her.

"But," Sally thought, "if I pray, the other girls will all laugh at me. They'll think I'm really different." She didn't dare to be different and Sally also ate without praying, but with a very guilty conscience.

Baptism is a mark of separation from the world. Could Sally's mark of baptism be clearly seen by others in this story? Why not?

Can your mark of baptism be clearly seen by others in the way you talk and act?

MEMORIZATION QUESTIONS

Holy Baptism

1. How are you incorporated into the Church of Christ?
   By Holy Baptism. .
2. In whose Name are you baptized?
   In the Name of the Father, of the Son, and of the Holy Ghost.
3. Who has instituted Holy Baptism?
   Christ, when He sent out His disciples to preach the gospel (Matthew 28:19).
4. Why did Christ institute baptism?
   To signify to us the washing away of sin.
5. Only to signify this?
   No; but also to assure us of the washing away of our sins (Acts 22:16).
6. How are our sins actually washed away?
   By the blood and Spirit of Christ (I Corinthians 6:11).
7. Do all who are baptized receive forgiveness of sin?
   No; only those who believe in Christ with their whole heart (Acts 8:37).
8. Why were you baptized as a child?
   Because my parents belong to the church of Christ and have God's promise.
9. What promise do your parents have?
   The same promise which God made to Abraham.
10. What must all baptized persons do?
    Believe in the triune God, love Him and serve Him.

— Donner's Catechism: Lesson XVIII,

157

CHECKING YOUR READING

1. How is a sacrament a:
   a. Sign? — _____
   _____

   b. Seal? — _____
   _____

2. Why was it necessary to change the form of the Old Testament sacraments in the New Testament? _____
   _____

3. Why is baptism administered only once in a person's life while the Lord's Supper may be used many times? _____
   _____
   _____

4. To be considered a legal baptism, what two requirements are necessary?
   a. _____
   b. _____

5. a. Name three methods of baptizing used by the New Testament church:
      1. _____
      2. _____
      3. _____
   b. Why are all three of these ways acceptable? _____
      _____

6. Why should the children of believing parents be baptized? List seven reasons:
   a. _____
   b. _____
   c. _____
   d. _____
   e. _____
   f. _____
   g. _____

7. List five reasons why your baptism is very valuable and a great privilege:
   a. _____
   b. _____
   c. _____
   d. _____
   e. _____

CHECKING YOUR READING

8. How do the blessings and privileges received in your baptism make you more responsible to God? _____

_____

_____

9. Why are only the outward benefits of baptism not sufficient for salvation?_____

_____

_____

10. Why is the Form for the Administration of Baptism written for the saved members of the Church Invisible when all children in the Church Visible are baptized?

a. _____

_____

b. _____

_____

■■■■■■■ EXTRA CHALLENGE QUESTIONS ■■■■■■■

1. a. From the story **How Was the Eunuch Baptized?**, explain how we do not know the manner in which the eunuch was baptized: _____

_____

b. Why is it not important nor necessary for us to know if the eunuch was baptized by sprinkling, pouring, or immersing? _____

_____

2. From the story **Citizenship**, describe the two ways in which a person may become a church member (a citizen):

a. _____

_____

b. _____

_____

3. How can a person:
a. Overvalue his baptism? _____

_____

b. Undervalue his baptism? _____

_____

4. What did Rev. Fraanje mean when he said, "Be not afraid to show the Lord your baptized forehead"? _____

_____

TESTING YOUR KNOWLEDGE

1. How are the means of grace:

   a. Undervalued — _____

   _____

   b. Overvalued — _____

   _____

2. Why are the means of grace very important? _____

   _____

3. To be brought up under the Word of God is both a great blessing and responsibility. Why?

   a. Blessing — _____

   _____

   b. Responsibility — _____

   _____

4. The three types of God's law found in the Bible are:

   a. _____

   b. _____

   c. _____

5. With what desire and motive must God's law be obeyed? _____

   _____

   _____

6. Each of God's Ten Commandments tell us what we _____ do and what we

   _____ do.

7. When and only when is it right to disobey a person who is placed in authority over you?

   _____

   _____

8. What does the word "gospel" mean? _____

   _____

TESTING YOUR KNOWLEDGE

9. Name the two requirements for a practice to be a New Testament sacrament:

   a. _____

   b. _____

10. Why were different New Testament forms of the Old Testament sacraments

    necessary? _____

    _____

    _____

11. a. Does the Bible clearly teach the manner of baptism that was used in the New

      Testament? _____

   b. Name the methods of baptizing that have been used by the church.

      1. _____

      2. _____

      3. _____

   c. Why is each of these three ways acceptable? _____

      _____

12. When a missionary minister begins his work in a new area, describe the steps that are

    followed regarding who and when he may baptize.

   a. _____

   b. _____

   c. _____

   d. _____

13. a. My outward baptism separates me from the _____, and places me in an

      _____ relationship to God's Covenant of _____. My baptism

      places me under God's _____ and includes me continually in the_____

      of the church. These are great blessings, but they are not sufficient for _____.

   b. Baptism applied inwardly by the power of the _____ seals the deepest

      truth of baptism in a person's life, which is the _____ through the

      blood of _____. This places a person in an _____ relationship

      to God's Covenant of _____.

CODED WORDS

Can you solve this code and find all of the Vocabulary Words from Chapters Seventeen and Eighteen? Each number stands for a letter. Write the correct Vocabulary Word on the blank below the coded word. Then place the letter of the best matching definition on the blank in front of the proper number.

6-13-24-11-21-20-7

_____ 1. _____

6-20-24-13

_____ 2. _____

12-20-24-11-6-10-19-18-7-24-22-20

_____ 3. _____

10-7-21-16-11-24-7-26

_____ 4. _____

22-16-3-16-13-13-24-2-6

_____ 5. _____

12-10-7-24-13-13-24-2

_____ 6. _____

22-10-11-5-20-11-5

_____ 7. _____

16-11-6-5-16-5-4-5-16-10-11

_____ 8. _____

22-13-20-24-11-6-16-11-18

_____ 9. _____

12-20-24-11-6

_____ 10. _____

6-24-22-7-24-12-20-11-5-6

_____ 11. _____

22-20-7-20-12-10-11-16-24-13-13-24-2

_____ 12. _____

10-19-19-16-22-16-24-13

_____ 13. _____

10-19-19-20-7

_____ 14. _____

22-10-11-19-16-7-12

_____ 15. _____

13-24-2

_____ 16. _____

9-7-16-3-16-13-20-18-20

_____ 17. _____

7-20-15-20-22-5

_____ 18. _____

16-12-12-20-7-6-16-10-11

_____ 19. _____

6-16-18-11

_____ 20. _____

A. Usual; normal

B. The act of placing something or someone entirely under water

C. The Bible and sacraments

D. Holy baptism and the Lord's supper

E. To refuse; cast away

F. A rule which tells us what we must or may not do

G. Something which confirms and guarantees the truth

H. Rules for everyday matters in society

I. Being satisfied with that which one has received

J. Lying to purposely hurt another person's reputation

K. Washing; making clean

L. Something presented to be accepted or rejected

M. A symbol; something we see which speaks of a deeper meaning

N. God's Ten Commandments

O. To settle or prove something beyond doubt

P. Something used to help accomplish a certain purpose

Q. Having proper authority

R. Israel's Old Testament religious laws

S. A favor or blessing given to some people

T. An organization established for some purpose

BIBLE STUDY QUESTIONS

Read the following chapters and write out the verse or verses which most clearly teach the following doctrinal truths:

1. The necessity of the Bible being inwardly blessed by God the Holy Spirit in our lives —
   I Thessalonians 1:_____ — _____

   _____

   _____

2. The first table of God's law requires love to God; the second table demands love to my neighbor —

   Mark 12:_____ (2 verses) — _____

   _____

   _____

   _____

3. Jesus Christ commanded His church to baptize — _____

   Matthew 28:_____ — _____

   _____

   _____

4. The promises of God in His Covenant of Grace include children —
   Genesis 17:_____ — _____

   _____

   _____

   Acts 2:_____ — _____

   _____

   _____

PROJECT IDEAS

1. Write a report on all the New Testament examples of baptism. Who was baptized? Where? By whom? Were only adults or also their households baptized?
2. Design a poster which explains various excuses people give for not using God's means of grace.
3. Make a poster and write a report on the three types of God's law. Give some biblical examples of each type.
4. Draw a chart which clearly shows the difference between an inward and outward relationship to the Covenant of Grace.

nd I will deliver
And they cove-
for thirty pieces

at time he sought
etray him.

first *day* of the
ened bread the
to Jesus, saying
e wilt thou that
thee to eat the

, Go into the city
nd say unto him,
h, My time is at
o the passover at
my disciples.

ciples did as Jesus
them; and they
passover.

n the even was
down with the

did eat, he said,
you, that one of
me.

were exceeding
began every one
nto him, Lord, is

hast said.

26 ℞ And as they were eating, Jesus took bread, and blessed *it*, and brake *it*, and gave *it* to the disciples, and said, Take, eat; this is my body.

27 And he took the cup, and gave thanks, and gave *it* to them, saying, Drink ye all of it;

28 For this is my blood of the new testament, which is shed for many for the remission of sins.

29 But I sa   to you, I will not drink hence   of this fruit of the vine, un   at day when I drink it ne   you in my Father's king

30 And when   g hymn, they w   mount of Olive

31 Then saith All ye shall be of me this night: I will smite the sheep of the f tered abroad.

32 But after will go before

33 Peter answe him, Though all

VOCABULARY

1. **Institute** — To set up; to start; to begin

2. **Replace** — To put in the place of

3. **Elements** — Parts or materials used

4. **Physical** — Material; natural; outward

5. **Administration** — The act of giving, serving, or managing

6. **Denying** — The act of refusing to believe; a statement that something is not true

7. **Examine** — To look into carefully

8. **Participate** — To take part in; to become involved in

9. **Celebrate** — To remember a special happening by participating in a certain ceremony or event

10. **Preparatory** — In preparation of; getting ready for

THE LORD'S SUPPER

Holy Baptism and the Lord's Supper are the two sacraments which the Lord Jesus Christ has given to His New Testament church. In the Bible, *the Lord's Supper* is referred to as the:

— Lord's Supper
— Lord's table
— Communion
— Cup of blessing
— Cup of the Lord
— Breaking of bread

The Lord Jesus instituted the Lord's Supper after He served the passover meal to His apostles. This took place during the last evening He spent with them before His crucifixion. We can read of this in the following verses:

> And as they were eating, Jesus **took bread,** and blessed it, and brake it, and gave it to the disciples, and said, Take, eat; this is My body.
> And He **took the cup,** and gave thanks, and gave it to them, saying, Drink ye all of it;
> For this is My blood of the New Testament, which is shed for many for the remission of sins.
> — Matthew 26:26-28

WHAT DO YOU THINK?

OTHER NAMES FOR THE LORD'S SUPPER

Which names are used for the Lord's Supper in each of the following verses? At times more than one name is used in a verse.

> When ye come together therefore into one place, this is not to eat the Lord's Supper.
> — I Corinthians 11:20

> Ye cannot drink the cup of the Lord, and the cup of devils: ye cannot be partakers of the Lord's table, and of the table of devils.
> — I Corinthians 10:21

> The cup of blessing which we bless, is it not the communion of the blood of Christ? The bread which we break, is it not the communion of the body of Christ?
> — I Corinthians 10:16

> And they continued stedfastly in the apostles' doctrine and fellowship, and in breaking of bread, and in prayers.
> — Acts 2:42

165

WHAT DO YOU THINK?

A FIRST LORD'S SUPPER

John Paton was a missionary to the New Hebrides. After being privileged to hold the first Lord's Supper with some natives from these islands, he described this blessed event by writing the following:

"The entire service took about three hours. The Islanders looked on in silent wonder. For the first time the Melbourne Presbyterian Sabbath School teachers' gift of a silver communion set was put to use. They gave it in faith, believing that we would need it and now their faith had not been put to shame. For three years we toiled, prayed, and taught, hoping for these fruits.

At the moment when I put the bread and wine into their dark hands, hands of cannibals which were once stained with human blood, but now were receiving the signs of the body and blood of the Savior, I had a foretaste of the glory of Christ which well-nigh broke my heart."

Why is the Lord's Supper such a wonderful sacrament? How does it speak of Christ's love and glory?

— Adapted from *3,000 Illustrations for Christian Service*

The Lord Jesus has lovingly commanded His New Testament church to continue to use this sacrament until He returns again at the end of time. We can read of this continuing command in the following verses:

> For I have received of the Lord that which also I delivered unto you, That the Lord Jesus the same night in which He was betrayed took bread:
> And when He had given thanks, He brake it, and said, Take, eat: this is My body, which is broken for you: **this do in remembrance of Me.**
> After the same manner also He took the cup, when He had supped, saying, This cup is the New Testament in My blood: **this do ye, as oft as ye drink it, in remembrance of Me.**
> **For as often as ye eat this bread, and drink this cup, ye do show the Lord's death till He come.**
> — I Corinthians 11:23-26

The New Testament sacrament of the Lord's Supper **replaces** the Old Testament sacrament of the Passover. Do you remember why the Old Testament sacrament forms had to be replaced after Christ died?

The **elements** used in the Lord's Supper are:

1. **Broken bread**

2. **Poured wine**

The **broken bread** testifies of Jesus' broken body and the **poured wine** points to Christ's poured-out blood. The bread and wine speak of the death of Christ's body as you can so clearly read in the previously quoted verses from I Corinthians 11.

Christ's *death* is His people's *life.* Christ died to deliver His children from death and to earn eternal life for them. Christ is their spiritual life.

To support our **physical** life and receive natural strength, we need food and drink. In New Testament times, bread was the main food and wine was the basic drink. These provided the necessary nourishment and strength required for physical life and health.

To support a true believer's spiritual life, spiritual "food" is also necessary. A true believer needs spiritual nourishment and strength in his daily walk on earth. His spiritual life and strength can only be found in his Savior, Jesus Christ.

The *signs* of bread and wine in the Lord's Supper point to the life and nourishment for true believers in the broken body and shed blood of Christ.

The Lord's Supper, as a sacrament, is not only a sign, but it is also a seal. The Lord's Supper **seals** to God's children:

1. That as surely as they see the broken bread and the poured wine, so sure is the truth that **Christ has died for them**

167

WHAT DO YOU THINK?

THE LIVING BREAD OF SPIRITUAL LIFE

After feeding five thousand men from five loaves of bread and two fish, the people wanted to crown Jesus as king. They wanted Him to provide bread from heaven for them just as God had provided manna for their forefathers in the wilderness.

Jesus answered them by saying,

Verily, verily, I say unto you, He that believeth on Me hath everlasting life.

I am the Bread of Life.

Your fathers did eat manna in the wilderness, and are dead.

This is the Bread which cometh down from heaven, that a man may eat thereof, and not die.

I am the living Bread which came down from heaven: if any man eat of this Bread, he shall live forever: and the Bread that I will give is My flesh, which I will give for the life of the world.

The Jews therefore strove among themselves, saying, How can this Man give us His flesh to eat?

It is the spirit that quickeneth; the flesh profiteth nothing: the words that I speak unto you, they are spirit, and they are life.

— John 6:47-52, 63

What type of king and bread did the people want? What type of "King" and "Bread" is Jesus? How does verse 63 help explain what Jesus meant in the previous verses?

2. That as certainly as they eat the bread and drink the wine, so certain is the truth that *God will spiritually feed and nourish their souls forever*

WHAT DO YOU THINK?

THE SIGN AND SEAL IN THE LORD'S SUPPER

Explain where the *sign* and *seal* of the Lord's Supper are spoken about in the:

Heidelberg Catechism

Q.75. How art thou admonished and assured in the Lord's Supper, that thou art a partaker of that one sacrifice of Christ, accomplished on the cross, and of all His benefits?

A. Thus: That Christ has commanded me and all believers, to eat of this broken bread, and to drink of this cup, in remembrance of Him, adding these promises: first, that His body was offered and broken on the cross for me, and His blood was shed for me, as certainly as I see with my eyes, the bread of the Lord broken for me, and the cup communicated to me; and further, that He feeds and nourishes my soul to everlasting life, with His crucified body and shed blood, as assuredly as I receive from the hands of the minister, and taste with my mouth the bread and cup of the Lord, as certain signs of the body and blood of Christ.

Form for the Administration of the Lord's Supper

That is, as often as ye eat of this bread and drink of this cup, you shall thereby as by a sure remembrance and pledge, be admonished and assured of this My hearty love and faithfulness towards you; that, whereas you should otherwise have suffered eternal death, I have given My body to the death of the cross, and shed My blood for you; and as certainly feed and nourish your hungry and thirsty souls with My crucified body, and shed blood, to everlasting life, as this bread is broken before your eyes, and this cup is given to you, and you eat and drink the same with your mouth, in remembrance of Me.

WHAT DO YOU THINK?

FOOD FOR STRENGTH

A general was preparing his men one morning for a battle which they would soon be fighting. His first concern was that all of his men would eat a good meal before the battle began. Why was this important?

Napoleon once said, "A soldier marches on his stomach!" What did he mean with this statement?

God's true children are also "soldiers." Against whom are they fighting? Who is their Captain? In this spiritual war, why is it necessary and helpful to God's children to eat and drink at the Lord's table? Why did God institute the Lord's Supper for His people?

In the Lord's Supper, the bread that is used is ordinary bread and the wine is normal wine. The bread and wine are used in a special manner at the Lord's table; they become signs which point to the body and blood of Christ. However, the bread remains bread, and the wine remains wine. The bread and wine **point to, represent,** and **picture** Christ's body and blood, but they **do not become, contain, or carry** Christ's actual body or blood.

There are church denominations which have different beliefs about the bread and wine used in the Lord's Supper. The Roman Catholic Church teaches that when the priest blesses the bread and wine, they actually change into the real flesh and blood of Jesus Christ. According to this belief, each person who receives the bread actually eats the physical body of Christ, and the priest, who drinks the wine for the people, actually drinks the physical blood of Christ.

WHAT DO YOU THINK?

THE ROMAN CATHOLIC MASS

In the Roman Catholic Church the Lord's supper service is often called the "mass." The bread, which is baked as small wafers, is believed to change, after the priest's blessing, into the body of Christ, even though it keeps its appearance of bread. This "changed bread" is called the "host." It is lifted on high by the priest and worshipped as Christ. It is taught that Christ is physically present and is sacrificed on an altar by a priest. The priest places one of the wafers on the tongue of each person receiving it. It is believed that the wafers, as the actual body of Christ, are too holy to be touched by anyone except the priest. The Roman Catholic Church teaches that the mass actually gives grace to those who receive it.

Can you understand why the bread is baked into a wafer for the mass? What would happen if normal bread were used and some crumbs dropped? Can you understand why only the priest drinks the wine? What would a true Roman Catholic believe if the wine were spilled?

Why is the mass:
— A lie?
— A practicing of idol worship?
— A **denying** of the one and only complete sacrifice of Christ?
— A denying that Christ's human nature is in heaven and not on earth?

Study the biblical texts on the next page for help in answering these questions.

WHAT DO YOU THINK?
THE BIBLE AND THE "MASS"

Explain how the following scriptural texts speak against the teachings and beliefs of the Roman Catholic Mass:

JOHN 6:53-56; 63

Then Jesus said unto them, Verily, verily, I say unto you, Except ye eat the flesh of the Son of man, and drink His blood, ye have no life in you.

Whoso eateth My flesh, and drinketh My blood, hath eternal life; and I will raise him up at the last day.

For My flesh is meat indeed, and My blood is drink indeed.

He that eateth My flesh, and drinketh My blood, dwelleth in Me, and I in him·

It is the spirit that quickeneth; the flesh profiteth nothing: *the words that I speak unto you, they are spirit, and they are life.*

MATTHEW 26:27

And He took the cup, and gave thanks, and gave it to them, saying, *Drink ye all of it.*

EXODUS 20:4-5a

Thou shalt not make unto thee any graven image, or any likeness of any thing that is in heaven above, or that is in the earth beneath, or that is in the water under the earth:

Thou shalt not bow down thyself to them, nor serve them:

JOHN 4:24

God is a Spirit: and *they that worship Him must worship Him in spirit and in truth.*

HEBREWS 9:25-26

Nor yet that He should offer Himself often, as the high priest entereth into the holy place every year with blood of others;

For then must He often have suffered since the foundation of the world: *but now once* in the end of the world *hath He appeared to put away sin by the sacrifice of Himself.*

HEBREWS 10:18

Now *where remission of these is, there is no more offering for sin.*

HEBREWS 10:10-12, 14

By the which will we are sanctified *through the offering of the body of Jesus Christ once for all.*

And every priest standeth daily ministering and offering oftentimes the same sacrifices, which can never take away sins:

But this man, after He had offered one sacrifice for sins for ever, sat down on the right hand of God.

For *by one offering He hath perfected for ever them that are sanctified.*

MARK 16:19

So then after the Lord had spoken unto them, *He was received up into heaven, and sat on the right hand of God.*

HEBREWS 1:3

Who being the brightness of His glory, and the express image of His person, and upholding all things by the word of His power, *when He had by Himself purged our sins, sat down on the right hand of the Majesty on high.*

WHAT DO YOU THINK?

THE BODY AND BLOOD OF CHRIST

Afoo was a native Malaysian boy who had been instructed by missionaries. One Sunday he witnessed a Lord's Supper service for the first time. A friend who was visiting the mission post, spoke with him after the service. He asked Afoo, "What did you see?"

"I see people eat bread and wine," he answered.

"What does it mean?"

"It mean the body and blood of Jesus."

"Is it really the body and blood of Jesus Christ?"

"No," he answered, "it not same — it keep in mind His body and blood. He die for sinners."

Afoo may not have spoken proper English, but did he have a right understanding about the bread and wine used in the Lord's Supper? How can you tell?

— Adapted from *The Shorter Catechism Illustrated*

171

While Martin Luther was a great reformer and servant of God, he also held a wrong idea about the body and blood of Christ being present at the Lord's Supper. This view is believed by most of the Lutheran churches yet today. Martin Luther did not believe that the bread and wine actually changed into the body and blood of Christ, but he taught that the bread and wine **actually contained and carried** the physical body and blood of Christ. Luther believed that **Christ's physical body came with, in, and under the bread** and His actual **blood came with, in, and under the wine.** To Luther, the bread remained bread and the wine remained wine, but in the Lord's Supper, Christ's actual body and blood **attached itself** to the bread and wine.

The Roman Catholic and the Lutheran churches base their beliefs on the following scriptural verses:

> And as they were eating, Jesus took bread, and blessed it, and brake it, and gave it to the disciples, and said, Take, eat; **this is My body.**
>
> And He took the cup, and gave thanks, and gave it to them, saying, Drink ye all of it;
>
> For **this is My blood** of the New Testament, which is shed for many for the remission of sins.
>
> — Matthew 26:26-28

Study the "What Do You Think?" on this page. Did Jesus actually mean His physical body here? How can you know? What did He mean?

WHAT DO YOU THINK?
AN ACTUAL OR SPIRITUAL MEANING?

Read: **Matthew 16:6** —

> Then Jesus said unto them, Take heed and beware of the leaven of the Pharisees and of the Sadducees.

Did Jesus mean here to be careful for the Pharisees' actual yeast or leaven? What did He mean?

Read: **John 4:14** —

> But whosoever drinketh of the water that I shall give him shall never thirst; but the water that I shall give him shall be in him a well of water springing up into everlasting life.

Did Jesus mean physical water and thirst in this verse? What did He mean?

Read: **John 4:31-32** —

> In the mean while His disciples prayed Him, saying, Master, eat.
> But He said unto them, I have meat to eat that ye know not of.

Did Jesus mean actual meat in these verses? What did He mean?

Read: **John 15:1** —

> I am the true Vine, and My Father is the Husbandman.

Did Jesus mean here that He was a physical vine? What did He mean?

Read: **John 10:7** —

> Then Jesus said unto them again, Verily, verily, I say unto you, I am the Door of the sheep.

Did Jesus mean that He was a physical door for sheep in this verse? What did He mean?

Read: **Matthew 26:26-28** —
(printed on this page)

Did Jesus mean here that the bread was actually His physical body and that the wine was actually His physical blood? What did He mean? Had Jesus died yet when He spoke these words? How can we know from this fact that He could not have meant His physical body and blood?

At the Lord's Supper service, the Lord Jesus is **not bodily present** in His human nature, but He **is spiritually present** in His divine nature.

WHAT DO YOU THINK?
JESUS' PRESENCE

How can Question and Answer 47 of the Heidelberg Catechism help explain how Christ is present at the Lord's Supper?

Q.47. Is not Christ then with us even to the end of the world, as He hath promised?

A. Christ is very man and very God; with respect to His human nature, He is no more on earth; but with respect to His Godhead, majesty, grace and Spirit, He is at no time absent from us.

To **properly observe** the Lord's Supper, our **Form for the Administration of the Lord's Supper** speaks of two necessary things. What are these two requirements?

> That we may now celebrate the Supper of the Lord to our comfort, it is above all things necessary,
> First. **Rightly to examine ourselves.**
> Secondly. **To direct it** to that end for which Christ hath ordained and instituted the same, namely, **to His remembrance.**

To **rightly examine ourselves** is necessary before participating in the Lord's Supper. Not everyone has a right to go to the Lord's table.

To properly attend the Lord's Supper a person must have:

1. A **church right**

2. A **divine right**

A **church right** to attend the Lord's Supper includes the following:

1. The person must be a **confessing member** of the church. A baptized member must wait until he becomes an adult and makes his personal confession of faith. This rule is generally followed to be certain that a person is old enough to properly examine himself

WHAT DO YOU THINK?

A FULFILLED DESIRE

A twelve-year-old girl was dying from a serious disease. She spoke to consistory members when they visited her and she told them how she longed to be at the Lord's Supper in her church before she died! The consistory gave its permission, and this girls, who was very weak by this time, came to the Lord's table.

This made a deep impression upon the entire congregation. Why, do you think? What exception to a normal rule did the consistory make when giving her permission to attend? Why did the consistory do this?

as God commands. Under special conditions, an exception to this rule can be made.

2. The person must **not be living in any public sin.** Anyone who is placed under silent or public censure by the consistory may not **participate** in the Lord's Supper. He is openly testifying that he is not walking in the way of God's Word.

Two elders stand at the table during the Lord's Supper with the minister. These elders are called "table waiters" or "table watchers." They are to:

1. Make sure that everyone who participates in the Lord's Supper has a **church right** to attend

WHAT DO YOU THINK?

MAN MUST BOW BEFORE GOD

Ambrose was serving as minister where the Roman emperor Theodesius attended church.

The emperor had left the city for some time to catch and punish some persons who had destroyed his statue and had committed other rebellious acts in another place. However, in his revengeful anger, he killed many innocent people in that city.

When he returned to church, the Lord's Supper was being held. However, Ambrose stopped the emperor from participating. Ambrose told him he must repent and confess his sins before he could participate.

Why was this action of Ambrose very dangerous for him? Why was it right for him to forbid the emperor to attend the Lord's table?

2. **to assist** the minister and persons attending

Those who are publicly living in sin or teaching false doctrine do not have a church right to attend the Lord's Supper. **The Form for the Administration of the Lord's Supper** forbids them to come to the table of the Lord with the following words:

FORM FOR THE ADMINISTRATION OF THE LORD'S SUPPER

Therefore, we also, according to the command of Christ and the Apostle Paul, admonish all those who are defiled with the following sins, to keep themselves from the table of the Lord, and declare to them that they have no part in the kingdom of Christ; such as all idolaters, all those who invoke deceased saints, angels or other creatures; all those who worship images; all enchanters, diviners, charmers, and those who confide in such enchantments; all despisers of God, and of His Word, and of the holy sacraments; all blasphemers; all those who are given to raise discord, sects and mutiny in church or state; all perjured person; all those who are disobedient to their parents and superiors; all murderers, contentious persons, and those who live in hatred and envy against their neighbors; all adulterers, whoremongers, drunkards, thieves, usurers, robbers, gamesters, covetous, and all who lead offensive lives.

All these, while they continue in such sins, shall abstain from this meat (which Christ hath ordained only for the faithful), lest their judgment and condemnation be made the heavier.

WHAT DO YOU THINK?

ACHAN PLAGUED ISRAEL

When God destroyed Jericho, He had forbidden any Israelite to take any spoils for himself. However, Achan found and took a costly garment, two hundred shekels of silver, and a wedge of gold, and hid them in the ground under his tent.

When Israel went to fight against Ai, the Israelites fled from them. Joshua asked the Lord why they were defeated and the Lord answered:

> Israel hath sinned, and they have also transgressed My covenant which I commanded them: for they have even taken of the accursed thing, and have also stolen, and dissembled also, and they have put it even among their own stuff.
>
> Therefore the children of Israel could not stand before their enemies, but turned their backs before their enemies, because they were accursed: neither will I be with you any more, except ye destroy the accursed from among you.
> — Joshua 7:11-12

The nation of Israel was unclean in God's sight; its sin had to be put away before God would again bless them.

Why is it important for a consistory not to knowingly allow those who are living in public sin to come to the Lord's table?

To properly attend the Lord's Supper a person must have a divine right as well as a church right. We cannot properly participate if we are only confessing members who are not living in public sin. We need to examine our hearts carefully to see if we also have a divine right to attend the table of the Lord.

A **divine right** means that we are one of God's true children, a true believer in Jesus Christ. It means that we have been converted from a heartfelt love of sin to God.

WHAT DO YOU THINK?

HEARING OR KNOWING?

A young, healthy-looking man had a complete physical examination. The results, however, showed that he had cancer! The doctor had to bring the sad report to this man!

The man, however, was not concerned about it. If people talked about cancer, he was not interested. He continued on in the same way as he had lived before. The man was told about and urged to use special medicines and treatments which had been used as a means to help several other people in the same condition; but the man felt no need to use these.

This man heard that he had cancer, but do you think he really "knew" it? Did he feel and experience the truth of it? Why not?

God's Word tells us that we have the deadly disease of sin. It informs us that Christ is the only Physician Who can heal us. But, if we go on uninterested in our sinful disease or in Christ; if these things are not a felt need and concern to us, do you think we really "know" or believe them? If we truly experience our sinful misery and need God's deliverance, how will this be seen in our lives, do you think?

What is the difference between having a head knowledge or an experiential knowledge of my misery, deliverance, and thankfulness?

When He instituted the Lord's Supper, Jesus said, "Take, eat; this is My body which is broken for **you,** this do in **remembrance of Me."** For whom did Christ die? Whom did He mean when He said "you"? Who only can truly "remember" or know Him as their Savior?

The Bible provides us with a very powerful warning that tells us that we may not participate in the Lord's Supper if we do not have a divine right. We may not eat and drink at the Lord's table if we are not yet His children through regeneration and conversion.

> Wherefore whosoever shall eat this bread, and drink this cup of the Lord, unworthily, shall be guilty of the body and blood of the Lord.
> But *let a man examine himself,* and so let him eat of that bread, and drink of that cup.
> For he that eateth and drinketh unworthily, eateth and drinketh damnation to himself, not discerning the Lord's body.
> — I Corinthians 11:27-29
>
> *Examine* yourselves, whether ye be in the faith; *prove* your own selves.
> — II Corinthians 13:5a

How must we examine ourselves? How can we know if we are regenerated and converted from sin to God? We must examine whether we know something in the experiences of our lives of our:

1. *Misery* in sin

2. *Deliverance* through Christ

3. *Thankfulness* unto God

We should examine whether our deepest longings and desires have been turned from loving and serving self, sin, the world, and Satan to loving and serving God. We must show the fruits of inward spiritual life in our lives by bringing forth good works of love to God and others.

When a person examines his own heart and life, he should prayerfully ask God for guidance and seriously ask himself the following questions:

— Do I know and feel something of the heavy burden of sinfulness? Have I learned that I am nothing but sin, a totally guilty and hell-worthy sinner? Have I painfully experienced that I cannot save myself, but that I only add to my sin continually?

— Do I know and feel a deep need for Jesus Christ as the only, perfect, and complete Savior for such a lost sinner as I am? Is He my only hope and trust for salvation? Do I need, believe, and hope in the forgiveness of my sins only through Christ's perfect sacrifice?

— Do I know and feel a love in my heart to God for the wonderful salvation He has provided for sinners such as I? Do I desire and strive to live my life in a way which is pleasing to God out of true love to Him?

WHAT DO YOU THINK?

SELF EXAMINATION

The Form for the Administration of the Lord's Supper speaks of true self-examination as follows: Can you find misery, deliverance, and thankfulness in this explanation?

The true examination of ourselves consists of these three parts:

First. That every one consider by himself, his sins and the curse due to him for them, to the end that he may abhor and humble himself before God: considering that the wrath of God against sin is so great, that (rather than it should go unpunished) He hath punished the same in His beloved Son Jesus Christ, with the bitter and shameful death of the cross.

Secondly. That every one examine his own heart, whether he doth believe this faithful promise of God, that all his sins are forgiven him only for the sake of the passion and death of Jesus Christ, and that the perfect righteousness of Christ is imputed and freely given him as his own, yea, so perfectly, as if he had satisfied in his own person for all his sins, and fulfilled all righteousness.

Thirdly. That every one examine his own conscience, whether he purposeth henceforth to show true thankfulness to God in his whole life, and to walk uprightly before Him; as also, whether he hath laid aside unfeignedly all enmity, hatred, and envy, and doth firmly resolve henceforward to walk in true love and peace with his neighbor.

— Do I know and feel a hating of and struggling against my spiritual enemies: sin, self, the lusts of the world, and Satan? Do I love to do that which is pleasing to God? If I sin, does it cause me pain in my heart that I have sinned against the One whom I love most in my life?

— Do I know and feel a wholehearted desire to obey God and to walk in His ways, not only because I am commanded to, but also because I love to serve Him with my whole heart?

If you would honestly examine yourself, alone today with God, how would you answer these questions?

The table waiters, or table watchers, are to make certain that everyone participating in the Lord's Supper has a church right. As men, they cannot perfectly judge the hearts of people to see if each person has a divine right. Only God can perfectly judge the heart. The careful examination regarding a person's divine right is a personal matter between the Lord and his own soul.

To properly **celebrate** the Lord's Supper we must rightly examine ourselves; but we must also direct everything to *the remembrance of Christ.*

The Lord's Supper speaks of Christ and His work. It pictures Jesus' death for His people and the spiritual life and strength He gives to them. The Lord's Supper is not to focus on nor glorify certain people, but to glorify Christ and His wonderful work.

No person is "worthy" or "good enough" to come to the Lord's table of himself. Those who are "worthy" have learned to find all their worthiness only in Jesus Christ. From their side, they are lost sinners. **The Form for the Administration of the Lord's Supper** explains this so beautifully in the following paragraph:

THE FORM FOR THE ADMINISTRATION OF THE LORD'S SUPPER

But this is not designed (dearly beloved brethren and sisters in the Lord), to deject the contrite hearts of the faithful, as if none might come to the supper of the Lord, but those who are without sin; for we do not come to this supper, to testify thereby that we are perfect and righteous in ourselves; but on the contrary, considering that we seek our life out of ourselves in Jesus Christ, we acknowledge that we lie in the midst of death; therefore, notwithstanding we feel many infirmities and miseries in ourselves, as namely, that we have not perfect faith, and that we do not give ourselves to serve God with that zeal as we are bound, but have daily to strive with the weakness of our faith, and the evil lusts of our flesh; yet, since we are (by the grace of the Holy Spirit) sorry for these weaknesses, and earnestly desirous to fight against our unbelief, and to live according to all the commandment of God: therefore we rest assured that no sin or infirmity, which still remaineth against our will, in us, can hinder us from being received of God in mercy, and from being made worthy partakers of this heavenly meat and drink.

The Lord Jesus commanded His Church to continually remember His death by celebrating His Supper until He returns at the end of the world. However, Christ did not say how often the Lord's Supper should be held. Most churches follow the rule of not holding the Lord's Supper so often that it becomes too common and not having it so seldom that it becomes too frightening or awesome.

> This cup is the New Testament in My blood: *this do ye,* as oft as ye drink it, *in remembrance of Me.*
> For as often as ye eat this bread, and drink this cup, ye do **shew the Lord's death till He come.**
> — I Corinthians 11:25b-26

The Lord's Supper is also called *"communion"*, which means "friendship", "togetherness", and "sharing."

God's children commune with Christ at His table, but they also commune with one another. They share as brothers and sisters in the riches of Christ that are graciously given to them. They are united as one body of Christ, their Savior.

> The cup of blessing which we bless, is it not the **communion** of the blood of Christ? The bread which we break, is it not the communion of the body of Christ?
> For we being many are **one bread, and one body:** for we are all partakers of that one Bread.
> — I Corinthians 10:16-17

It is important that all those who commune with Christ at His table and receive His love, walk in true love and communion with one another. To make certain of this, previous announcement of the Lord's Supper is given in the congregation, so that anyone who has difficulties with or hard feelings toward another can visit that person and clear away their problems.

> **If a man say, I love God, and hateth his brother, he is a liar:** for he that loveth not his brother whom he hath seen, how can he love God whom he hath not seen?
> — I John 4:20

A consistory meeting is also held before the Lord's Supper is served. This provides an opportunity for members to speak with the consistory about any continuing problems which should be settled before the Lord's Supper would be held.

The entire congregation should attend the church service when the Lord's Supper is served, not only those who plan to participate. The Lord's Supper pictures the gospel. When it is served, everyone can hear and see that Jesus died to give spiritual life and strength to needy sinners. Everyone must place himself under the means of grace that God has given and earnestly pray that God would bless these means savingly in his heart. Everyone is called to spiritually examine himself.

Every member makes a confession when the Lord's Supper is served. By participating, a person confesses that he knows something of sinful misery, deliverance through Christ, and a life of thankfulness to God. By not participating, a person confesses that he is yet a stranger of true misery, deliverance, and thankfulness in his life. He confesses that he is yet unregenerated and unsaved. Why are both of these confessions very serious ones?

WHAT DO YOU THINK?

LOOKING AT THE WRONG PERSON!

Mrs. Sands carefully watched each person who attended the Lord's table. "For 'that man' and 'those ladies' it was true," she thought, "but not for 'that person!' Why, just last week I heard 'this' and 'that' about her! How did she dare to go to the table?"

What is frightfully wrong with Mrs. Sands' attitude during the Lord's Supper service? Why are her thoughts very sinful? Whom should she be looking at and examining very carefully?

WHAT DO YOU THINK?

THE VISIBLE GOSPEL IS BEING SHOWN

Mike is in church and the Lord's Supper is being served, but his thoughts are quite different from that which is taking place in the service.

"Why do I have to be here?" he thinks. "It is not for me anyway. Even if I could go, I'm not old enough. Besides, it takes so long, too."

What is clearly wrong and sinful with Mike's attitude during the Lord's Supper service? Whose person and work is being pictured in the Lord's Supper? Why should everyone in the congregation attend the church service when the Lord's Supper is being served?

The time of preparation and self-examination for the Lord's Supper can be a difficult time for a child of God. At times, he can be torn between God's loving command, "Do this in remembrance of Me," and God's powerful warning, "He that eateth and drinketh unworthily, eateth and drinketh damnation to himself."

A **preparatory** sermon is preached in church the Sunday before the Lord's Supper is held to help everyone in preparation for the Lord's Supper. To help each person examine himself according to the Word of God, this sermon clearly presents the scriptural marks of conversion (misery, deliverance, and thankfulness) and its fruits (love to God and others).

When the Lord's Supper is served, there can be six groups of people in the church. These groups are listed in the following chart:

When the Lord's Supper is served there can be people who:	
1. *Have a divine right and attend,* properly following Christ's loving command	4. *Do not have a divine right and attend,* unworthily
2. *Have a divine right but do not attend* due to fear of self, personal sin, and self-deceit	5. *Do not have a divine right and do not attend,* but have burning consciences and painful hearts that they cannot properly participate
3. *Have a divine right but do not attend* due to fear of others — that which others might think or say	6. *Do not have a divine right and do not attend,* but have no concern about their condition

If you were a confessing member with a church right, and the Lord's Supper was served in your church next Sunday, into which of these six groups would you place yourself?

MEMORIZATION QUESTIONS

HOLY SUPPER

1. What did Christ institute besides Holy Baptism?
The Holy Supper.
2. When did Christ institute this?
In the last night of His life when He was betrayed (Matthew 26:20-29).
3. What did Christ use in the Holy Supper?
Christ took bread and wine, and gave them to His disciples to eat and to drink.
4. What does the bread and wine signify in the Lord's Supper?
The body and blood of Christ (Matthew 26:26-28).
5. What did it signify that Christ brake the bread and poured out the wine?
That His body was to be so broken on the cross and His blood poured out.
6. To what purpose did Christ institute this Holy Supper?
In remembrance of His suffering and death.
7. How must we remember His suffering and death in Holy Communion?
Thus; that through His suffering and death He has obtained the forgiveness of sins for us (Matthew 26:28).
8. Who are true communicants?
All who realize their sinfulness aright, believe in Christ, and desire to live for Him.
9. Until what time shall the Lord's Supper be celebrated in the church of Christ?
Until Christ comes again (I Corinthians 11:26).

— Donner's Catechism: Lesson XIX: Q. 1-9

CHECKING YOUR READING

1. Name the elements that are used in the Lord's Supper and describe what they point to as signs:

   a. _____ — _____

   _____

   b. _____ — _____

   _____

2. What wonderful truths are sealed to God's people in the Lord's Supper?

   a. _____

   _____

   b. _____

   _____

3. Why is the Roman Catholic mass:

   a. A lie?_____

   _____

   b. An idolatry? _____

   _____

   c. A denying of the one, only, and complete sacrifice of Christ?_____

   _____

4. Describe the wrong idea that Martin Luther believed and taught concerning Christ's body and blood at the Lord's Supper: _____

   _____

   _____

5. To properly partake of the Lord's Supper we need both a _____ right and a _____ right.

6. A church right includes both of the following:

   a. _____

   _____

   b. _____

   _____

7. Of what three things should I know something in my life's experience to properly participate in the Lord's Supper?

   a. _____ b. _____ c. _____

CHECKING YOUR READING

8. a. Are the table waiters or watchers at the Lord's table to judge whether a person is regenerated or not? _____

    b. What is their duty at the Lord's table? _____

9. The Lord's Supper is often called "communion." With whom do God's people experience communion?

    a. _____   b. _____

10. Give three reasons why everyone in the congregation should be in attendance in church when the Lord's Supper is served.

    a. _____

    b. _____

    c. _____

11. Why is a preparatory sermon preached the Sunday before the Lord's Supper will be administered? _____

_____

━━━━━ EXTRA CHALLENGE QUESTIONS ━━━━━

1. From the story **Food for Strength**, explain why it is necessary and helpful for God's people to eat and drink at the Lord's table. _____

_____

_____

2. From the story **Hearing or Knowing?**, describe how a "head knowledge" and an "experiential knowledge" of my misery, deliverance, and thankfulness are different. _____

_____

_____

3. Why are **bread** and **wine** used as signs when we observe the Lord's Supper? Why not other foods? _____

_____

_____

4. What did Jesus mean when He said "This is My body" and "This is My blood" when serving the first Lord's Supper? How can you prove this? _____

_____

_____

CHAPTER 20

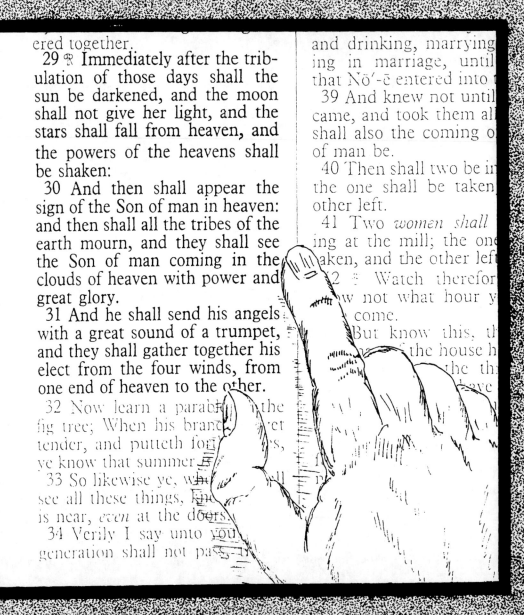

...ered together.

29 ℞ Immediately after the tribulation of those days shall the sun be darkened, and the moon shall not give her light, and the stars shall fall from heaven, and the powers of the heavens shall be shaken:

30 And then shall appear the sign of the Son of man in heaven: and then shall all the tribes of the earth mourn, and they shall see the Son of man coming in the clouds of heaven with power and great glory.

31 And he shall send his angels with a great sound of a trumpet, and they shall gather together his elect from the four winds, from one end of heaven to the other.

32 Now learn a parable of the fig tree; When his branch is yet tender, and putteth forth leaves, ye know that summer is nigh:

33 So likewise ye, when ye shall see all these things, know that it is near, even at the doors.

34 Verily I say unto you, This generation shall not pass, till...

and drinking, marrying and giving in marriage, until the day that Nō'-ē entered into the ark,

39 And knew not until the flood came, and took them all away; so shall also the coming of the Son of man be.

40 Then shall two be in the field; the one shall be taken, and the other left.

41 Two women shall be grinding at the mill; the one shall be taken, and the other left.

42 ℞ Watch therefore: for ye know not what hour your Lord doth come.

43 But know this, that if the goodman of the house had known in what watch the thief would come, he would have...

THE SOUL AFTER DEATH
CHRIST'S SECOND COMING
THE RESURRECTION OF THE DEAD
THE FINAL JUDGMENT
ETERNITY

VOCABULARY

1. **Passageway** — A means of passing from one place to another

2. **Reunite** — To bring together again; to join after separation

3. **Deceive** — To lie; to cause someone to believe that which is not true

4. **Visibly** — Being seen with the eye

5. **Triumphantly** — Joyfully rejoicing in a victory

6. **Executioner** — One who puts to death those who have been condemned to die

7. **Dismay** — A loss of courage because of distress or fear

8. **Famine** — An extreme lack of food; a condition of starvation

9. **Persecution** — The act of hurting and harming others

10. **Torment** — Extreme pain or torture of body or mind

THE SOUL AFTER DEATH

WHAT DO YOU THINK?

"AND HE DIED"

Mr. Henry Goodear, a London businessman, never attended church and often mocked with the Bible and its teachings. However, one Sunday morning, just to please his niece, Mary, he went to church with her.

Mary was most pleased that her uncle had come to church, but she was very disappointed when her minister read Genesis 5 that morning. She thought, "This chapter is only a long list of names; it will have nothing to say to my uncle." She wondered why God had permitted such an uninteresting chapter to be read on this special Sunday morning.

However, Mr. Goodear was silent as they walked home from church. Each step he took seemed to repeat the words of that chapter, "... and he died, ... and he died." In his room that night, when the clock chimes sounded, it seemed to pronounce "... and he died." The next morning he could not concentrate on his work; "... and he died" kept going through his mind. Mr. Goodear could find no relief. "And he died" would also become true for him, and what then? He trembled.

God the Holy Spirit blessed these words "... and he died" from Genesis 5 to the soul and conversion of Mr. Goodear. Why is death most serious? Will the statement "... and he died" be true for you also one day? What will take place after death? We hope to examine this question in this final chapter.

— Adapted from *3,000 Illustrations for Christian Service*

Death is the result of sin. Sinful man must die.

> For the wages of sin is *death.*
> — Romans 6:23a

> And as it is appointed unto men once *to die,* but after this the judgment.
> — Hebrews 9:27

However, there is a great difference between death for the righteous or the wicked. For those who are saved by Jesus Christ, death is a **passageway** from this sinful world into a sinless heaven. But for those who die in their sins, death is their eternal punishment.

When a person dies physically, his soul separates from his body. His body returns to the dust in the grave, but his soul returns to God, and is sent by God to heaven or hell.

> Then shall *the dust return to the earth* as it was: and the *spirit shall return unto God* who gave it.
> — Ecclesiastes 12:7

> And fear not them which kill the body, but are not able to kill the soul: but rather fear Him which is able to *destroy both soul and body in hell.*
> — Matthew 10:28

> And Jesus said unto him, Verily I say unto thee, *To day* shalt thou be with Me *in Paradise.*
> — Luke 23:43

> That he may take part of this ministry and apostleship, from which Judas by transgression fell, that he might *go to his own place.*
> — Acts 1:25

God's judgment of each soul is unchangeable. After the great resurrection takes place, a person's body will be **reunited** with his soul and each person will be sent to his eternal place with both body and soul.

We may not pray for people who have died. Their souls have been judged by God and sent to their eternal places. Their place is unchangeable. How do the stories of David's child who died and the rich man and Lazarus teach this truth?

WHAT DO YOU THINK?

THE DEATH OF DAVID'S LITTLE CHILD

In II Samuel 12, we can read of David and Bathsheba's baby who was very sick. David fasted, prayed, and lay all night upon the earth. His servants tried to comfort him and to get him to eat with them, but he would not. However, after the child died, David arose, washed himself, changed his clothes, and went to the House of the Lord to worship. His servants found his behavior strange and asked him why he did this. David answered,

While the child was yet alive, I fasted and wept: for I said, Who can tell whether GOD will be gracious to me, that the child may live?

But now he is dead, wherefore should I fast? can I bring him back again? I shall go to him, but he shall not return to me.
— II Samuel 12:22-23

How can we see from this story that after death each soul is sent by God to heaven or hell and that this state is unchangeable? Is it right to pray for a person who has died? Why not?

WHAT DO YOU THINK?

THE RICH MAN AND LAZARUS

In Luke 16 we read about a rich man and a beggar:

There was a certain rich man, which was clothed in purple and fine linen, and fared sumptuously every day:

And there was a certain beggar named Lazarus, which was laid at his gate full of sores,

And desiring to be fed with the crumbs which fell from the rich man's table: moreover the dogs came and licked his sores.

And it came to pass, that the beggar died, and was carried by the angels into Abraham's bosom: the rich man also died, and was buried;

And in hell he lift up his eyes, being in torments, and seeth Abraham afar off, and Lazarus in his bosom.

And he cried and said, Father Abraham, have mercy on me, and send Lazarus, that he may dip the tip of his finger in water, and cool my tongue; for I am tormented in this flame.

But Abraham said, Son, remember that thou in thy lifetime receivedst thy good things, and likewise Lazarus evil things: but now he is comforted, and thou art tormented.

And beside all this, between us and you there is a great gulf fixed: so that they which would pass from hence to you cannot; neither can they pass to us, that would come from thence.
— Luke 16:19-26

How can we see from this story that each soul is sent by God to heaven or hell immediately after the person's body died? How do we know from this story that the place of each soul is unchangeable?

MY DEATH — HOPE OR DESPAIR?

When the famous emperor Napoleon Bonaparte was dying, he confessed, "I die before my time; and my body will be given back to the earth, to become the food of worms. Such is the fate which so soon awaits the great Napoleon!"

How is this confession very different from Job's testimony, "For I know that my Redeemer liveth, and that He shall stand at the latter day upon the earth: and though after my skin worms destroy this body, yet in my flesh shall I see God" (Job 19:25-26)?

What caused these two men to make such different confessions when viewing their death? What lesson should this teach us?

Some church denominations teach that souls after death can still be saved or brought into heaven. Others teach that those who die unsaved will be given another chance to be saved. Why are these teachings very **deceiving** and dangerous?

God strictly forbids any attempts to communicate with the spirits of people whose bodies have died.

There shall not be found among you any one that maketh his son or his daughter to pass through the fire, or that useth divination, or an observer of times, or an enchanter, or a witch,

Or a charmer, or a **consulter with familiar spirits,** or a wizard, or a **necromancer.**

— Deuteronomy 18:10-11

Why is the time of your life on earth very valuable? Do you highly value this time and use it to seek God through the means of grace He has given?

WHAT DO YOU THINK?

THE RICH FOOL

We can read the "Parable of the Rich Fool" in:
Luke 12:16-21

And He spake a parable unto them, saying, The ground of a certain rich man brought forth plentifully:

And he thought within himself, saying, What shall I do, because I have no room where to bestow my fruits?

And he said, This will I do: I will pull down my barns, and build greater; and there will I bestow all my fruits and my goods.

And I will say to my soul, Soul, thou hast much goods laid up for many years; take thine ease, eat, drink, and be merry.

But God said unto him, Thou fool, this night thy soul shall be required of thee: then whose shall those things be, which thou hast provided?

So is he that layeth up treasure for himself, and is not rich toward God.

Why did this person think that he was rich? Why was he actually very poor? Why does God call him a "fool"?

CHRIST'S SECOND COMING

The Bible speaks of both a first and *second coming* of Jesus Christ to this earth, physically. These two are described and compared in the chart below:

CHRIST'S FIRST COMING	CHRIST'S SECOND COMING
1. The first step of His humiliation: — His humble birth	The last step of His exaltation: — His coming to judge the world
2. As a humble servant, lying in a manger	As the King of kings, sitting upon His glorious throne
3. At the close of the Old Testament and the beginning of the New Testament	At the close of the New Testament and the beginning of eternity

What will the second coming of Jesus be like?

1. Christ will come *personally* and *bodily.*

> Which also said, Ye men of Galilee, why stand ye gazing up into heaven? *this same Jesus,* which is taken up from you into heaven, *shall so come in like manner* as ye have seen Him go into heaven.
>
> — Acts 1:11

> When *Christ,* who is our life, *shall appear*, then shall ye also appear with Him in glory.
>
> — Colossians 3:4

2. Christ will come *visibly;* every person shall see Him.

> *Behold, He cometh* with clouds; *and every eye shall see Him,* and they also which pierced Him: and all kindreds of the earth shall wail because of Him. Even so, Amen.
>
> — Revelation 1:7

> And *ye shall see the Son of man* sitting on the right hand of power, and *coming in the clouds of heaven.*
>
> — Mark 14:62b

3. Christ will come *gloriously* and *triumphantly.*

> And then shall appear the sign of the Son of man in heaven: and then shall all the tribes of the earth mourn, and they shall see the Son of man coming in the clouds of heaven *with power and great glory.*
>
> — Matthew 24:30

> And then shall they see the Son of man coming in a cloud *with power and great glory.*
>
> — Luke 21:27

4. Christt will come *suddenly.*

And then shall He send His angels, and shall gather together His elect from the four winds, from the uttermost part of the earth to the uttermost part of heaven.

But of *that day and that hour knoweth no man,* no, not the angels which are in heaven, neither the Son, but the Father.

— Mark 13:27, 32

For as in the days that were before the flood they were eating and drinking, marrying and giving in marriage, until the day that Noe entered into the ark,

And *knew not until the flood came, and took them all away; so shall also the coming of the Son of man be.*

— Matthew 24:38-39

When Christ physically returns to the earth, time will end and eternity will begin. We all must be prepared, for no one knows when Christ will return. Neither does anyone know when he will die. The day of a person's death is his "final day"; his "judgment day." Therefore we must always be prepared.

Blessed are those servants, whom the lord when he cometh shall find watching: verily I say unto you, that he shall gird himself, and make them to sit down to meat, and will come forth and serve them.

And if he shall come in the second watch, or come in the third watch, and find them so, blessed are those servants.

And this know, that if the goodman of the house had known what hour the thief would come, he would have watched, and not have suffered his house to be broken through.

Be ye therefore ready also: for the Son

of man cometh at an hour when ye think not.

— Luke 12:37-40

But of *that day and that hour knoweth no man,* no, not the angels which are in heaven, neither the Son, but the Father. *Watch* ye therefore.

— Mark 13:32, 35a

Therefore *be ye also ready: for in such an hour as ye think not the Son of man cometh.*

— Matthew 24:44

Jesus Christ encourages His children to look forward with desire to the time of His second coming; to eagerly hope for this great day. What a glorious and wonderful day this shall be for God's children! Then they shall see and forever be with their Savior, the One whom they love above all! But, what a fearful and terrible day it shall be for those who are unregenerated and still living for self, sin, world and Satan! Who will be able to stand before the righteous anger of the Almighty God in his own strength?

And then shall they see the Son of man coming in a cloud with power and great glory.

And when these things begin to come to pass, then *look up, and lift up your heads;* for your redemption draweth nigh.

— Luke 21:27-28

For what *is our hope, or joy, or crown of rejoicing?* Are not even ye in the presence of our Lord Jesus Christ at His coming?

— I Thessalonians 2:19

Behold, He cometh with clouds; and every eye shall see Him, and *they also which pierced Him:* and all *kindreds of the earth shall wail because of Him.*

— Revelation 1:7a

And said to the mountains and rocks, Fall on us, and hide us from the face of Him that sitteth on the throne, and from the *wrath of the Lamb:*

For the great day of His wrath is come; and *who shall be able to stand?*

— Revelation 6:16-17

WHAT DO YOU THINK?

LORD SHACKLETON'S RETURN

When Lord Shackleton went to search for the South Pole, he once had to turn back, leaving some of his men on Elephant Island amid the ice and snow. He promised to come back for them. He finally reached South Georgia, where he secured another ship and more supplies, and then went back to get his men. He tried to reach Elephant's Island, but failed time after time.

Suddenly one day there appeared an open place through the ice leading to the island! Quickly he sailed his ship through the open place, got his stranded men on board, and came out again, just before the ice crashed together. It was all done in half an hour.

When the excitement was over, he asked one of the men who had been on the island, "How did it happen that you were all packed and ready for my coming? You were standing on the shore ready to leave at a moment's notice."

The man replied, "Sir, you said that you would come back for us, and we never gave up hope. Whenever the sea was partly clear of ice, we rolled up our sleeping bags and packed our things, saying, 'Maybe Shackleton will come today.' We were always ready for your coming."

How should this story be an example for us? How should we "always be ready"? How should we show this "being ready" in our lives? How does a person's "being ready" show true faith in the Lord?

— Adapted from *The NRC Banner of Truth*

WHAT DO YOU THINK?

HE COMES AGAIN!

A Christian king of Hungary once became very sad and depressed. His brother, a very jolly man, asked why he was so sad and gloomy.

"O, Brother," said the King, "I have been a great sinner against God, and know not how to die or appear before Him in judgment!"

His brother made a joke of it, saying, "Why do you think such gloomy thoughts? You must not concern yourself with such things." To this, however, the king made no reply.

It was the custom in Hungary that if the king's **executioner** sounded a trumpet before the door of any man, that person would be promptly led away to die. During that same night, the king sent his executioner to blow his trumpet in front of his brother's door. What fear and **dismay** filled his brother's heart when he heard that sound and saw the messenger of death! He hurried into the presence of the king, begging to know in what way he had offended him.

"O, Brother," said the king, "you have never offended me. Is the sight of my executioner so dreadful? Yesterday you laughed about my fear and sadness, but should not I, who have greatly offended the Lord of heaven and earth, be much more fearful to be brought before the judgment seat of Christ?"

What lesson should this story teach us about appearing before God without a Savior?

— Adapted from *The NRC Banner of Truth*

While no man knows exactly when the Lord Jesus will return, the Bible does mention various signs that clearly point to His second coming. These signs are listed in the chart below:

BIBLICAL SIGNS WHICH POINT TO CHRIST'S SECOND COMING	
SIGNS	*EXAMPLE TEXTS*
1. Knowledge and travel will increase.	But thou, O Daniel, shut up the words, and seal the book, even to the *time of the end:* many shall *run to and fro,* and *knowledge shall be increased.* — Daniel 12:4
2. Dangers, wars, **famines,** and earthquakes will multiply.	This know also, that in the *last days perilous times* shall come. — II Timothy 3:1 For *nation shall rise against nation,* and kingdom against kingdom: and there shall be *famines,* and *pestilences,* and *earthquakes,* in divers places. — Matthew 24:7
3. Sin will publicly increase and abound.	*But as the days of Noe were, so shall also the coming of the Son of man be.* For as in the days that were before the flood *they were eating and drinking, marrying and giving in marriage,* until the day that Noe entered into the ark, And knew not until the flood came, and took them all away; so shall also the *coming of the Son of man be.* — Matthew 24:37-39
4. Love and concern for others will generally grow cold.	And because iniquity shall abound, the *love of many shall wax cold.* — Matthew 24:12
5. Mission work will expand throughout the entire world.	And this *gospel* of the kingdom shall be *preached in all the world* for a witness unto all nations; and *then shall the end come.* — Matthew 24:14
6. Severe **persecution** of God's church will take place.	Then *they shall deliver you up to be afflicted, and shall kill you:* and ye shall be hated of all nations for My Name's sake. For then shall be *great tribulation,* such as was not since the beginning of the world to this time, no, nor ever shall be. And, except those days should be shortened, there should no flesh be saved: but for the elect's sake those days shall be shortened. — Matthew 24:9, 21-22
7. Spiritualism and devil worship will be present.	Now the Spirit speaketh expressly, that in the *latter times* some shall depart from the faith, giving heed to *seducing spirits,* and *doctrines of devils.* — I Timothy 4:1
8. False "saviors" and "christs" will arise. Various cults will deceive many.	And Jesus answered and said unto them, Take heed that no man deceive you. For *many shall come in My Name, saying, I am the Christ; and shall deceive many.* — Matthew 24:4-5
9. A great falling away from the truth shall be evident.	Let no man deceive you by any means: for *that day shall not come, except there come a falling away first.* — II Thessalonians 2:3a
10. The Anti-christ shall appear.	*Let no man deceive you by any means: for that day shall not come, except* there come a falling away first, and *that man of sin be revealed, the son of perdition;* *Who opposeth and exalteth himself above all that is called God,* or that is worshipped; so that he as God sitteth in the temple of God, shewing himself that he is God. — II Thessalonians 2:3-4

THE RESURRECTION OF THE DEAD

When the Lord Jesus returns upon the clouds of heaven, all people who have ever lived on the earth shall arise out of their graves. This event is called the **resurrection.**

Marvel not at this: for the hour is coming, in the which all that are in the graves shall hear His voice,

And shall come forth; they that have done good, unto **the resurrection of life;** and they that have done evil, unto **the resurrection of damnation.**

— John 5:28-29

Now if Christ be preached that He rose from the dead, how say some among you that there is no **resurrection of the dead?**

But if there be no resurrection of the dead, then is Christ not risen:

And if Christ be not risen, then is our preaching vain, and your faith is also vain.

— I Corinthians 15:12-14

But this I confess unto thee, that after the way which they call heresy, so worship I the God of my fathers, believing all things which are written in the law and in the prophets:

And have hope toward God, which they themselves also allow, that there shall be a **resurrection of the dead, both of the just and unjust.**

— Acts 24:14-15

Jesus saith unto her, Thy brother shall ris . again.

Martha saith unto Him, I know that he shall rise again in the **resurrection at the last day.**

— John 11:23-24

And I saw the dead, small and great, stand before God; and the books were opened: and another book was opened, which is the book of life: and the dead were judged out of those things which were written in the books, according to their works.

And the **sea gave up the dead** which were in it; and **death and hell delivered up the dead** which were in them: and they were judged every man according to their works.

— Revelation 20:12-13

For if we believe that Jesus died and rose again, even so **them also which sleep in Jesus will God bring with Him.**

— I Thessalonians 4:14

All those who have died shall arise; the righteous as well as the wicked. All people who are living on the earth at that time shall be changed into their eternal bodies in a moment.

Behold, I shew you a mystery; **We shall not all sleep, but we shall all be changed,**

In a moment, in the twinkling of an eye, at the last trump: for the trumpet shall sound, and the dead shall be raised incorruptible, and **we shall be changed.**

For **this corruptible must put on incorruption, and this mortal must** **put on immortality.**

So when this corruptible shall have put on incorruption, and **this mortal shall have put on immortality,** then shall be brought to pass the saying that is written, Death is swallowed up in victory.

— I Corinthians 15:51-54

For the Lord Himself shall descend from heaven with a shout, with the voice of the archangel, and with the trump of God: and the **dead in Christ shall rise first:**

Then we which are alive and remain shall be caught up together with them in the clouds, to meet the Lord in the air: and so shall we ever be with the Lord.

— I Thessalonians 4:16-17

WHAT DO YOU THINK?

DECAYED MATERIALS RESTORED

A person once visited a large paper mill. He saw tons of waste, shredded, and scrap paper and rags being washed, mashed, shaped, and formed into long rolls of clean white paper.

While he was surprised and impressed by the beautiful and useful paper which was produced in the plant, another thought struck him. "If man can produce such clean, excellent, and useful paper from wasted scraps, certainly God can turn the dust of wasted and decayed forms into beautiful resurrected bodies!"

What truths regarding God's resurrection of the dead are taught in this example? Describe various ways in which the miracle of God's resurrection of the dead exceeds and cannot be compared with re-cycled paper.

WHAT DO YOU THINK?

JESUS' RESURRECTED BODY

After His resurrection, Jesus appeared to Thomas and instructed him accordng to that which we read in the following verses:

And after eight days again His disciples were within, and Thomas with them: then came Jesus, the doors being shut, and stood in the midst, and said, Peace be unto you.

Then saith He to Thomas, Reach hither thy finger, and behold My hands; and reach hither thy hand, and thrust it into My side: and be not faithless, but believing.

And Thomas answered and said unto Him, My Lord and my God.
— John 20:26-28

What evidence can you find in these verses that Jesus' resurrected body is the same body that He had before He died? What evidence can you find in these verses that His resurrected body has more spiritual qualities than it did before?

What can we read about the resurrected bodies of God's children in:

Philippians 3:20-21?

For our conversation is in heaven; from whence also we look for the Saviour, the Lord Jesus Christ:

Who shall change our vile body, that it may be fashioned like unto His glorious body, according to the working whereby He is able even to subdue all things unto Himself.

After the resurrection, a **person's body** will be:

1. **The same.** A person's body will not be a new body; it will be his own body brought back to life. It will not be newly created, but a resurrected body.

For I know that my redeemer liveth, and that He shall stand at the latter day upon the earth:

And **though after my skin worms destroy this body, yet in my flesh shall I see God:**

Whom **I shall see for myself, and mine eyes shall behold,** and not another; **though my reins be consumed within me.**
— Job 19:25-27

Thy dead men shall live, **together with my dead body shall they arise.** Awake and sing, ye that dwell in dust.
— Isaiah 26:19a

2. **Different.** A person's resurrected body will be a never-aging and never-dying body. It will be more spiritual. God's children will arise with glorious bodies fitted for their new heavenly home. They will never experience tiredness, sickness, or pain anymore.

So also is the resurrection of the dead. It is sown in corruption; it is **raised in incorruption:**

It is sown in dishonour; it is **raised in glory:** it is sown in weakness; it is **raised in power:**

It is sown a natural body; it is **raised a spiritual body. There is a natural body, and there is a spiritual body.**

And so it is written, The first man Adam was made a living soul; the last Adam was made a quickening spirit.

Howbeit that was not first which is spiritual, but that which is natural; and afterward that which is spiritual.

The first man is of the earth, earthy: the second man is the Lord from heaven.

As is the earthy, such are they also that are earthy: and as is the heavenly, such are they also that are heavenly.

And as we have borne the image of the earthy, we shall also **bear the image of the heavenly.**

Now this I say, brethren, that flesh and blood cannot inherit the kingdom of God; neither doth corruption inherit incorruption.

Behold, I shew you a mystery; We shall not all sleep, but we shall all be changed,

In a moment, in the twinkling of an eye, at the last trump: for the trumpet shall sound, and the **dead shall be raised incorruptible, and we shall be changed.**

For this corruptible must put on incorruption, and this mortal must put on immortality.
— I Corinthians 15:42-53

WHAT DO YOU THINK?

FROM CATERPILLAR TO BUTTERFLY

Andrea, a young girl who truly loved God from her heart, had to suffer much from a crippling disease which increasingly deformed her body. Often she was troubled by the thought that she might have her crippled body forever — even in heaven.

Andrea's bed was placed near a window through which she could watch a rather unattractive caterpillar eating and crawling on the leaves of a nearby bush. Later, she saw this caterpillar gradually disappear into the chrysalis which it spun around itself. It appeared to be dead for some time, but one beautiful, sunny morning she saw movement and life again. A beautiful, brilliantly-colored butterfly unfolded its gorgeous wings to dry them in the sunlight!

God used this insect to teach Andrea the lesson found in: **I Corinthians 15:42-44**

So also is the resurrection of the dead. It is sown in corruption; it is raised in incorruption:

It is sown in dishonour; it is raised in glory: it is sown in weakness; it is raised in power:

It is sown a natural body; it is raised a spiritual body. There is a natural body, and there is a spiritual body.

What lesson did Andrea learn? How did this lesson apply to Andrea's situation?

THE FINAL JUDGMENT

The final judgment of all people will immediately follow their resurrection. Jesus Christ will judge all people, both the righteous and the wicked.

For *we must all appear before the judgment seat of Christ;* that every one may receive the things done in his body, according to that he hath done, *whether it be good or bad.*

— II Corinthians 5:10

For the Son of man shall come in the glory of His Father with His angels; and then He *shall reward every man according to* his *works.*

— Matthew 16:27

But why dost thou judge thy brother? or why dost thou set at nought thy brother? for *we shall all stand before the*

judgment seat of Christ.

— Romans 14:10

And, behold, I come quickly; and My reward is with Me, *to give every man according as his works shall be.*

I am Alpha and Omega, the beginning and the end, the first and the last.

— Revelation 22:12-13

Christ will send His angels to separate the righteous from the wicked. All those who truly love God and have graciously found their righteousness in Christ, will be separated from those who still love themselves, Satan, sin and the world — and who must still give an account for themselves. What a great separation this will be!

So shall it be at the end of the world: *the angels* shall come forth, and *sever the wicked from among the just.*

— Matthew 13:49

The Son of man shall send forth *His angels,* and they shall

gather out of His kingdom all things that offend, and *them which do iniquity;*

And shall cast them *into a furnace of fire:* there shall be wailing and gnashing of teeth.

— Matthew 13:41-42

And He shall send *His angels* with a great sound of a trumpet, and they shall *gather together His elect* from the four winds, from one end of heaven to the other.

— Matthew 24:31

WHAT DO YOU THINK?

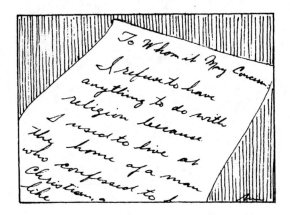

A WORTHLESS EXCUSE

A minister once visited a young man who told him that he never wanted to have anything to do with religion.

"Why?" asked the minister.

"I will tell you why," the young man answered. "For a few years I was in the home of a man who confessed to be a Christian. I said some things he didn't like and he became so angry that he swore at me and kicked me out of his house. From that day I decided never to have anything to do with religion; it's all hypocrisy."

"I understand," said the minister slowly, thinking of how he could respond to this young man. "Would you please write down your reason clearly on paper and sign it for me?" he asked.

The young man was surprised by this request, but did as the minister asked and gave it to him.

But the minister handed it back to him and said, "Take this, and when you are called before God on the final judgment day, give this to Him as your excuse."

The effect of this instruction altered this young man's life and he began to attend church regularly.

What will happen to all the excuses of every sinner when they stand before a holy, righteous, and almighty God on the final judgment day?

God's children will be gathered and united with their Savior, Jesus Christ. What an eternally wonderful union that will be! Those who have suffered for Christ's sake in their lives on earth shall then live and reign with Him forever. All God's children will join in the righteous pronouncement of God's judgment.

> Do ye not know that *the saints shall judge the world?*
> — I Corinthians 6:2a

> And Jesus said unto them, Verily I say unto you, that *ye which have followed Me,* in the regeneration when the Son of man shall sit in the throne of His glory, ye also shall sit upon twelve thrones, *judging the twelve tribes of Israel.*
> — Matthew 19:28

All those who remain outside of Christ, the only Savior of lost sinners, will have to give an account of all their own thoughts, words, and deeds. God will open their consciences and in a moment of time, their entire lives will come into remembrance and pass before them.

> For God shall *bring every work into judgment,* with every secret thing, whether it be good, or whether it be evil.
> — Ecclesiastes 12:14

> But I say unto you, That *every idle word* that men shall speak, they shall *give account* thereof in the *day of judgment.*
> — Matthew 12:36

What shall it be to stand before a perfectly Holy God, without Christ as our Substitute, to answer to God for all our sins?

As Judge, Christ will pronounce His righteous sentence upon all people. He will say to those on His right hand:

> **Come,** ye blessed of My Father, *inherit the kingdom* prepared for you from the foundation of the world.
> — Matthew 25:34b

Then He will turn and condemn those on His left hand, saying:

> **Depart,** from Me, ye cursed, *into everlasting fire,* prepared for the devil and his angels.
> — Matthew 25:41b

God will perfectly and righteously judge all people according to His law and gospel. Those who never received or heard the Bible will be judged by the law of God as it was written in their consciences. Those who had the great blessing of hearing God's Word will be judged accordingly. God will judge fairly and perfectly. Each person will be judged according to the blessings and privileges he has received.

> But he that **knew not,** and did commit things worthy of stripes, shall be beaten with *few stripes. For unto whomsoever much is given, of him shall be much required:* and to whom men have committed much, of him they will ask the more.
> — Luke 12:48

> For as many as have sinned without law shall also perish without law: and as many as *have sinned in the law shall be judged by the law;*
> For when the Gentiles, which have not the law, do by nature the things contained in the law, *these, having not the law, are a law unto themselves:*
> *Which shew the work of the law written in their hearts, their conscience also bearing witness,* and their thoughts the mean while accusing or else excusing one another.
> — Romans 2:12, 14-15

WHAT DO YOU THINK?

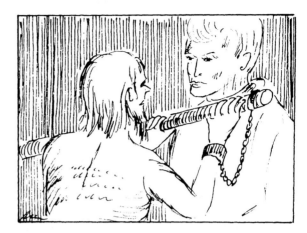

THE GUILTY GALLEY SLAVE

To be punished as a slave on a galley ship was a terribly cruel punishment. Galley slaves were chained to both their seats and oars and commanded to row for great lengths of time. When a galley slave died, another was chained in his place.

A German prince once visited a harbor where several boats were stationed and toured a galley ship. To celebrate this special occasion, he would release one galley prisoner and allow him to go free. The prince, wishing to make the best choice, spoke to several of the galley slaves individually. He asked each one why he was sentenced to this cruel punishment. The one answered that he was accused falsely; another, that he was mistreated; another, that his friend who escaped was more guilty while he only went along and was caught; and so on. In short, all felt they were innocent or had been overpunished.

At last the prince came to a galley slave who answered, "Sir, I have no right to complain. I lived a sinful life and committed a terrible crime. I knew better but I did it anyway and this is no more than a just punishment. Actually, I deserve to be killed."

To the shock of the other galley slaves, the prince said in a loud voice to the commander of the ship, "Release this man. He is such a terrible man that we cannot leave him on this boat. All the others around him are such 'good' people that he would certainly corrupt them!"

What did the prince really mean by this remark? Those who confess their guilt and hell-worthiness to God will never need to be punished in hell. Why not? When we truly learn and feel our misery, we will need and seek for the Savior. Why? Why is this a most important lesson for each of us to learn?

— Adapted from *The Shorter Catechism Illustrated*

WHAT DO YOU THINK?

THE BROAD AND NARROW WAYS

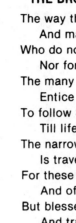

The way that leads to death is broad
    And many travel there
Who do not heed the voice of God
    Nor for His precepts care.
The many pleasures of this world
    Entice the sinner on
To follow Satan's flag unfurled
    Till life and hope are gone.
The narrow way that leads to life
    Is traveled by but few
For these must enter into strife
    And oft' their faith renew.
But blessed is he who fears the Lord
    And travels on this way
For he by grace will be restored
    And live with God for aye.
Upon which road are you traveling?

ETERNITY

After Christ has pronounced His righteous sentence upon all people, they will be brought or sent, with soul and body, to their eternal homes. Christ will bring all His children into heaven, and the angels shall cast all the ungodly into hell. This great difference will not exist for only a few years, but it will be *eternal;* it will be forever. How is this great difference between people pictured in "the Parable of the Tares?"

WHAT DO YOU THINK?

THE PARABLE OF THE TARES

We can read of the "Parable of the Tares" (or Weeds) in:

Matthew 13:24-30:

Another parable put He forth unto them, saying, The kingdom of heaven is likened unto a man which sowed good seed in his field:

But while men slept, his enemy came and sowed tares among the wheat, and went his way.

But when the blade was sprung up, and brought forth fruit, then appeared the tares also.

So the servant of the householder came and said unto him, Sir, didst not thou sow good seed in thy field? from whence then hath it tares?

He said unto them, An enemy hath done this. The servants said unto him, Wilt thou then that we go and gather them up?

But he said, Nay; lest while ye gather up the tares, ye root up also the wheat with them.

Let both grow together until the harvest: and in the time of harvest I will say to the reapers, Gather ye together first the tares, and bind them in bundles to burn them: but gather the wheat into my barn.

What is meant by the field, the good seed, the tares, the enemy, the harvest, the reapers, the burning of the tares, and the gathering of the wheat into the barn? (See Matthew 13:36-43 for these answers.) How does this parable picture the great difference which will be seen on the final judgment day?

HELL

Those who are not saved by Jesus Christ will be cast away into *hell* forever as just punishment for their sins. The Bible speaks of hell as a place:

— Of *everlasting fire* prepared for Satan and his angels
— Where the worm, or *conscience, never dies* and the fire is never put out
— With no end, as *a bottomless pit*
— Full of great *darkness*
— Of *torment* in fire and brimstone
— Of continual *weeping and pain* with no rest

And shall cut him asunder, and appoint him his portion with the hypocrites: there shall be *weeping and gnashing of teeth.*
— Matthew 24:51

Where their worm dieth not, and *the fire is not quenched.*
— Mark 9:44

But the fearful, and unbelieving, and the abominable, and murderers, and whoremongers, and sorcerors, and idolaters, and all liars, shall have their part in *the lake which burneth with fire and brimstone:* which is the second death.
— Revelation 21:8

And he opened the *bottomless pit;* and there arose a smoke out of the pit, as the smoke of a great furnace; and the sun and the air were darkened by reason of the smoke of the pit.
— Revelation 9:2

Raging waves of the sea, foaming out their own shame; wandering stars, to whom is reserved the *blackness of darkness for ever.*
— Jude:13

The same shall drink of the wine of the wrath of God, which is poured out without mixture into the cup of His indignation; and *he shall be tormented with fire and brimstone* in the presence of the holy angels, and in the presence of the Lamb:
And the smoke of their torment ascendeth up for ever and ever: and *they have no rest day nor night,* who worship the beast and his image, and whosoever receiveth the mark of his name.
— Revelation 14:10-11

WHAT DO YOU THINK?

IS THERE ANYTHING BEYOND DEATH?

Before Christopher Columbus discovered the "New World" of the Americas, the Spanish coat of arms bore the motto: "Ne Plus Ultra" which means "There is Nothing Beyond." Three miles west of their coastline was believed to be the end of the world with nothing beyond.

After Columbus's discovery, the "Ne" was dropped from the Spanish coat of arms leaving the words "Plus Ultra" meaning "There is More Beyond!"

Some people believe that death is "Ne Plus Ultra," that "there is nothing beyond." Why is it ignorant and deceiving to believe and teach this? Does the Word of God speak of death as "Ne Plus Ultra" or as "Plus Ultra"? Realizing that death is not the end, but that there is an eternity beyond it, why is your life on earth so important?

Scripture teaches us that hell is a place of great torment and painful suffering. The fire of God's wrath and their guilty consciences will burn and torment those in hell forever. This suffering will be in both soul and body, for those in hell have sinned against God in both soul and body.

It is impossible to fully describe what hell will be like just as it is impossible to explain how awful sin is, in its open rebellion against God, the eternal Creator of all things.

Therefore, God warns us so clearly and seriously to flee from sin for His wrath will be poured out upon sinners. He instructs us to take refuge in Jesus Christ, for it will be terrible to fall into the hands of a holy and justly angry God.

It is a **fearful** thing to fall into the hands of the living God.

— Hebrews 10:31

O generation of vipers, who hath warned you to flee from the **wrath to come?**

— Luke 3:7b

The **punishment** of those condemned to hell will include:

1. A total **separation from any blessing of God**

2. A total **separation from** any of **God's children**

3. Being **with devils and haters of God** forever

4. Being **tormented by their consciences** continually forever

5. Suffering **under the wrath of God,** which is poured out upon them forever, because of their rebellious sins against him

The punishment of those in hell will continue forever with no resting nor ending. They have sinned and continue to sin against an infinite and eternal God. Their just sentence requires an infinite and eternal payment — a payment that will never be fully repaid, which will never end.

Then shall He say also unto them on the left hand, Depart from Me, ye cursed, into **everlasting fire,** prepared for the devil and his angels:

— Matthew 25:41

And these shall go away into **everlasting punishment:** but the righteous into life eternal.

— Matthew 25:46

The same shall drink of the wine of the wrath of God, which is poured out without mixture into the cup of His indignation; and he shall be tormented with fire and brimstone in the presence of the holy angels, and in the presence of the Lamb:

And the smoke of their torment ascendeth up **for ever and ever:** and they have no rest day nor night, who worship the beast and his image, and whosoever receiveth the mark of his name.

— Revelation 14:10-11

HEAVEN

All those who are saved by Jesus Christ will be gathered and brought into *heaven.* As we cannot fully explain the terribleness of hell, so we cannot fully describe the wonderfulness of heaven.

Heaven is a place of continual and eternal joy. God's children will be full of perfect joy there because heaven is a place of:

1. *Perfect Salvation.* In heaven, God's people will be perfectly delivered from their enemies: Satan, world, sin, and self. In heaven there will be no more tears, pains, sorrows, temptations, weaknesses, old sinful natures, or deaths. Jesus Christ, their King, has perfectly saved and delivered them from all their enemies, and He shall wipe away all tears from their eyes forever.

2. *Perfect Activities.* In heaven, the saved will perfectly worship God. They will sing and praise His wonderful Name and serve God perfectly without sin. God's children will reign with Christ in heaven. They will be with the saints and angels and will continually learn more of God and of His greatness. They will perfectly and securely rest in God forever.

NOT THE MANSION BUT THE SAVIOR!

A church elder once visited an older, dying child of God. He asked her, "Shall I read you the most beautiful verse in the Bible?"

"Yes, certainly," was her reply.

He then read John 14:2, "In My Father's house are many mansions: if it were not so, I would have told you. I go to prepare a place for you."

"No," said the woman, "the next verse is yet more beautiful. Please read on!"

The elder then read the next verse: "And if I go and prepare a place for you, I will come again, and receive you unto Myself; that where I am, there ye may be also."

"That," said the woman, "is more beautiful. It is not the mansion I desire but the Savior Himself!"

What truth regarding heaven is taught in this story?

3. *Perfect Beauty.* Heaven will be a place of great beauty which will not be spoiled or damaged by sin. It will be a place of many mansions prepared by Christ for His people. It will always be "day" with no "night" there, and the saved shall live in the most wonderful and beautiful surroundings.

4. *Perfect communion.* For God's people, the greatest joy of all shall be that heaven will be a place of perfect communion with God, There they will be with God forever. There they will enjoy knowing, seeing, loving, praising, serving, and communing with God forever. In heaven, there will be no sin and therefore no separation from the felt presence of God, but God's children will forever live in the warmth of God's smile, bathe in God's glory, and feast in God's presence.

And he shewed me a pure river of water of life, clear as crystal, proceeding out of the throne of God and of the Lamb.

In the midst of the street of it, and on either side of the river, was there the tree of life, which bare twelve manner of fruits, and yielded her fruit every month: and the leaves of the tree were for the healing of the nations.

And there shall be no more curse: but the throne of God and of the Lamb shall be in it: and *His servants shall serve Him:*

And they shall see His face; and His Name shall be in their foreheads.

And there shall be no night there; and they need no candle, neither light of the sun; for the Lord God giveth them light: and *they shall reign for ever and ever.*

— Revelation 22:1-5

In *My Father's house* are many mansions: if it were not so, I would have told you. I go to prepare a place for you.

— John 14:2

After this I beheld, and, lo, a great multitude, which no man could number, of all nations, and kindreds, and people, and tongues, stood before the throne, and before the Lamb, *clothed with white robes, and palms in their hands;*

And I said unto him, Sir, thou knowest. And he said to me, These are they which came out of the great tribulation, and have washed their robes, and made them white in the blood of the Lamb.

Therefore are they before the throne of God, and *serve Him day and night in His temple:* and He that sitteth on the throne shall dwell among them.

They shall hunger no more, neither thirst any more, neither shall the sun light on them, nor any heat.

For the Lamb which is in the midst of the throne shall feed them, and shall lead them unto living fountains of waters: and *God shall wipe away all tears from their eyes.*

— Revelation 7:9; 14-17

But ye are come unto mount Sion, and unto the city of the living God, the heavenly Jerusalem, and to an innumerable company of angels,

To the general assembly and church of the firstborn, which are written in heaven, and to God the Judge of all, and to the spirits of just men made perfect.

And to Jesus the mediator of the new covenant, and to the blood of sprinkling, that speaketh better things than that of Abel.

— Hebrews 12:22-24

In heaven, all God's children will receive the deepest longing and desire of their hearts, to perfectly love, serve, and praise God without sin.

Where will you stand on the great judgment day? Where will be your eternal home? There are only two possibilities — heaven or hell. What is your deepest longing and desire? Are you painfully learning the sinfulness of your thoughts, words, and actions? Do you need Jesus Christ as your Savior above anything else in your life? Do you love Him and desire to perfectly and sinlessly serve Him as your King? Then continually pray and use the means of grace to grow in faith, love and obedience to God.

Is your deepest purpose still to love and serve yourself, sin, and the lusts of this world? Oh, then pray and cry unto God! Use the means of grace God has given and ask God to bless them savingly in your heart. You cannot save yourself. Therefore, continually ask the Lord to convert you from loving sin to loving Him, for He is almighty and He delights to save sinners. God urges you to seek Him and to plead for salvation from Him. Do not rest until, by God's grace, you may rest in Him.

Ho, every one that thirsteth, *come ye to the waters,* and he that hath no money; *come ye,* buy, and eat; yea, *come,* buy wine and milk without money and without price.

Wherefore do ye spend money for that which is not bread? and your labour for that which satisfieth not? *hearken diligently* unto Me, and eat ye that which is good, and let your soul delight itself in fatness.

Incline your ear, and come unto Me: hear, and your soul shall live; and I will make an everlasting covenant with you, even the sure mercies of David.

Seek ye the LORD while He may be found, *call ye upon Him* while He is near:

Let the wicked forsake his way, and the unrighteous man his thoughts: and let him *return* unto the LORD, and He will have mercy upon him; and to our God, for He will abundantly pardon.

— Isaiah 55:1-3, 6-7

WHAT DO YOU THINK?

HEAVENLY JOY FOR YOU?

The teenage son of a God-fearing mother was not living in the way his mother desired. He was drawn away by the temptations of the world and was living in sin.

One Sunday morning when he went to church with his mother, the minister preached on the joy, beauty, and communion to be found in heaven. The boy noticed that his mother was crying during the sermon and that she was very depressed on the way home from church. He finally asked her, "Mother, why are you sad about what you heard this morning? Of all people, I think you should be the most happy!"

"Yes," answered his mother, "but I was thinking about you. Will you be there, or will you be cast out forever, my dear son?"

What important truth and lesson is taught in this story? Where will **you** be?

MEMORIZATION QUESTIONS

The Resurrection of the Dead

1. What will take place at the second coming of Christ?
   The resurrection of the dead and the last judgment.

2. Shall the dead rise again?
   Yes; there will be a resurrection of the dead, both of the just and of the unjust (Acts 24:15).

3. Who shall raise them?
   Christ, for the hour cometh in which all that are in the graves shall hear His voice (John 5:28).

4. What shall the bodies of the righteous then be made like unto?
   They shall be made like unto the glorious body of Christ (Philippians 3:21).

5. Of what nature shall the bodies then be?
   Incorruptible and immortal, for death shall be no more (1 Corinthians 15:54-55).

6. Shall heaven and earth be renewed also?
   Yes: John saw a new heaven and a new earth (Revelation 21:1).

7. Are all these things possible?
   Yes: with God, who did create all things, nothing is impossible.

8. What purpose shall the new heaven and the new earth serve?
   So that the redeemed in Christ shall serve God therein forever.

The Last Judgment

1. What will Christ do at His second coming besides raising the dead?
   Christ will execute judgment also (John 5:27).

2. How is this judgment called?
   The last judgment.

3. Shall Christ then appear bodily in His human nature?
   Yes; for every eye shall see Him; and they also which pierced Him (Revelation 1:7).

4. Shall Christ then appear in great glory?
   Yes: "For the Son of Man shall come in the glory of His Father, with His angels" (Matthew 16:27).

5. Who shall then be judged by Christ?
   All mankind, for we must all appear before the judgment seat of Christ (2 Corinthians 5:10a).

6. According to what shall we be judged?
   According to what we have done in this life, whether it be good or bad (2 Corinthians 5:10b).

7. Shall the believers then be acquitted because of the good works which they have done?
   By no means, but rather these works prove that they have believed in Christ and loved Him (Matthew 25:40).

8. To what place shall Christ direct the unbelieving and unrighteous?
   Into everlasting fire, prepared for the devil and his angels (Matthew 25:41).

9. And what will Christ say to the believers?
   "Come, ye blessed of My Father, inherit the kingdom prepared for you from the foundation of the world" (Matthew 25:34).

Eternal Life

1. Will not the lot of those who are lost, be most terrible?
   Yes; because they will suffer punishment in hell, even everlasting destruction.

2. Of what shall that punishment consist?
   In exclusion from God's blessed communion and in suffering God's unbearable wrath (2 Thessalonians 1:8-9).

3. Shall this punishment ever come to an end?
   No: for Christ says: "Where the worm dieth not, and the fire is not quenched" (Mark 9:44).

4. But on the other hand, will not the lot of the saved be most blessed?
   Yes; for in heaven they shall eternally rejoice and be happy.

5. Will all mourning and sorrow have an end in heaven?
   Yes; "God shall wipe away all tears from their eyes" (Revelation 21:4).

6. Will there be no more sin or imperfection?
   No; there can be no sin in heaven, and there all things shall be perfect (1 Corinthians 13:10).

7. Wherein shall the redeemed find their greatest blessedness?
   In the service and enjoyment of the Father, who did elect them; of the Son, who did redeem them, and of the Holy Ghost, who did prepare them for everlasting bliss (Revelation 5:9-10).

— Donner's Catechism: Lessons XX, XXI, XXII

CHECKING YOUR READING

1. Describe what death is for:
   a. The wicked — _____

   _____

   b. The righteous in Christ — _____

   _____

2. Why are we forbidden to pray for people who have died? _____

   _____

   _____

3. Christ's first coming to earth marks the _____ step of His

   state of _____. Christ's second coming to earth will mark the

   _____ step of His state of _____.

4. Name four characteristics of Christ's second coming.
   a. _____
   b. _____
   c. _____
   d. _____

5. Why is the day of our death actually our "sentencing day"?

   _____

   _____

6. Draw a line to match the following signs of Christ's second coming with its best matching text.

SIGNS	TEXTS
1. Knowledge and travel will increase	**A. Matthew 24:12** And because iniquity shall abound, the love of many shall wax cold.
2. Mission work will expand throughout the world	**B. Matthew 24:7** For nation shall rise against nation, and kingdom against kingdom: and there shall be famines, and pestilences, and earthquakes, in divers places.
3. Love and concern for others will grow cold	**C. II Thessalonians 2:3a** Let no man deceive you by any means: for that day shall not come, except there come a falling away first,
4. A great falling away from the truth shall take place	**D. Daniel 12:4** But thou, O Daniel, shut up the words, and seal the book, even to the time of the end: many shall run to and fro, and knowledge shall be increased.
5. Dangers, wars, famines, and earthquakes will increase	**E. Matthew 24:14** And this gospel of the kingdom shall be preached in all the world for a witness unto all nations: and then shall the end come.

CHECKING YOUR READING

7. Describe how the resurrected bodies of God's children will be:
   a. The same — _____
   _____

   b. Different — _____
   _____

8. What will happen to all those who must stand to give an account of their own thoughts, words, and actions? _____
_____

9. Each person will be judged fairly and perfectly according to the _____ and _____ he has received from God during his life on earth.

10. The punishment of those in hell will include:
    a. _____
    b. _____
    c. _____
    d. _____
    e. _____

11. God's children will be full of perfect joy in heaven because heaven will be a place of:
    a. _____ c. _____
    b. _____ d. _____

━━━━ EXTRA CHALLENGE QUESTIONS ━━━━

1. a. From the story **The Guilty Galley Slave**, what did the prince actually mean when he said, "He is such a *terrible* man" and "The others around him are such *good* people"? _____
_____

   b. Does God forgive *innocent* sinners or *guilty* sinners? _____ Why? _____
_____

2. From the story **How Do People Want to Die?**, what truth can we learn from many who want to die differently from how they want to live? _____
_____

3. Why must the punishment of sinners in hell be eternal? _____
_____

4. Why would the torment of suffering under the "fire" of God's wrath and one's conscience be even more painful than suffering in actual fire? _____
_____

5. Explain the meaning of the following statement, "Heaven is a prepared place for a prepared people." _____
_____

TESTING YOUR KNOWLEDGE

1. Concerning the bread and wine used in the Lord's supper, what is taught by the following church denominations:

    a. The Roman Catholic Church? _____

    _____

    _____

    b. The Lutheran churches which follow Luther's view? _____

    _____

    _____

    c. The Reformed churches? _____

    _____

    _____

2. What is meant by the bread being "broken" and the wine being "poured out"?
    _____

    _____

3. Describe the Roman Catholic Mass: _____

    _____

    _____

    _____

    _____

4. What are the duties of the table waiters or watchers at the Lord's table?

    a. _____

    b. _____

5. What is meant by a "divine right" to attend the Lord's supper?

    _____

    _____

6. How are we to examine ourselves to know if we are regenerated or not? What are the scriptural marks of regeneration and conversion?

    _____

    _____

    _____

7. a. Can a person be "worthy" in himself to partake of the Lord's supper?_____

    b. How can a person be "worthy"? _____

    _____

8. Death is the result of _____

TESTING YOUR KNOWLEDGE

9. When a person dies a physical (corporal) death, what happens to his:
   a. Body? _____

   _____

   b. Soul? _____

   _____

10. When will people be in heaven or hell with:
    a. Their souls (or spirits) only? _____

    _____

    b. Both their souls and bodies? _____

    _____

11. Christ's first coming to earth took place at the close of the _____ time

    and the beginning of the _____ time. Christ's second coming

    will take place at the close of the _____ time and the

    beginning of _____

12. Name the biblical signs of Christ's second coming which are described in the follow-
    ing two texts:

Texts	Sign·

    a. **Matthew 24:9**
       Then shall they deliver you up to be
    afflicted, and shall kill you: and ye shall be
    hated of all nations for My Name's sake.

    a. _____

    _____

    _____

    b. **Matthew 24:4-5**
       And Jesus answered and said unto
    them, Take heed that no man deceive you.
       For many shall come in My Name, say-
    ing, I am Christ; and shall deceive many.

    b. _____

    _____

    _____

13. Which "fires" will burn in hell with the greatest torment? _____

    _____

    _____

14. What is meant by heaven being a place of **perfect** salvation? _____

    _____

    _____

15. How will God's people receive their deepest longings and desires in heaven? _____

    _____

    _____

FILL IN THE MISSING BLANKS

Fill in the missing letters to complete each of the Vocabulary Words in Chapters Nineteen and Twenty. Then place the letter of the best matching definition on the blank provided.

_____ 1. _ _ _ _ e _ u _ _ _ _

_____ 2. _ _ _ _ a _ e _ _ _

_____ 3. _ _ e _ e _ _ _

_____ 4. _ _ _ t _ _ i _ _ _ _

_____ 5. _ _ r _ e _

_____ 6. _ _ p _ _ c _ _

_____ 7. _ e _ e _ _ _

_____ 8. _ _ _ i _ i _ _ _ _ _ _ _

_____ 9. _ i _ i _ _ _

_____ 10. _ h _ _ _ c _ _

_____ 11. _ _ m _ n _

_____ 12. _ _ _ u _ i _ _

_____ 13. _ n _ _ i _ _ _

_____ 14. _ _ a _ i _ _

_____ 15. _ i _ a _

_____ 16. _ _ n _ i _ _

_____ 17. _ _ i _ _ _ h _ _ _ _

_____ 18. _ _ e _ _ a _ _ _ _

_____ 19. _ _ e _ u _ _ _ _ _

_____ 20. _ _ l _ _ a _ _

A. The act of refusing to believe; a statement that something is not true

B. Being seen with the eye

C. Parts or materials used

D. The act of afflicting and harming others

E. To take part in; to become involved in

F. To set up; to start; to begin

G. To lie; to cause someone to believe that which is not true

H. To look into very carefully

I. One who puts to death those who have been condemned to die

J. Getting ready for; in preparation of

K. Extreme pain and torture of body or mind

L. To remember a special happening by participating in a certain ceremony or event

M. An extreme shortage of food and a condition of starvation

N. Natural; outward; material

O. A means of passing from one place to another

P. To put in the place of

Q. To bring together again; to join after separation

R. A loss of courage because of distress or fear

S. The act of giving, serving, or managing

T. Joyfully rejoicing in a victory

BIBLE STUDY QUESTIONS

Read the following chapters and write out the verse or verses which most clearly teach the following doctrinal truths:

1. Jesus commanded His Church to observe the Lord's Supper in remembrance of Him
    I Corinthians 11:_____ — _____
    _____
    _____
    _____

2. We must carefully examine ourselves that we do not attend the Lord's Supper unworthily —
    I Corinthians 11:_____ (2 verses) — _____
    _____
    _____
    _____
    _____
    _____
    _____

3. When a person dies, his body is buried, his soul returns to God who sends it to heaven or hell —
    Ecclesiastes 12:_____ — _____
    _____
    _____

4. No person knows exactly when Christ's second coming will be —
    Mark 13:_____ — _____
    _____
    _____

PROJECT IDEAS

1. Write a report on the Roman Catholic Mass; what is believed, how it is performed, and what its errors are.

2. Make a chart which clearly shows the differences between the Roman Catholic, Lutheran, and Reformed teachings about the signs used in the Lord's Supper.

3. Draw a poster which shows the biblical signs that point to Christ's second coming and the end of the world.

4. Look up and write out ten texts which speak about heaven and ten texts which speak about hell. Place these in two columns on a large chart. Describe the important lesson this presents to us.

MEMORIZATION QUESTION INDEX

PRIMARY SOURCE: *Simple Instructions in Bible Truths for Catechising*   Rev. J.H. Donner

SECONDARY SOURCES: *Bible History in Questions and Answers for Beginners*   Rev. P. Dyksterhuis

Simple Questions for Children   Rev. L.G.C. Ledeboer

Rev. Donner's **Lesson Number**	Bible Doctrine for Older Children's **Chapter** Number
1	1
2-3	2
4	4
5	5
6	6
7	7
8,10	8
9	9
11-13	10
14	13
15	14
16	15
17	16
18	18
19	19
20-22	20

Rev. Ledeboer's **Question Number**	Bible Doctrine for Older Children's **Chapter** and **Question** Number
15	7-15

Scriptural Memorization Passages

Passage	Bible Doctrine for Older Children's **Chapter**
Romans 9:11-16	3
Ephesians 2:1-9	11
Exodus 20:1-11	17

Rev. Dyksterhuis' **Lesson Number**	Bible Doctrine for Older Children's **Chapter** Number
31	12

DIRECTORY OF SOURCE CREDITS

The Banner of Truth
Rev. J.R. Beeke, Ed.
Banner of Truth
1422 Tamarack Ave. N.W.
Grand Rapids, Michigan
49504

Bible History Presented in Questions and Answers for Beginners

Rev. P. Dyksterhuis
NRC Book and Publishing Committee
1020 N. Main Street
Sioux Center, Iowa
51250

The Broad and Narrow Way
Marshall, Morgan & Scott
London, England

Explanation of Reformed Doctrine
Rev. C. Hegeman
NRC Book and Publishing Committee
1020 N. Main Street
Sioux Center, Iowa
51250

The Little Gleaner
W. H. & L. Collingridge,
Aldersgate Street
London, England
1867-69

NRC Banner of Truth Tract Committee
Elder J. De Bruyne, Ed.
540 Crescent St. N.E.
Grand Rapids, Michigan
49501

1001 Stories for Children and Children's Workers
Alice M. Knight
Wm. B. Eerdman's Publishing Co.
255 Jefferson Ave. S.E.
Grand Rapids, Michigan
49503

Religious Stories for Young and Old Vol. I, IV
NRC Book and Publishing Committee
1020 N. Main Street
Sioux Center, Iowa
51250

A Selection of Hymns
William Gadsby
Gospel Standards Publications
63 Hampden Way
Southgate, London, 1965

The Shorter Catechism Illustrated
John Whitecross, Ed.
The Banner of Truth Trust
78b Chilton Street
London, England

Simple Catechism Questions for Children
Rev. L.G.C. Ledeboer
NRC Book and Publishing Committee
1020 N. Main Street
Sioux Center, Iowa
51250

3,000 Illustrations for Christian Service
Walter B. Knight
W.B. Eerdman's Publishing Co.
255 Jefferson Ave. S.E.
Grand Rapids, Michigan
49503

2,400 Scripture Outlines, Anecdotes, Notes and Quotes
A. Noismith
Baker Book House
P.O. Box No. 6287
Grand Rapids, Michigan
49506

Youth's Living Ideals
Glen Berry, Ed.
Youth's Living Ideals
Rt. 2
Elon College, N.C.
27244

ASSIGNMENT RECORD

Assignment	Due Date	Completed ✔

BIBLE DOCTRINE SCORESHEET

Student's Name: _____

Year: _____

BIBLE DOCTRINE FOR OLDER CHILDREN
BOOK B — CHAPTERS 11-20

CHAPTER CHECK-UP AND REVIEW PAGES

	11	12	REVIEW	13	14	REVIEW	15	16	REVIEW	17	18	REVIEW	19	20	REVIEW
A A															
A-															
B B+															
B															
B-															
C C+															
C															
C-															
D															
E															

CHAPTER TESTS

	11	12	13	14	15	16	17	18	19	20
A A										
A-										
B B+										
B										
B-										
C C+										
C										
C-										
D										
E										

Parent's Signature _____ Unit 2 _____ Unit 6 _____

_____ Unit 4 _____ Unit 8 _____

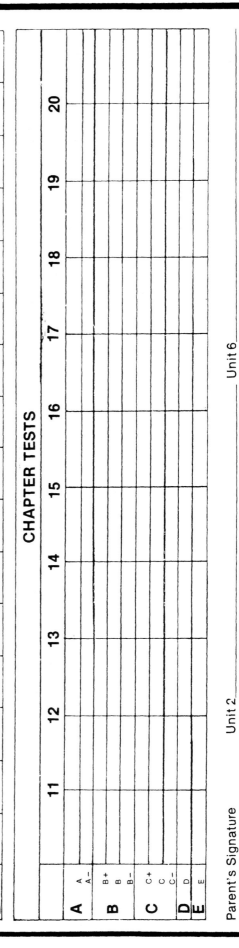